LURES FOR LUNKER BASS

By:
Bud Andrews
and
W. Horace Carter
Pulitzer Prize Winning
Journalist

I

Copyright 1989 by
W. Horace Carter
First Printing 1989
Second Printing 1991

Printed in the United States of America

Published by
W. Horace Carter
Atlantic Publishing Company
P. O. Box 67
Tabor City, North Carolina 28463

Library of Congress Card Number 89-084506

ISBN Number 0-937866-20-2

All Photographs by the author, DuPont, Skeeter Boats, Tim Tucker and Douglas Hannon.

Front Cover Photo by the author

Back cover photo by Homer Circle
Fishing Editor, *Sports Afield*

INTRODUCTION

When you finally make the decision to write a book, you know that there are months and months of painstaking effort putting together the paragraphs and pages that hopefully will appeal to readers. If it is an outdoor book, as this one is, you are determined to make it attractive to those hunters and fishermen around the country who occasionally relax in their favorite den chair and read rather than watch another fishing show or another sporting event.

We decided this book should be written two or three years ago because the 321 trophy bass discussed here were generally caught using a unique technique little imagined by the lay fisherman or the professional bass angler. Indeed this highly successful technique is the discovery of the author of the book who feels he should share his secrets with other bass fishermen throughout the land. Because of his obsession to share his expertise, he badgered me to put the words together in this book that I have chosen to name *Lures for Lunker Bass*. That is exactly what the book is about—the attraction that artificial bass baits have for trophy size fish when handled expertly and astutely by the weekend angler and the best of the pros on the cast-for-cash circuits.

It is the sincere wish of Bud Andrews and me that the reader will learn something here that has never been revealed to him anywhere else. If it makes the fisherman catch more big bass and if he will carefully release those trophies to thrill another generation, we will not have spent our time in vain. All but a very few of the many wallmounts caught by Bud Andrews were weighed, documented and turned loose to strike an angler's lure on another fishing adventure.

With those thoughts in mind, start reading Chapter 1, "How I Learned to Catch Big Bass." Unless we have failed miserably, you'll be glad you did and you'll not stop reading until you reach "The End."

W.H.C.

III

ACKNOWLEDGEMENTS

We are indebted to a number of companies and individuals for their cooperation in providing the authors with biographical and technique material and photographs that appear in this book. We are particularly appreciative of the material on the professional bass fishermen provided by Skeeter High Performance Bass Boats and The DuPont Company. *Fishing Facts* magazine, *Bassmaster* magazine, *Woods and Waters*, *Florida Bass* and other publications have graciously permitted us to use information from their books. We appreciate the help from Douglas Hannon and Tim Tucker in some of the mechanics of putting this book together.

Public relations departments from Bass Pro Shops, Cabela's and lure manufacturers have also assisted in providing good information on new and old lures that catch big bass.

FOREWORD

Charles (Bud) Andrews walked along the marshy canal shoreline on the fringe of the massive Everglades jungles in South Florida. Three stoic Seminole Indians were dragging big fish out of the dark waters, piling them in a homemade reed basket and they were obviously happy to have such successful pursuit of another seafood dinner for the tribe that lived in this remote wilderness.

Unsophisticated cane poles with six-inch live baits were enough for these native Americans to catch fish. Few owned rods and reels and they didn't really need them as these narrow tributaries were full of hungry fish. Fish would quickly bite anything that looked like a meal that came within striking distance.

"What kind of fish are you fellows catching?" Andrews inquired, having never been in these swamps before, and knowing nothing about freshwater fish of the South.

"These are trout," a skinny, suntanned fisherman grunted, and he didn't seem particularly anxious to volunteer any more information. He went right back to his fishing pole and soon another nice fish flounced on the surface. He dragged a two-foot long, big-mouth fish out on the grassy bank.

"I thought you caught trout in the mountain streams," Andrews pushed his first question.

"We don't know nothin' about the mountains. We been living here in these Everglades for generations and we catch these trout in these potholes and canals all over the place," the same Indian fisherman mumbled again.

After an hour of observing, Bud marveled at the success these natives were having and it was infectious. He wanted to catch some of those "trout." On a lightweight rod and reel, it would certainly be a lot of fun and more sport than any of the adventures he had had back in New Jersey before he joined the U.S. Air Force.

That experience of watching the Indian anglers was on a Saturday. The next day Andrews returned to the canal with the lazy water flow with his fishing equipment and half a dozen redfin shiners he had bought from a local bait shop. He didn't know how to impale them on a hook and there were no other fishermen around to advise him. He just hooked a big 8/0 steel hook through the lips of a wriggling bait and flipped it a dozen yards across the canal.

He didn't have time to take a few breaths that he needed from fighting his way through the undergrowth to reach this honey hole where the"trout" were so plentiful 24 hours previously. His line straightened and headed upstream. He yanked with all the gusto that his light line would stand. Suddenly, he had a devil on the hook. Ten minutes later he almost miraculously pulled a monster to the shoreline, got his hands around the big fish and lifted it out of the water. Bud looked down upon the first Florida largemouth bass he had ever seen and he didn't know what it was until he left the canal and asked about the species at a nearby bait shop.

"The Indians said these fish they were catching were trout. Is that what I have here?" he asked the proprietor.

"No, this is a Florida strain of largemouth bass, but a lot of Southerners here and in other states call them trout. It's a great gamefish and these waters around the Everglades are loaded with big ones. Let's see how much your fish weighs," the accommodating bait shop operator volunteered.

On the grocery store-type scales, Bud's first bass weighed exactly ten pounds. He smiled as he looked at his trophy. It changed his life. He was thoroughly stung with the ambition to catch more and more of these great fighting lunkers. He would complete his tour with the Air Force and return home to his good sales position with Ford in New Jersey. But in the back of his mind, he had that penchant to spend his life catching big fish, like this Florida bass.

He never lost that desire, that motivation instilled by that first ten-pounder from the bank of an Everglades canal. He did go back to New Jersey and was a successful salesman for a time. But opportunity knocked and in 1976 he returned to Florida, bought a modest fish camp motel on credit and began learning how to catch and help others catch trophy size largemouth bass. He abandoned the live bait technique of the Indians. He chose the more challenging artificials and began experimenting with various lures in Little Lake Henderson and other water near his fish camp at Inverness on the Tsala Apopka chain, a hop and skip from the Gulf of Mexico in Citrus County.

He soon learned where the big fish were and in time discovered a unique technique for catching these lunkers, both on the surface and on the bottom. He continues to catch big bass today and this talented angler has helped hundreds of clients over the past 15 years land a wall mount fish while personally catching and releasing 321 trophies.

He is the Muhammad Ali of artificial lure big bass fishing. All of his trophies except that first one in the Indian territory, have been caught on artificial lures and all have been caught in public water of Florida. In modern times, he is the champion trophy bass fisherman with artificial lures and his novel technique has made him a legend in our time. With the increased fishing pressure on largemouth Florida bass and modern tackle, boats and electronics, there may never again be a fisherman with a documented record of so many wallmount-size bass. Andrews may be the last angler to catch so many once-in-a-lifetime trophies, at least one in a lifetime for many. These dream bass will never again be caught in such numbers.

Bud Andrews unlocked the secret of fishing lures for big bass. His technique works as his experiences almost daily attest. He followed a dream to the end of the rainbow and he is a winner.

by W. Horace Carter

ABOUT THE AUTHORS

Charles (Bud) Andrews is primarily a bass fishing guide, although he has written angling columns for several local publications as his reputation for catching trophy size bass in Florida has received national attention.

Articles about his expertise have appeared in *Fishing Facts, Bassmaster, Florida Sportsman, Game & Fish, Florida Bass, North Carolina Outdoorsman, Woods & Waters, Field & Stream, Sports Afield,* among other publications.

In recent months, Andrews has made frequent appearances on national television outdoor shows and has been featured at numerous seminars and fishing schools that have attracted widespread participation by hundreds of Floridians.

He and his wife Kathy live at Cypress Lodge, a fish camp motel on Highway 44 East near Inverness, Florida. They moved to Florida from New Jersey where Bud held a sales position with Ford Motor Company for a number of years.

W. Horace Carter is a writer, although he fishes too. He won a Pulitzer Prize in North Carolina as a newspaper editor and publisher. For the past 15 years, he has been a full-time free lance writer for the outdoor magazines and has sold more than 2,000 stories on fishing and hunting. His articles have appeared in every national and many regional and state magazines. He has written 11 books on the outdoors, two of them with Doug Hannon (The Bass Professor). Both these books rank among the best-selling bass books of all time. *Big Bass Magic* is a first place award winner in the Southeast.

A North Carolinian from Stanly County, Carter is now a Floridian and lives at Cross Creek in Alachua County with his wife Brenda. He is a journalism graduate of the University of North Carolina at Chapel Hill.

Carter writes about both fresh and saltwater fishing from Maryland to Texas and is assisted in the photography by his wife. He is a past president of the Florida Outdoor Writers Association, three terms; the Southeastern Outdoor Press Association; and has served six years on the board of Directors of the Outdoor Writers Association of America. He is a member of the North Carolina Journalism Hall of Fame, and in 1953 was named "One of the Ten Most Outstanding Young Men in America" by the U.S. Junior Chamber of Commerce.

**Baseball legend Ted Williams and Bud Andrews
Catch a Big One**

TABLE OF CONTENTS

ANDREWS' PROWESS EARNED HIM A PLACE ON TROPHY BASS CATCHING LADDER

The first national publicity that Charles (Bud) Andrews ever received for his championship record of catching trophy bass appeared in *Fishing Facts* magazine, January 1988. That story is reprinted here with a few updates of his record. Since then, he has been lauded in virtually every national and regional outdoor publication in the country.

By **W. Horace Carter**

Using a unique dead-in-the-water lure presentation, Charles (Bud) Andrews, Inverness, Florida, has compiled a fantastic trophy largemouth catch of 321 over 10-pounds in a dozen years. Moreover, all his giant bass were caught on artificial lures and in public waters of Central Florida. While there are no offices that keep records certifying individual landings of trophy bass over a period of time, and while this articulate guide makes no claim to fame, it is generally conceded that few, if any, other anglers anywhere have amassed such a fantastic big-bass record in the second half of the twentieth century.

There are those who challenge Andrews' lunker-landings claim, but writers, tourists and natives acquainted with this busy guide's angling prowess concede that his novel expertise has earned him a place high on the ladder of successful trophy bass anglers in the era of modern fishing history.

Andrews makes every effort to document this sensational giant-bass record and provides the skeptic with three pages of names, addresses and phone numbers of clients with whom he fished who vouch for his outstanding success. He also notes some of his fishing-partner witnesses have died or moved and he cannot contact them. He has pictures of virtually every one of his trophy lunkers made before the bass was released. His sponsor and long-time associate at Cypress Lodge in Inverness, John (Jake) Chastain, says he has weighed in all of Bud's trophy bass and the number is actually well over 400. Andrews refuses to count those lunkers landed when he was fishing alone. Only

1

those caught when he had witnesses are tallied in the 321 count. He vows that every one of this number was caught in the presence of an observer and that each was caught by him, not one of his clients. His record appears to be unimpeachable.

"I never count any fish except those that I personally land. I never fish live bait and I do not fish in private waters. My trophy fish were all caught in public lakes and streams and all on artificial lures that I fish considerably differently from most guides and professional bass fishermen," Andrews says.

"I release all of my 10-pounders and most smaller bass too. I have mounted only 12 of my 321 big fish; eight are on my wall now. All the others were released after I brought them in to the dock and weighed them, except for a few that died. I had some of those mounted or given to the children's hospital for the kids to admire. Those mounts were a good promotion and advertising for Cypress Lodge too. Sometimes a gut-hooked bass will not survive regardless of how hard I try to save it, and these casualties end up on the walls of the hospital for the children. I believe in catch-and-release of all bass that I or my clients land and the paying customer is made aware of that before we start fishing," says Andrews.

Acknowledging Andrews' remarkable big-bass success, the St. Petersburg *Times* selected him as the top largemouth angler in Florida in 1982. Not only is his personal record for catching big bass enviable, he almost daily helps his customers find trophy bass. Hundreds of his clients return to Central Florida every year to stalk wallmount-size bass with this successful guide. Andrews and his seven associates guide from 700 to 1000 anglers every year. "If we don't have at least 750 customers, we consider it a bad year," says Andrews. He and his guides charge $150 a day and up for their services.

Where did Andrews catch his 321 giant bass?

"I caught six of the trophies in Lake Okeechobee and a few others in the Kissimmee chain. Some came out of the Withlacoochee, Rainbow, Homosassa, Crystal, Hall and St. Johns rivers. Others came from the Rodman Reservoir on the Oklawaha River. But mostly I caught these bass in Lakes Jackson, Plaza, June, Josephine, Lochloosa, Orange, Rousseau, Weir and Holly, the latter in the Ocala National Forest. I also caught a few in the Clermont chain. All came from waters within driving distance of my home in Inverness in Central Florida, but 60% of my catches were pulled right out of this Tsala Apopka area where

2

Cypress Lodge is located. They came from these small lakes, namely Henderson, Davis, Spivey, Little Henderson and others. This sprawling Tsala Apopka complex stretches from Floral City in the south to Hernando to the north and is a labyrinth of lakes, canals, ditches, creeks and ponds with a great deal of aquatic growth that is great bass cover. There are many fine grassy points to fish and the eddies and currents around the tributary mouths provide great bass-feeding areas. I do catch about 40% of my big bass from other surrounding areas but mostly I fish right here in Citrus County. When I do fish other areas, I look for the same kind of habitat that has been so good for me here. That's cover along shorelines, in water from about four to eight feet deep. If you have grass, weeds, or lilies along the banks of these shallow lakes, there will be big bass feeding there.

"We are blessed with a lot of water here and good cover. Remember, this Tsala Apopka chain alone has 50 lakes in it that cover about 24,000 acres. When you learn to fish holes in the cover, the creek mouths and weedy shallows, you'll find the big bass, " says this transplanted New Jersey native who worked with Ford Motor Company in Atlantic City before moving to Florida.

"When I was younger, I used to spend some time every year in Florida fishing and hunting. I had a great time then. But I went back to New Jersey where I had a lucrative position with Ford Motor Company. But that was not what I wanted to do. My wife and I headed back to look for a fish camp to operate. We bought Cypress Lodge in 1975, and we think we've been in heaven ever since. The lodge is on Lake Henderson, a few miles south of Inverness on State Road 44, 55 miles north of Tampa and 12 miles off I-75."

In those early days Bud was a regular on several of the professional bassing circuits, including National, American and United, among others. He placed high in the money several times but dropped off the pro trail when he felt there was some dishonesty and collusion that tainted the tournaments. But operating the fish camp and guiding for lunkers was Bud's first love, and he has capitalized upon that opportunity to reach a pedestal today. Some writers have referred to him as the Muhammad Ali of bass fishing.

Perhaps the most remarkable thing about Bud's record catch of trophy bass is the fact he never fishes with live bait and he opposes all kinds of largemouth fishing on the nests of the

3

spawners. He feels that it takes an unfair advantage of the bass, admitting that years ago he did use shiners, crawfish, and other live morsels. When he began his guiding career, he turned entirely to artificials and all his big bass hit some type of artificial lure. He knows how to put BIG fish in the boat.

It was one of Tom Mann's Razorback lures that he cast in 1978 and reeled in a 15-pound, 3-ounce bass that broke the old Tsala Apopka lake record. That's one of the fish he has mounted at Cypress Lodge now.

Reminiscing, Bud thinks back to the 1950's when he was stationed at Homestead Air Force Base in Florida. He began observing the natives fishing for bass in the area, including two young Seminole Indians. He was fascinated with the way they caught fish with shiners, frogs, grass shrimp and crawfish. The plastic worm was coming to the forefront then and he bought a few of the new gadgets that had three exposed hooks, some beads and even a propeller. He caught a few bass on that antique lure but soon began experimenting with other worms and minnow-like artificials and he quickly unlocked the secrets for landing lunkers in Florida. The expertise he learned then, and after his return to civilian life in 1960, has served him well over the past 14 years.

"While I was working those ten years for Ford in New Jersey, I fished whenever I had an opportunity and kept learning. I remember well the 6-pound, 8-ounce bass I caught in New Jersey, a real nice fish for that state. By the time I got back to Florida and bought our lodge, I knew that I had mastered a unique system of catching big bass on plastic worms and plugs. It was different and most people laugh at my technique, but the hundreds of clients who have fished with me know that I can catch big fish. I call my two kinds of bass fishing the 'bumping worm,' and 'dead lure,' and virtually all my big fish were caught on one of those two lures," says this accomplished trophy-catcher who wouldn't swap his lifestyle for the Presidency of the United States.

While most plastic-worm fishermen cast often and twitch their lure along the bottom and sometimes all the way back to the boat, Andrews casts his wiggle-tail worm, a flat, curly tail Culprit about eight or ten inches long, and lets it lie on the bottom. Often he will not move it for half-an-hour. Or maybe he will dip the rod tip just enough to make it wriggle but not move the body of the worm from where he flipped it.

4

"Bass are a lot like people and they can be provoked or irritated. If you put that worm in front of a bass and leave it there long enough, four out of five fish will eventually pick it up. I'm sure they perceive it as a dead worm that is not going anywhere and they gulp it down. They will bite that 'dead worm' even when their belly is full and they may not be hungry. I think they just get tired of looking at it in their territory. It takes patience and self discipline to fish a 'dead worm,' but it will pay off if you stick with it. I actually stumbled on this secret of not moving my worm on the bottom. Several times when I stopped fishing to eat a sandwich or drink a Coke, I left my worm on the bottom. Then off would go the line and I grabbed the rod and set the hook. I realized that I hadn't moved the bait at all. The bass had inhaled it when it was totally inactive. That was the start of my dead-worm or bumpin' worm system," Bud reveals.

"Of course, you have to know where to cast that worm and let it stay put for as much as 15 minutes or more. You can't catch bass if there are none there. But I know in these Central Florida lakes that bass often feed around the grass and lilies where the water is pretty shallow, two feet to about seven or eight feet. We don't have many deep coves or sharp drop-offs in the waters I fish. I have to concentrate on the shorelines and creek mouths mostly. Where I can find some structure in deeper water, that is a fine place to plant a 'dead-in-the-water' worm and let it stay there. There are often concentrations of bass in the deep holes where there is a bottom structure. Unfortunately, this Tsala Apopka chain doesn't have much of that kind of habitat. Some lakes like Lochloosa, about an hour-and-a-half from Inverness, have a lot of cypress trees and knees along the shoreline in a couple of feet of water. Worms left on the bottom around this cover will catch big fish too.

"Often some of my clients are impatient with the slow way I move the boat to where they have cast a worm. I tell them to cast ahead of the boat and not to pick up the worm until we get to it. I may take ten or 15 minutes or even longer getting the boat to their bait. But patience with this dead-worm system will pay off. I move the boat forward at a snail's pace," Bud divulges another productive guiding secret.

"My other unorthodox way of catching big bass is just a variation of the 'dead-in-the-water' worm fishing, except that I leave them dead in the water on the surface. I fish topwaters mostly but I may use a crankbait when I think it is right for the place and the time. Sometimes I may pull the crankbait lip off so it looks more like a real topwater lure and I do not crank it. I want it to float peacefully on the surface. I fish Rapalas frequently and I let the lure appear dead. I like the No. 11 gold or silver with black back. I always tie a two-inch loop in my line if there is no split ring at the front of the lure. It gives the plug better action. I never tie the loop knot in the line directly to the lure if there is a split ring in it. The ring will give it action without the loop.

"I cast the minnow-shaped floater near the grass, overhanging bushes or tree cover and let it float like it was an injured minnow for five to ten minutes without twitching or moving it in any way. The loop in the line makes it more life-like and the bass will find it. If it is a tough fishing day and the strikes are few, after several minutes of watching the lure float, I will point the tip of the lure down with my rod and walk the lure in. It's the way many anglers maneuver the well known Zara Spook. Occasionally that walk will turn bass on when the dead-in-the-water lure isn't working. But most of my 10-pounders (and over) hit the worm or the lure when it was still, or dead in the water. Even if the bass are schooling and active, there is no need for jerking and yanking the lure. But sometimes they won't hit anything dead or alive.

"I also have another unconventional way of catching big bass. I cast some of the sinking-type plugs made by Rebel, Storm, Norman and others in the holes and along the fringes of the aquatic growth where the water is several feet deep. Again, I revert to my dead-in-the-water practice. I let those lures lie on the bottom just like I do a worm. I may not twitch or move it for ten minutes or longer. I put the lure where I think there's a fish and leave it in her territory. I think the big bass look it over and eventually decide it's dead and should be moved. That's when I catch some of my trophies.

"I like the looks of some crankbaits and, while I don't crank them, I may fish them anyhow because they look like real forage fish. Most crankbaits won't sink but you can wedge a few split-shot between the treble hooks and they will fall slowly to the bottom. I leave them there motionless like I do the plugs designed to sink. I don't move them until I get ready to cast again, often as long as 15 minutes or more.

"I believe one of the reasons I have good success with plugs on the bottom is my using the lightest possible line. I never use anything heavier than eight- or ten-pound test. I use that same light line when I'm fishing the Rat-L-Trap, Brokenback Jitterbug, Tiny Torpedoes, Bombers and PT Spoons dead-on-the-surface. The lighter the line the more strikes I get. I can get a lot of distance casting a lure on light line, sometimes when the water is shallow, getting it far enough from the boat so that the bass can't possibly see me," Bud says.

"I lose a few big fish because of the light line that I use. But I know that I get many more big bass strikes than I could get using heavier line. Sometimes I freeline the Rat-L-Traps in Apopka. This lure is bright, shiny and looks like glass when you let it float to the bottom in the sunshine. Recently I left a half-ounce plug lying on the bottom and a fine 6-1/2-pound bass nosed it up and nailed it. That bass inhaled the lure when it was perfectly still but reflecting a lot of light.

"Almost every bass fisherman at one time or another has caught a nice fish when it seemed accidental. He was doing something else and the fish got on the hook when he was not looking. I know that doing nothing brings me more strikes from bass than any action that I initiate. And that's how I catch a lot of fish on lures that look like forage fish. Many people give the lure a lot of action from the time it hits the water until it is back in the boat, but that isn't the best technique for me," says this big bass catcher who certainly ranks among the top successful artificial bait bassers in the country.

"I also believe I catch more big bass than some fishermen because I watch the alligators, otters, birds and insects. Anytime I see the 'gators and otters moving about, I know there are some fish in that spot and they are there looking for a meal. I fish where they fish. Then if there are many flying or swimming insects in an area, I know these will attract bait minnows and other small forage fish. Where those little fish school, big bass will not be far away. I like to put my baits where the insects are gathered. I have confidence in those places," he reveals.

"I have tried to educate myself on bass fishing. I have read everything I could get my hands on about how to catch big bass. Some of it has helped, but generally I have had to learn for myself. I make notes of my success and try to learn from every experience on the water. And I try to learn from the experience of other good bass anglers on the water. I still remember vividly the first trophy bass I ever caught in Florida. I was in a little 11-foot jonboat and had no trolling motor. I was sculling the boat along with a paddle and had a yellow Beetle Spin on the line. It was right here on the Tsala Apopka chain. I got a strike and landed a 12-1/2-pound bass that was 29 1/2-inches long. That was the start of my successful big-bass career that has now reached 321," Andrews remarks.

"I will never fish a bass spawning bed if I know it is there. I am opposed to all bed fishing for bass. I'll never eat a bass unless it was gut-hooked and I cannot keep it alive. While I fish five days a week with my clients and we catch fish every day (Andrews has never yet been skunked in his guiding career), I will not lose more than two or three fish a week from gut-hooking. A few will die. I use a chemical called Catch and Release and take every precaution to release my bass well and healthy. I want to protect the resource for my young son and others in the next generation.

"I believe that the future of big-bass fishing in Florida is in jeopardy. There is too much chemical spraying to kill aquatic growth. When the water hyacinths and pepper grass are killed, the bass will quickly decline and fishing goes downhill. I do not believe that we should ever kill what Mother Nature puts in the water," Andrews points out.

While there are writers and guides who question Bud Andrews' record number of trophy largemouths, he talks with sincerity and confidence. His sponsor and close friend, Jake, declares he has weighed in at least 400 of Bud's 10-pounders. More than half-a-hundred clients vouch for the bulk of the 321 caught on artificials in public waters claimed by this astute artificial-lure champion. Bud himself says he has caught at least 40 or 50 others in the trophy class but does not count them because he had no witness that he did catch the fish and on an artificial lure. His wife, Kathy, has personal knowledge of almost every trophy fish and confirms Bud's enviable big fish record. Those who have fished with him testify quickly to his expertise and uncanny success with "dead" lures.

Bud was once a dreamer in New Jersey who was doing well with a major industry. But his dream was to return to Florida and bass fishing. It has all come true and, indeed, this 49-year-old former Yankee lives with a smile on his face. Catching big bass and getting paid for the effort is like finding the pot of gold in the sun and he has carved a Utopian career for which he is grateful.

For those who would like to fish with this trophy bass-hunter, a real artificial lure innovator whose success in this generation may be unsurpassed, he can be reached at Cypress Lodge, 1025 Highway 44 East, Inverness, FL 32650; phone 904-726-1272

HOW I LEARNED TO
CATCH THE BIG ONES

It was mid-morning in the spring of 1977. Fishing was slow and I sat in my Ranger boat off a grassy point in Little Lake Henderson alone. Fog shrouded the surface as the temperature of the air and the water contrasted. I knew that there were plenty of largemouth bass in this Tsala Apopka chain. I lived on the western shore at Cypress Lodge and during the few short months I had operated the fish camp, dozens of monster bass had been brought in by natives and tourists. Someone knew how to catch those trophies and if I was ever to be a recognized, successful fishing guide, I had to unlock the secret and catch these big wallmounts. I had to be able to catch them before I could show someone else how. I wanted to be a big bass guide.

I looked down in my livewell at two foot-long bass that breathed calmly in the aerated box. I had caught them an hour earlier around a cypress tree. They were pretty but they were not the dream fish at the end of the rainbow. You don't call home to brag about two-pounders you caught in Florida. That size isn't a conversation topic at the 19th hole or at the bait and tackle shop where cronies meet to talk bass fishing. In the yesteryears when outdoorsmen sat around pot-bellied country stoves at liar's corner stores rehashing the past summer's bassing success, no one talked about a stringer of yearlings. It was that old reprobate with the 10-pounder on the wall whose slow words fell on attentive ears. He was everyone's envy.

The paying customers from far away states don't come to Florida to catch yearlings. They want eight and 10-pounders or above. There are plenty of little bass in New York, Illinois, Ohio and everywhere. It's the giants of the Florida strain that attract the wintertime anglers to the Sunshine State.

I mulled that obvious conclusion over in my mind, reached in the livewell and lifted my yearlings to freedom. They flipped on the surface an instant and then headed for the bottom , where a foot of green, healthy hydrilla sprouted from the muck and the sand. It was home for these fish that by instinct and experience knew forage food flitted in the aquatic weeds on the bottom, even when it was 15 feet below the surface. There must be a lesson in that for me, I thought. If the yearlings like that bottom cover way out here in the open water, then the giants must like it too. I have to discover how to get those monsters on the hooks instead of the little fellows.

I had caught my share of small fish around the grassy shoreline and off shallow points during many vacation weeks when I loved to visit Central Florida during time off from my sales job with Ford Motor Company in New Jersey. I had been a pretty good Yankee bass fisherman, once holding the New Jersey smallmouth record with a 6-pound, 8-ounce fish for several months. My challenge was to learn how and where to catch the big bass in Florida and the success of my fish camp and career in general hinged on that discovery.

Those reflections that May morning changed my fishing style and indeed my very life. Big bass do like to maraud in the deep water where there is bottom cover. It doesn't have to be real deep, there are not many lakes in Florida that are deeper than 15-20 feet. But big bass do stake out territories in six to ten feet of water and challenge their smaller cousins to invade it and partake of the food supply. The real lunkers are cannibalistic, eating other bass that are not too big to swallow when they venture into the giant's domain. Indeed, this characteristic of eating others of the same species is one of the reasons some bass grow to wallmount size. They grow to giant proportions at the expense of their own kind.

The territorial domination of the monsters had been planted in my mind some years earlier by Douglas Hannon, the Bass Professor of Odessa, Florida, who has documented catches of more than 400 bass weighing 10-pounds or more. He caught his fish mostly on live shiners but he is a respected authority on the life styles of big bass. If these big fish lived most of their lives near the bottom in relatively deep water, I had to learn a technique that would make them strike. Once that was clearly established, I would be on my way to catching big bass and guiding others to similar success.

I cranked my motor and slowly returned to the dock that morning. I didn't have a fish in the boat, but I had a lot of new ideas running rampant in my head. I wondered if the seed for success would evolve from those thoughts. Time would soon tell. I sat down at the lunch table and began discussing my thoughts that morning with Kathy.

"You know, Kathy, I believe if I am ever to be a success at guiding fishermen for big bass, I have to do something that other anglers are not doing. Mostly, the guides here move along the grass and cypress lines, casting plastic worms, topwaters and crankbaits around the cover. They catch some fish and even a giant every now and then. But I believe there are more big fish out there than most people realize. I have to devise a system for getting them to strike. I'm going to start fishing for the big ones in deeper water than I have in the past," I said with more seriousness than I had ever talked about fishing with her before.

Two days later, with no guiding parties booked, I went back on Lake Henderson to try my new idea. I watched my depthfinder and finally anchored in a hole about a dozen feet deep where there was some obvious weed growth sprouting that almost covered the bottom in a house-size area.

I strung on my favorite Culprit, curly-tailed blue worm with a half-ounce bullet slip sinker for a head and flipped it 30 feet off the bow of the boat. I watched the 10-pound test Stren run off the reel and then the bait hit the bottom. I tightened the line a little, twitched it a few times and slowly retrieved. Nothing happened. I cast again and again and again in all directions. But there was not a strike to be had. Perhaps the big fish didn't like this particular deep hole. I cranked and moved to another similar spot a half mile away.

With the anchor secure on the bottom, I repeated my enticing lure presentation again. I twitched it on the bottom, retrieved it at half a dozen speeds and even let it drop straight down and flipped and flitted it in the top of the hydrilla over and over. The vertical jigging attracted no attention. Nothing worked. Not one fish touched the lure as I experimented for hours, hoping to hang a lunker. I knew at least one big fish was in that second hole because she crashed once on the surface, attacking a scared crawfish that had ventured out of the grass and tempted a big mama. She chased the crustacean to the top and gulped it down in a feeding frenzy before diving back to her haven on the bottom. I was discouraged when I got out of the boat at the dock and went inside.

"You have any luck with your new ideas?" Kathy asked, but from the sober look on my face she knew the answer without any doubt.

"Nothing, absolutely nothing. I didn't even get a strike from a yearling. I may be barking up the wrong tree but I'll give it another try or two before admitting it," I told her.

A week passed before I was back on the lake experimenting. I hadn't had that much guiding to do, but maintenance and book work had kept me tied up. But all the time my mind was churning with the idea that I could catch big wallmount bass in the deeper water where there was good cover if I knew just how to fish that territory. The idea had to be sound. What must I do to prove it?

I awoke to a clear and pretty bluebird Monday. There was only a trickle of wind on the lake. Few boats disturbed the quiet and calm after the chaos that was everywhere you looked on the warm weekend just passed. I'll go fishing again, I decided, and minutes later I was rushing over the lake to one of those deep holes that I knew about.

Again I started casting my worm lure and with more confidence than on previous days. Somehow, I felt this was the day I would vindicate my beliefs. But at 10:00 A.M. my confidence had dwindled. Not one bass had dared touch my enticing morsel, even though I had fished it everywhere and every way. I might as well give up.

I flipped my lure out from the boat, laid the rod on the deck and pulled out my sandwich bag from under the console. If I couldn't get the fish to bite, at least I could enjoy watching the herons and ospreys arguing about the minnows in the grass and the grackles and redwing blackbirds competing for the bonnet worms on the spatterdock lilies. This abundance of wildlife made every fishing trip a success whether I caught fish or not. But when I was being paid to guide tourists after a big fish, catching or skunking did become important. And today it was significant because I was trying to prove a theory that might help me the rest of my guiding career.

I munched on the sandwiches for nearly half an hour and marveled at the acumen of the wild birds that worked so feverishly for a morning meal. When I swallowed the last drop of the Diet Coke and carefully stuffed the bottle and papers in the trash bag, I was ready to start fishing again. I picked up the rod and looked out at my line. It was yards away from where I had left it. I reeled ever so carefully. The line tightened. I felt the tap-tap of something alive on the hook. It was the tell-tale assurance. With gusto, I yanked the rod tip over my head and the 6-foot fiberglass Fenwick rod bowed like a Fred Bear big game hunting weapon. This was no yearling. I had a fish to write home about.

I had been considered a good bass fisherman for years from having been somewhat successful in several of the professional bassing circuits before I got into serious guiding. Even my competitors were complimentary of my ability. But I had never really caught any huge fish. This thing I had on the line was going to be a first for me. It was. I slowly and carefully led the monster to the gunnels. The fish was too big to lip land. I slid my net under the monster and lifted her aboard. She was a giant, the largest one I had ever seen, much less caught.

I put the bass in the livewell, making sure the aerator was working well, and the fish had plenty of fresh water. The big mama looked healthy and contented despite her challenging struggle to unbutton my worm hook. I pulled in the anchor and headed for home. The smile on my face revealed my success to Kathy even before I opened my mouth.

"How big is she?" she yelled before I opened the livewell. I lifted the fish out and smiled some more.

"That's really a beauty," she said with obvious pride. And so it was. The scales showed the monster weighed 12-pounds, 9-ounces. My largest bass ever at that time.

But far more importantly, I learned that morning how to catch big bass in Florida. The secret was putting something in the territory of the fish that would look out of place to the bass. Then leave it there for a long time, often as much as half an hour without any bait movement by the fisherman. The only movement would be that of the worm's tail in the slight current. It would stand on its head and to all observers, including the big bass, it would look like a dead worm had settled on the bottom. No self-respecting wallmount-size largemouth would leave a dead object in its territory forever. She would get tired of the invasion, pick it up and carry it away. Only when it was there too long for her to put up with it, did she bother to nose it around. Its presence eventually irritates the bass and she moves it away. That lure that falls in her face and soon is reeled away is not her nemesis. She didn't even bother to strike one that was wriggling up and away. She wasn't always that hungry anyway. But she would not tolerate a dead worm messing up her staked-out haven. She would drag it away.

That revelation has made me a big bass fisherman. Of course, I use some other techniques, particularly with topwaters and crankbaits, but the principle remains the same. Big bass are protective of their territory. When you challenge their right to it, they can't stand the competition. You'll catch the giants because of their pride and determination to stop the invasion by an object that isn't just passing through; it is there to stay for a long time.

Patience becomes the factor that is the difference between success and failure. You'll catch the really big fish when you can cast a worm in a good spot and leave it there for half an hour or more. I discovered this while eating lunch and leaving my bait unmolested on the bottom. Since then I have landed 321 bass 10-pounds or heavier, all on artificial lures, and in almost every case, success came from unusual patience. I have trouble getting my clients to cast and leave their worm lures on the bottom for long periods of time. I deliberately troll and stop, troll and stop, often moving only a few boat lengths in half an hour. This keeps my clients fishing the same spots with patience. But many get fidgety and anxious to move along before I am convinced the lunkers are not eyeballing their worms and deciding whether they are in the way or not.

I know that patience is the name of the game when worm fishing for trophy bass. I don't fish live baits like most of the wallmount fish are caught with in Florida, but that requires patience, too. Big lunkers are not usually real anxious to hit something quickly. They take their time. But if you are not in a hurry, you can catch that fish of your dreams on an artificial lure, in public waters and have something to tell your grandchildren about.

Try it! You'll be glad you did.

FAKING OUT
BIG BASS

I cut the outboard and tipped the trolling motor prop into the water. Immediately I began casting in the middle of Little Lake Henderson and my client looked at me as if I had lost my mind. This was a most unlikely spot to catch a largemouth bass, the quizzical eyes of my customer relayed the message. There was not a cloud in the sky, not a blade of grass in sight and the August heat hung over the water like a shroud.

This Tsala Apopka lake is in my backyard at Inverness. I had caught many of my 10-pounders here. I knew what I was doing but to the stranger in these parts, it obviously was an unorthodox bassing location.

I handed my customer a rod and reel with a brown, curly-tail Culprit worm looped in the line below a 1/2-ounce black bullet sinker. Then I picked up a similar one from the rack on the side of my Ranger boat and we were ready for action.

I believe my customer would have been ready to go back to the dock at that moment had he not heard of my success catching Central Florida bass. He reasoned that I must have a little intelligence and he would be patient with me. I suppose two hours later he was thankful that he kept his mouth shut. We had pulled in 15 nice bass from that 12-foot deep water and lost half that many that came unbuttoned.

I remarked to the client that I studied bass every day of the year and knew something about where they hung out, even on hot August mornings like this. He was convinced.

What my partner that morning didn't know was that a good stand of hydrilla covered the bottom of the lake at this point. And where there is good bottom cover in these lakes, the bass

15

congregate to forage on the minnows, frogs, crawfish and other edible creatures that live here. You have to be aware of these factors to find fish at times when many veteran bassers declare that you can't buy a bite.

I know my ABC's of bass fishing. After fishing the pro circuit for several years and guiding for more than a dozen others, some years spending over 300 days on the water, I have gained from experience. I make it my business to know where bass are active and what months, days and nights they are striking lures. If I didn't study these bass habits and characteristics, I would strike out. But I don't.

This particular spot in Henderson is always a productive hole in August and September. Bass stay here because the water is between 69 and 72 degrees, an ideal temperature for Florida bass, and that's the range that much of the lake water of the Sunshine State is this time of year in the deeper holes.

While much of my success is focused on how I know where to find fish, that isn't complete reason for landing so many lunkers. I have the expertise to catch fish with a unique system of patience with topwaters and worms on the bottom. That day I tried to share some of that technique with my skeptical customer after he was convinced I knew **where** to fish in Lake Henderson. I had to show him I knew the **how-to.**

When I am using a topwater and the lure does not have a swivel, I tie the lure on the line by looping it in the eye ring. I use a two-inch loop for better lure action.

I use a topwater differently from most other guides. I cast it near cover and let it stay there for unusual lengths of time, sometimes for more than 15 minutes. Really big bass suspend off the bottom and eyeball the lure a long time before striking. They get nervous and bust it. That's how I catch a lot of my trophy bass, I told my client that morning. He was amazed.

When bass seem to have lockjaw and don't go for my topwater, then I shift to the plastic worm. It goes down where the fish are and if it is rigged right and you fish it my way, you'll never get zipped. I like everything dark; hook, sinker, and worm. I don't want any shiny hook or bright-colored hardware. I want my worm on the bottom to look like a natural dead snake, eel or worm and none of these are shiny. Four out of five bass that see a dark worm on the bottom will strike it. Knowing how to properly fish a plastic worm separates the men from the boys.

You never fish a worm with a tight line. You give the line

16

at least one dip, a reel turn of slack and let it flutter to the bottom. Then my dead-worm technique comes into play. I learned it by accident when I let the worm rest on the bottom while I ate a sandwich a dozen years ago. When the line was at a different place from where I left it ten minutes earlier, I knew something had taken it away. I set the hook and came in with a 10-pounder. As I have said before, that changed my life, at least my fishing life.

Since I learned that worms fished dead on the bottom, like my "dead" topwaters, catch more fish than "live" ones, I also found out that they catch **bigger** bass too. Yearlings bite the lively, active plastic worms and other lures that you twitch and retrieve. But often the giants won't touch it until they get tired of seeing the intruder in their territory and bust it from frustration or anger. Every experienced basser at one time or another has caught or at least hooked a big bass when he left his lure in the water for what seemed like an unreasonable length of time while he did something else. He got a strike. That was no accident. The bass thought she was striking something dead.

This is not to say that every strike comes on the "dead" worm. I get about one-fourth of my strikes on a falling worm that is sucked up before it gets to the bottom. But those are usually smaller bass, not the trophies like the 321 I have landed.

My ability to catch big bass, and yours, hinges upon successfully finding the fish, presenting the lure properly and using the best equipment for that particular time and place. I use Stren clear line in clear water and the brown Royal Bonnyl in cider-colored water. I know these are good monofilaments for me. I have fished hundreds of different plastic worms. I know that the 7-1/2 inch Culprit with the wagging tail and natural moccasin color produces for me. Sometimes Jake's black worm gets strikes and I may stray away from dark colors on a bluebird, bright sunny day. I may loop on a pastel blue on the bright day and maybe an orange color on an overcast day. I don't want to ever be so absolute as to fight change. You may have to get away from the norm and your preference to entice bass on particular days at various times and places. You must adapt to change when it is necessary and the usual fails.

I like the blue 4/0 Mustad hook and I sometimes use TruTurns too. They must be razor-sharp. I sharpen them myself before looping on the line. I hide the brightness on the sharpened point by sticking it into the worm. I don't want that brightness showing.

17

Every time that I catch a fish, I analyze my situation. What technique did I use? What was the water depth? What was the time of day and the phase of the moon? I put these factors together to establish a pattern for each week of the year. That's how I can go out on these lakes any week of the year and be fairly sure I'll catch some bass. I have a history of the bass I catch. It is a kind of guarantee of success.

You must remember that you will never catch all the bass that strike a worm. I stick about four out of five but I miss some like everyone else. Reflexes must be pretty good for you to be a proficient worm fisherman. When I feel that familiar tap-tap, sometimes ever so lightly, I take up the line slack and let the fish run. I delay more than some fishermen do. I want to make sure the bass has the worm in her mouth before I set the hook. That often means patience and waiting for about a three second count.

A bass will not normally spit out a worm unless she feels tension. But if the line gets tight, she will spit it out. I hold my line with one finger when the worm is lying on the bottom and I feel almost anything that touches it. Occasionally a bass will pick it up without my feeling it, but that's unusual.

I prefer a casting rod and reel to spinning tackle. And I try to have my fish straight ahead of me when I set the hook. I don't like sidewise hook setting.

In a nutshell, these are my words of advice to worm anglers: Leave a little slack in the line. Point the rod tip toward the surface when you feel the tap-tap. Take up the slack slowly until you feel tension and then cross her eyes with a gusto hook setting. Drop the rod tip back toward the surface and keep the line coming in. Be patient and practice self-discipline.

When you are fishing a worm on the bottom, you seldom hang up even when there is a lot of aquatic growth. It's a lure that you can use in cover. But you should change worms frequently, especially after every strike. Every time I get a strike I change worms whether I hooked the fish or not. I want the worm to be free of tooth marks and scratches. It may make you buy a few more worms, but you'll catch more bass than you will on a tattered and torn bait.

I doubt if any of the fish attractor scents on the market actually draw bass to the lure because of the chemical. But I believe it will camouflage and cover up some of the human odors and that may make the scents worth trying by at least not running the fish away. I put a few drops of the attractor in a plastic bag with a handful of worms when I start out in the morning. It may help me get a few more strikes.

If I go several minutes without a strike when I have been casting the worm in the weeds and grass, I retrieve it and re-oil or put on a new worm with oil on it. I don't take a chance of my smell spooking a bass.

I am sure that bass communicate with each other, and maybe even between species. When I lose two strikes in the same place, I move to another spot. Other fish there will not bite. But if you don't miss a strike, the other bass there will continue to hit. It's not the bass that you catch that stop the strikes. It's those that get away. They become suspicious when they take a bite of your bait, don't get to swallow it and it suddenly disappears. By sound, sight or action, they relay a message that the worm you see on the bottom is dangerous and others better leave it alone. I'm sure the bass talk to each other.

As a guide, I must keep on doing my homework daily. When I am on vacation, which isn't very often, it takes me several days when I return to find the fish. They have homes down there where they live, find food and stay close to their refrigerators, just like people do. If the refrigerator is locked, they will stay close by. I have to keep up with where the forage fish are. They school and often are in a frenzy in an area. That's the refrigerator of the bass and I must know where it is located.

Circles on the water on still, calm mornings are a dead give-away. If there are no circles, there are no minnows or insects, thus there are no bass. There's nothing for the fish to eat. Locate the surface circles and you have found the bass. Often you'll see the predators making noisy, mad dashes for the food supply. They'll bite if you get the right lure in their faces.

The circles are harder to see when there is wind and ripples are on the surface. But you may still be able to see the minnows and hear the strikes of the predators. Herons may give bass away by wading the shallows and pecking on minnows that the bass share with the birds. Wallowed-out holes in the grass and weeds may be a feeding ground for bass where the alligators stalk their food. The 'gators wouldn't live there if the food supply wasn't available. In Florida, anywhere that you see a 'gator is a good spot to make a few casts. Bass may be hanging around. All wildlife know where food can be found and I take a cue from these creatures of nature with great instincts and know-how.

I lost the biggest fish I ever hooked. I was casting from my pier at Cypress Lodge and trying to show a youngster from Kentucky how to cast. I cast a big worm well out into the lake and

19

let it settle. I wasn't expecting a hit but I got one. I knew it was a big fish. That bass jumped twice, clearing the water with its gills flared, head shaking. It was a monster. I kept playing the fish and getting her closer to the pier. The kid grabbed a net and was about to scoop up the bass but the fish had other ideas. She turned toward the open water and I could see her no more than a yard from the dock. She headed into the lake and straightened my 5/0 steel hook. She was unbuttoned and escaped.

I'm sure the bass was three feet long and I am satisfied she weighed 17 or 18 pounds. I had no idea that a bass that size was right here in my back yard on Lake Henderson. But I saw the fish close up. She was a real giant. She rolled over once right at the dock and her eyes looked as big as silver dollars. I could have cried. But maybe she is still out there for someone to catch. By now she ought to be a world record.

I don't know how many 10-pounders and above I can catch if I continue guiding the rest of my life. There are still a good number of those trophies in Central Florida. There are also many of them in Texas and California, maybe other states too.

Today I'm not concentrating on catching more and more trophies. I have proven that I can catch them. Now I simply know that my greatest reward is the satisfaction I get from letters and calls from satisfied clients. It maintains my enthusiasm and my determination to do the very best job that I can for my customers. At 49 years of age, I should have time to make a lot of other people happy who come to Florida to catch a big bass.

My wife Kathy and my sponsor Jake Chastain deserve a lot of credit for any fishing success that I have enjoyed. Their encouragement has kept me on my toes, always trying to learn more about the lifestyles of bass so I can hopefully out-think the trophies that we seek.

My last bit of advice to bass anglers: Whether you are a worm fisherman, crankbait enthusiast, spoon, jig or spinner expert, your success depends upon how you apply your techniques. You can't just charge off a morning of bad luck and no strikes to fish having lockjaw. Most fishermen make their own good or bad luck. Build up a defense against the time when bass are not biting and turn to other spots and techniques. Learn your ABC's of bass fishing and you'll seldom be skunked. Confidence, patience and self-discipline along with a bass behavior education will make the difference in the fishing stories you will tell back at the ramp at the end of the day and to your grandchildren next Christmas.

BUMPING WORM VARIATION GETS LUNKERS

While my dead-worm-on-the-bottom technique has proven highly productive over my guiding years and many veteran bassers have adapted to the system, I have varied the details and many times enticed lunkers to bite that otherwise rejected the bait. The refining of the dead-worm-on-the-bottom to my bumping worm fishing is the same concept, but instead of never moving the worm, I make it dance on its head in the same location for long periods.

Like my dead-on-the-bottom technique taught me, bass often strike for reasons other than hunger. I refined the technique based on my theory that big bass will not tolerate an invader in their territory—not even a dying worm.

When I am reasonably sure that there is a lunker in an area and I cast my worm bait, I let it filter to the bottom and stay there for many long minutes without a tap-tap of any kind. I give it slight twitches of my rod tip every few seconds. I strive not to move the worm that's standing on its head on the bottom. I just want to put enough action on the line so the curly tail of the worm will wiggle. That's the bumping worm.

Often when the bass has just nosed around and observed the dead worm and not made a decision to get it out of her way, she will see the tail curl a time or two right in her face. From frustration, anger or curiosity, she will pick it up and start to swim away. That's when I cross her eyes and hope I have set the hook. Often when other fishermen are coming in with a tale of woe about the fish having lockjaw, I can show off another trophy that decided to inhale my bumping worm. The system works the year around in Central Florida.

When I first came to Florida to start my guiding career after first fishing the professional circuits for a few years, I learned about largemouth habits and lifestyles, I knew you had to fish for the trophies differently than you did the yearling keepers. And I knew that tourist fishermen who came to Florida were trying for giants, not a stringer of eating-size bass. I also knew that the

21

really big wallmounts were under a lot of pressure and the clients I would guide had to agree to catch-and-release. They could keep a single fish for a wallmount but all the rest had to go back in the lake. There would be no bass kept for the dinner table unless we had some yearlings that succumbed to the hooking and could not swim away if released. I had to do everything that I could to preserve the species, particularly the giants.

It was with that premise that I sat out to perfect a system for catching big fish. The system consisted of my dead-worm-on-the-bottom, dead-in-the-water topwater and the bumping worm techniques. These unorthodox methods have been the difference in success and failure for me over the years and I expect to continue successfully catching and releasing giants. I never wanted to fish shiners or any other live bait for bass. I wanted the challenge of catching big bass that I had coaxed into making a mistake and to feel her strike a man-made morsel. That's still a big thrill to me after landing 321 wallmount-size fish.

You can't let lady luck dictate your fishing success. You have to know something about the bass you stalk and study their behavioral patterns, territorial protective instincts, migration and preference of cover to be able to catch large fish regularly.

Douglas Hannon is one of the bass fishermen I admire the most. While he is primarily a shiner fisherman, he has documented catches of more than 400 bass weighing 10-pounds and above. He perfected a system of live bait fishing. He doesn't fish for bedding bass and he is a great proponent of catch-and-release. He tags and releases all the bass he catches, landing some of the same giants as many as six times. I am the same kind of resource conservationist that he is. I want to do everything I can to preserve the resource even while making a living guiding customers and assisting them in catching a trophy bass, even sharing my three techniques of bass fishing that have been so successful.

My bumping worm fishing is done with a 5-1/2 foot rod, because a longer one moves the worm too much when it is twitched. I flip an eight or nine inch curly tail worm, sometimes a Tom Mann black grape color and at other times the moccasin-colored Culprit with the curly tail. Sometimes I use a clear blue. I like my 8-pound test line and I'm usually fishing in water ten to 20 feet deep. I like to fish the bottom where there is a growth of hydrilla or some other weed. I pick them up on my depthfinder. But sometimes I find these big bass on sandy bottoms near aquatic growth.

Andrews With Another Lunker

When fishing the bumping worm, I finger the line hoping for the tap-tap. When I feel it, I take up the slack, lower the rod tip, bend my body down in the boat so it has a low profile and after a count of three, I set the hook with gusto.

But my success with this technique results from how I rig and fish the bumping worm. When the worm hits the bottom, I have it weighted so it will stand on its head. With it lolling on the bottom, I continue to flick the rod tip just enough to make the curly tail wriggle. I don't want that worm moving out of its place by even an inch. When the bass are dormant, they will strike the bumping worm while ignoring it fished any other way.

I am a drummer and it takes both hands and versatility to be a good drummer. I use the drummer's rhythm to catch fish with the bumping worm. I feel the tap-tap and then it is one, two and three. I set the hook and the rhythm continues as I reel in with a four, five and a six. About 60 percent of my big bass catches come from this bumping worm and dead-on-the-bottom worm techniques.

I believe that by just jarring the worm, you antagonize the bass. If you establish a worm-jarring rhythm, it's kind of like a disco dancer or drummer. The big bass loses her cool. That bumping worm system got me started and it still works well today.

My biggest problem as a guide trying to help clients catch a big fish is their reluctance to let the worm stay put. They always want to move the worm as soon as the ripples disappear on the surface from the splashdown. That's exactly opposite from my recommendation. It's that old "grass is better on the other side of the fence" syndrome.

Another difference in me and most other guides in Central Florida is the months that I prefer to fish. I recommend August, September and October. Most guides pick the spawning months of February and March. I don't want to take a chance of catching a big mama off the beds and destroying thousands of eggs and fry that may grow up to thrill today's children when they are teenagers.

YOU CAN'T HURRY A TOPWATER

George Perry cast his Creek Chub lure near a log in Georgia's Lake Montgomery, let it float a while and then watched it disappear when he reeled. He thought he was hung but then the line moved, a bass exploded and Perry says he had "hung a fish as big as a sack of flour." No one knows how long his Creek Chub floated on top, perhaps for minutes, maybe seconds. But he made bassing history with that plug and his 22-pound, 4-ounce world record has stood since 1932. It was an historic catch with the minnow-like Creek Chub lure. We will never know how long Perry left the lure on top.

But I do know some of the interesting facts about the largest bass ever caught in Orange Lake, one of the places where I have landed several of my 321 trophies over 10-pounds. The facts surrounding that catch helped me devise my topwater strategy that has made me better with topwaters.

Orange Lake is a 13,600 acre shallow lake with a mucky bottom. In past years, it had numerous floating islands, up to 30 acres and even larger, all covered with dense green bushes, weeds, grasses and some 40-foot high gum trees. Some even had marsh rabbit populations that were hunted with dogs.

On a spring morning when business was slow at Campbell's Holiday Fish Camp on U.S. Highway 441, on the west side of the lake, R. W. Campbell, who was a deputy sheriff in Mississippi for nine years, locked the doors of his bait shop and went fishing. He had taken over the fish camp after losing his deputy's job. Campbell loved to fish and he bought the camp facilities and was enjoying life. He went fishing that mid-March morning and got his name in the local record books.

Campbell anchored his homemade, plywood batteau on the windy side of one of these boggy, floating marshes where numerous lunker bass had been caught, some old-timers saying a 9-pounder then was so commonplace that it might not even be a keeper, and he cast a topwater jitterbug called a "Paw-Paw." It only went about half the distance to the little nook in the island where Campbell had aimed. Like something that even the professionals will do on occasions, Campbell had a massive backlash, his lure plopping in an open hole 20 feet from the cover.

Old fishing lines of cotton or silk were difficult to untangle and Campbell struggled with the bird nest for at least half an hour. Finally, he had the tangle straightened out and began winding the line back on his reel. When it tightened, he was surprised to feel something alive on the hook. He was even more surprised an instant later when a giant rolled on the surface and almost yanked the rod out of his hand. He later said that he thought one of the many playful otters on the island was on his hook, little suspecting a record bass.

Despite Campbell's surprise hookup, he eventually reeled his bass to boatside, scooped it up in his hands and sat on it as he hurried toward camp and the scales. The monster weighed 17-pounds, 4-ounces, still the Orange Lake record and one of the largest bass ever caught on a topwater by anyone anywhere. A tree growing near where he caught his fish is still known as the "Paw-Paw" tree.

The uniqueness of Campbell's strike and catch, is the foundation of my system of fishing for trophy bass on top today. He let his lure lie still for a long time. He later said it might have been more than half an hour after the backlash before he started reeling in his line.

That's my style now. I believe that really big bass despise an intruder in their territory, even if it is dead. If a lure doesn't move for a long period, the wallmounts apparently figure this is a dead fish that floats on the surface and must be dragged away. They will often do this even when they are not hungry and absolutely disinterested in any kind of food, artificial or natural. They will eyeball it for many minutes and make no move to strike it. But after awhile, they mouth the lure and start off with it, often hanging themselves on the multiple hook arrangement.

I fish Rapalas, Rebels, Bagleys and other topwater lures in Orange Lake, the Tsala Apopka chain, the Withlacoochee River and several small ponds in the Ocala National Forest territory. I catch some giant bass in all of those places by fishing big topwaters near cover. Generally, I cast, take the slack out of my line and let the lure float free for as much as half an hour if I am satisfied it is in a good spot and if the current isn't taking it away.

A hungry lunker there may strike the lure the instant it splashes on the surface. Indeed, I have seen big fish dive after a lure while it was in the air, coming to the spot it hits before the lure gets there. They definitely can see and do go after lures before they are in the water. But a big fish that is just lolling around with his stomach full often cares nothing for food. She will strike for some other reason, one of which is to remove an unwanted dead object from her haven. A topwater that is still minute after minute sometimes irritates the big mamas and you get a chance to add another wallmount catch to your statistics. Many of my big fish were caught after I watched a do-nothing topwater long enough to go to the bathroom or eat my lunch.

How many times on a slow day have you said to your fishing partner, "Well, I'll eat my lunch and sure as shooting I'll get a strike when I'm not expecting it?" You do. Most fishermen have experienced this many times.

Maybe your arm is tired from a thousand unsuccessful casts. You plop the lure out there in a hole, decide to drink a Coke or smoke a cigarette, leaving it floating quietly. Then bingo! The water explodes and your lure is gone. Most of the time it is so unexpected that you lose the fish. Generally those are lunkers that hit the dead-in-the-water lure because they wanted it moved out of their bailiwick. When you learn patience and fish these topwaters like you have the time to wait all day, you'll catch giants in places where most anglers fail to get a rise.

When I start out fishing early in the morning on lakes or streams where there are shorelines laced with lilies, weeds, overhanging bushes or cypress trees out in the water, I look for surface circles. These are little ripples caused by gambusia minnows or insects on the surface. If there are plenty of these little circles breaking up the calmness on a windless day, it means there is a lot of food in the area. If the forage fish are there, you can be sure the predators are not far behind. I cast along the fringes of this cover. If there's a hungry lunker around, I may get immediate action. If a lazy old mama is hiding with the territory staked out, I may have to let that Devilhorse float along for several minutes. Sometimes in canals, branches and creeks, you can't leave your lure alone. It drifts away and you have to cast much more rapidly than you would need to in a lake where there is little or no current or wind to push your topwater away from the cover.

I don't spend a lot of time in those areas after the sun rises an hour or so. I usually leave the topwater areas and go to the deeper holes where there is bottom cover. I can catch fish with my dead-on-the-bottom plastic worm system in those spots. Keep in mind that I am talking about catching big bass. The yearlings do not keep you waiting.

27

Whether it's topwater or worms on the bottom, patience is the name of the game and you have to learn to wait and wait and wait if you are after trophy bass and not just another yearling that may strike anything, anywhere and anytime. The really big ones are more persnickity than the youngsters that have not been educated.

Certainly R. W. Campbell's experience on Orange Lake was a lesson for all topwater anglers. His accidental delay in recasting resulted in his unusual catch. It taught me a lesson that I use every day. Big fish do not always strike from hunger but from frustration and good housekeeping instincts. If you understand the lifestyles and instincts of these monster bass, it goes a long way toward making you a successful big fish catcher. A totally unversed basser may catch a giant occasionally, but only those experienced wallmount catchers who study behavioral patterns and adapt their techniques to those lifestyles will record trophy catches year after year and in dozens of different waters.

Catching big bass is a learning experience and only the patient, motivated and determined fisherman will grasp the knowledge and eventually succeed.

You can be one of the successful. Just learn about the eyes, ears and noses of big bass and why they do what they do. The more knowledge you have of these factors, the better basser you'll be.

- - -

Many avid bass fishermen do not believe that fish go after a topwater lure **before** it hits the surface. But an expert like Douglas Hannon, of Odessa, Florida, says he has seen a big bass part the lilies and the grass seconds before it splashed down. They can see the object overhead and mistake it for a bird, frog or jumping forage fish and they can meet it on the surface with their mouths open, gulping it down before the slower predators get there. They have an amazing ability to forecast the exact splashdown spot from the trajectory that they observe.

Visual proof of the ability of fish to see an object in the air and give chase to it from their submerged position while it is still sailing overhead, can be observed daily at the Homosassa Attraction on U.S. Highway 19, in Citrus County, not far from where I live at Inverness.

28

The fishbowl at the attraction where millions of guests watch 32 species of fresh and saltwater fish cavort in the warm spring water as they come in from the Gulf of Mexico and the Homosassa River, is filled with jack crevalle, snook, sheepshead, mullet and other saltwater species as well as many freshwater fish. Attendants sell small herrings to tourists who feed them to the milling throng of expectant fish. You can toss one of these herring high in the air over the water and literally dozens of big fish will split the water and rush to where the bait comes down. You can try to fool them by faking a throw and not a fish will move. But once that herring is in the air, every predator in the area will fight for space at the end of the trajectory. It's absolute proof of how fish see and anticipate food even when it is fully airborne.

Topwaters Still Catch The Big Ones

I LEARNED A BASS LESSON
IN CAROLINA TOURNAMENT

Fifteen years ago I was following one of the professional bass fishing trails and an event at Currituck on the North Carolina coast carried me to that famous sound. This is a shallow water inlet separated from the Atlantic by a narrow spit of sand. This huge body of water has long been known as one of the finest bass fishing holes in the country. But when a northeast wind huffs and puffs over the dunes, it blows a lot of the water out of the sound. Often the water level will drop four or five feet in a few hours. It is dangerous then to have a boat in the water. You may not be able to get back to the dock or the launching ramp.

I was fishing the bass tournament on Currituck when one of these dangerous squalls hit and brought chaos to the more than 400 bassers competing. Bad weather has always been a challenge to me. The squall motivated me to do well despite the inclement weather and I putt-putted out into the sound to do my thing. Like so many other seemingly insignificant events in my life, that experience in the squall helped me to be a better bass fisherman.

Close to shore I saw a number of waist-deep wade fishermen. They were casting into the shallow holes in the thick milfoil, an exotic weed similar to hydrilla but not normally quite as difficult to fish as a healthy stand of hydrilla.

Despite the storm, you could see those waders dragging in bass regularly. They knew what they were doing. What kind of lure were they using? That was the foremost question in my mind. I kept waiting and watching patiently. Then I saw that the lure they were using was a bright, shiny thing that looked like a minnow and they were swimming it across the top of the milfoil, seldom hanging up. I quickly knew what that lure was.

Moments later I tied on a silver Johnson Spoon to my 10-pound test line. I eased my bass boat near shore and with the whitecaps breaking almost over the gunnels, I cast that spoon into the cover. Not before and never since have I seen such active bass strikes as I got that morning. A bass hit that spoon viciously on almost every cast.

I had to anchor the boat to stay in the area and several times I moved a few yards. But at no time did the action slow down. I landed 70 keepers in the milfoil that day, releasing all but the 14 I was allowed to weigh in. It was that day when I began loving the milfoil and the hydrilla. Bass were in the aquatic growth by the thousands and I cast and caught bass until I was totally fatigued.

The waders along the bank had caught fish all day, too. Everyone was casting and reeling. It was unbelievable. I learned that day to adapt to the lures and styles the natives liked. And I learned to fish the dense cover even if it did mean getting hung up a lot and losing some fish in the tangles. The milfoil held many bass as hydrilla does today.

I began operating Cypress Lodge on Lake Henderson, Highway 44 East of Inverness, Florida, in 1975. I was obsessed with bass fishing with artificial lures then as I am now. I was opposed to live bait fishing for bass as it seemed unchallenging to catch a fish with bait it ate normally. I wanted to catch my fish on manmade morsels that led the bass to make mistakes. I wanted to outsmart them. Now I know I have succeeded in my quest to become a good big bass angler.

After fishing in many states for years, I made my decision to rise or fall as a bass fishing guide in Central Florida. It was a lifestyle I coveted and I moved my family to Inverness. Today many of my clients say I am the "greatest artificial bait bass catcher in the world." I don't know whether I can appropriately wear that accolade or not. I don't want to identify myself with such greatness. I do know I can catch big bass on worms and topwaters. I think I have unlocked the secrets of fishing those lures.

I have caught all my big fish on eight to 10-pound test line. I believe you get more good strikes on the lighter test monofilament. I have mounted only 12 of my 321 trophy bass. I have released all of the others except a few that were gut hooked and died. I gave most of those to hospitals where they were enjoyed by the patients and my family ate a few that did not live. A few were mounted and donated to schools in the hope it would help create some fishing enthusiasts among the youngsters. But my policy is to release every bass I catch as long as it is healthy and my clients can keep only one trophy for their den walls. I believe we must preserve the resource and catch and release is one way of doing that.

32

My biggest fish was a 15-pound, 4-ounce giant I caught using my dead bait worm theory right in my back yard, Lake Henderson.

Some of my critics say I use line that is too light. I admit I do lose a few big fish that part the line and leave me fussing. But most of my bass are hooked in open water, often where there is submerged hydrilla, and if I use patience and know-how, along with good equipment and proper drag setting, I save most of the lunkers that I get on my hook. Anyhow, it is more fun to catch fish with light tackle than with well-windlass reels, broomstick rods and cowboy ropes for a line.

Dozens of outdoor newspaper and magazine writers have fished with me over the last 15 years. Generally, they are amazed at my unique dead-in-the-water lure technique. But it works as they often attest. It not only works for me, it is productive for my guiding associates and it will work for you if you have a little patience, nay, have considerable patience. Just locate the fish and stay with the pattern. You'll eventually succeed if the bass are there and no one can catch them by any technique if they are not.

Too many people want to carry home every fish they catch, size not withstanding. Too many people want to carry home a cooler full of bass fillets. And there is too much chemical spraying of the weed growth by wildlife agencies. What mother nature puts in the water ought to be left there, but obviously exotic transplants from other countries do throw nature out of balance. But when chemicals kill the pepper grass, water hyacinths and much of the other aquatic growth, you seal the doom of freshwater bass fishing. Bass must have the weeds and grass cover to reproduce and grow. I believe a lot of good habitat has been lost because of excessive chemical spraying. A little weed control is necessary in some spring-fed lakes with no dams or system for draw-downs, but when too much cover is destroyed bass populations suffer.

Thousands of bass anglers live a lifetime dreaming of the day they will catch one 10-pound bass just like hunters stalk gobbler turkeys for life and never get one in their sights. I use patience with knowledge of where fish can be found and that helps me put the giants in the boat. My 321 trophies may or may not be a record. Most people think it is, especially when you confine your technique strictly to artificials and public waters. But record or not, it has given me many great thrills and I believe you can catch those wallmount lunkers too. It's up to you to learn patience and technique and then get those lures where the bass are. If you are determined to get a big bass, you will. Confidence goes a long way toward success.

EMORY CATCHES GIANTS
FLYRODDING SHORELINES

Mark Emory is a unique Floridian who guides for salmon in Alaska in the summer, works with Sports City in Ocala in the winter, and fishes for bass every time he gets a chance. And he catches fish with a flyrod and big popping minnow topwater lures.

Emory catches a lot of fine bass with his flyrod equipment. He sometimes wades and at other times he casts from a boat. Always he fishes the weed or lily lines along the shore and bass gulp down his chartreuse and white bugs with gusto, sometimes splashing so loudly you can hear them a half football field away.

Emory likes Rat-L-Traps, Rebel and Bagley crankbaits when he is using casting or spinning tackle, but when he goes after the largemouths in Central Florida with a flyrod and popping bug, that's when he has all the confidence in the world.

CENTRAL FLORIDA
BASS BELT—FISHING PARADISE

By **Susan Cramer**
as told by
Bud Andrews

I think bass are the most challenging freshwater fish there are to catch, especially if you are a purist and do all your bassing with artificial lures. While it is challenging to catch bass, angling for the species is more than that. It teaches patience and appreciation for the great beauty of the outdoors. Those are plusses over and above the challenge to put a bass in the boat.

You can fish all day without catching a fish and still go home happy and without disappointment. You can admire the birds, the flowers, the alligators, in Central Florida and experience a rewarding day. Landing a bass is a bonus.

Yet, there is no denying that there is a special thrill in catching a big trophy bass with a manmade lure that is perfect enough to entice this important species into making a mistake. And that's what happens when you catch a fish on an artificial lure, you fooled her, you outsmarted one of nature's most remarkable creatures.

Some people wonder what inspires so many outdoorsmen to go after largemouth bass with a rod, reel and a piece of wood, plastic or rubber on a hook. And go after them they do, bass topping all of the 675 U.S. freshwater species among angling enthusiasts. This fish is the primary interest of 71 percent of licensed anglers in Florida where there are 115 species.

Central Florida is the real "Bass Belt," an angler's paradise. Fishermen in the Sunshine State spend $615 million a year stalking bass. The estimate is that 22,952,500 fishing trips a year in Florida have bass as the primary objective. These trips average costing the bass angler $26.79.

Bass anglers are confronted with many confusing decisions. What equipment will they buy? What rod, reel, line, lure? Remember, man caught fine bass in the yesteryears with a cane pole, hand-braided cotton line and some rustic homemade lures when he couldn't get a natural bait. While there has been a lot of sophistication of tackle and equipment, there is plenty of fun

35

for the novice with nothing much but desire. Humble techniques sometimes are successful.

But for most bassers, it takes patience and self-control. You must know where the bait fish are and that keeps you in control and successful. Beginners could find the array of tackle so confusing that the decision becomes a chore. But the more dedicated veterans of bass fishing enjoy trial and error and the success or failure of the products they buy while trying to lure a big bass to the boat. The multi-million dollar fishing tackle industry challenges the outdoorsman to select the best products for him and to put bass in the boat that are bigger than those caught with competing gimmicks.

My friend Doug Hannon, known widely as the "Bass Professor," lives at Odessa, Florida. He delves into the mysteries of this intriguing species and has devoted his life to freshwater bass. As a scientist and conservationist, he studies the species and understands how it sees, hears, feels and even smells. He has shared his research with anglers around the world and he notes that understanding the lifestyle is far more apt to make you a better bass catcher than having a tackle box full of lures and a boatload of electronic equipment.

He has designed lures, anchors, props, moon clocks, hook sharpeners and potions to help anglers in their pursuit of bass. But he says knowing where bass will be each of the seasons and at various times of day are more important than anything else in catching fish. He also recommends wearing muted colors, camouflaging your boat, keeping quiet and maintaining a low profile by sitting down.

Observing in a new river or lake by taking a few trips before you start fishing can be helpful. Acquaint yourself with the location of weed beds, canals, points and bottom cover. Think like a fish. If you were a bass , where would you be in this body of water at this time of year early, late and in the middle of the day? Just what spot would a bass be most likely to hide and catch a swimming bait fish for dinner?

Topographical maps of lakes and rivers are a help. If studied carefully, they may help you pick a spot where bass congregate and feed.

Often the best money you can spend when fishing a new lake or river is what you pay a knowledgeable guide. He will know every nook, slough and hole in the area and where fish are season by season and in good and bad weather. You may learn more in one day than you would in months without his services.

I can always tell an experienced bass angler from a novice when I go fishing with him. The experienced fisherman will want to know where the bait fish are. The novice will inquire about what color worm he should use. Bass will always be where the best supply of natural food can be found.

Unlike Hannon, I do not fish with live bait. I catch all my fish with artificial lures. It is more challenging to me. While most fishermen assume that a bass strikes a lure because she is hungry, I believe most of them strike from the irritation of a distracting foreign object in their feeding territory.

The artificial lure gets the attention of the bass by movement, sound, color and presentation. With my own unique technique, it gets the fish's attention by being out of place in what the bass considers his homeland. The fish doesn't like to have an intruder, even a dead one, cluttering up his domain. After a long wait, she drags it away.

Some artificial lure anglers believe that bass caught on these man-made baits can be removed from the fish after she is caught better than you can the hooks in natural baits. They are not swallowed as deeply and can be removed without as much danger to the life of the bass. The released bass has a better chance of surviving.

Releasing bass has become the vogue in this generation. Damage to bass populations from pressure, pollution, chemicals, housing developments, and excessive weed harvesting, among other things, has curtailed catchable bass numbers almost everywhere. In an effort to replenish the population, catch and release has become popular among bassers since the 1960's.

If you ask a dozen fishermen what is the best lure on which to catch a bass, you'll probably get a dozen different answers. The opinions vary greatly. But the majority would agree upon the plastic worm. It can be fished many different ways. The Texas Rig is popular with the worm fished on the bottom behind a sinker. The Swimmin' Worm retrieved slowly in shallow water catches fish. The Do Nothin' Worm catches bass by lolling around on the bottom or being twitched.

Topwater lures come in an endless variety and many bass anglers consider a strike on the surface more thrilling than any other kind of hit. You get the thrill of sight and sound. Propeller types like Devilhorse and Heddon Tiny Torpedo are hard to beat.

37

Hoppers and chargers like Zara Spook and Burke's Top Dog are producers. Professional Charlie Campbell is among the more famous bassers for catching fish on the Zara Spook. The wobblers like the Jitterbug catch fish and the minnow-types are legend. Rapala, Rebel, Storm, Norman, Bagley and dozens of others make successful minnow replicas that catch big bass. Generally, the minnow-types are more successful in shallow water when the temperature is warm in spring and fall. They are also good for night fishing.

Trolling is a desirable form of bass fishing for a few avid sportsmen who swear by the system. This society of bassers uses some form of crankbait that imitates fish or crawfish. Among the most popular are the Hellbender and Bomber. These lures are deep divers that wobble as they move over obstructions. White and red and white are the most popular. Wilbur Haymaker, who lives in Alachua County, Florida, prefers the big gold Rat-L-Trap for trolling and he has caught more than 3,000 bass on that lure. He also likes used, battered lures better than new ones.

Spinner baits are among the most productive lures in the spring. They excite sluggish, lazy bass. Fitted with a multitude of colored skirts that camouflage hooks, bass often go after spinners when other lures fail. The gold colored spinner is generally considered best for dingy water while the silver blade is better in clear water. Spinner baits are ideal in holes in grass beds, lily pads and near brush and log cover.

Artificial lures require special techniques in various depths of water, seasons, temperatures and other factors. But there are many that excel when properly presented by experts.

Live bait bass anglers use everything from native wild shiners in Florida to tiny turtles and crawfish. Shiners are by far the most popular of the live, natural baits. Shiners caught in the river or lake where you are fishing still have the fear instinct and react with panic to the presence of bass or other predators in the area. This prompts vicious strikes. Live baiters generally insist that you will be the most successful with live shiners if you catch them in the water where you are fishing. Bait fish raised in tanks commercially will not work as effectively, many bass catchers insist. There are those who disagree. Steve Lloyd, a veteran live bait bass guide at Roland Martin's Marina at Clewiston, Florida, says that while native shiners at times are superior, he has seen seasons when the domestic variety were more productive than the wild native baits. Perhaps they were easier for the predators to catch.

Florida has a record bass listed at 20-pounds, 2-ounces. It was caught by Frederick Joseph (Fritz) Freibel in a private pond in Pasco County in May of 1923. Before that fish was recognized, W.A. Witt, of Tarpon Springs, held the bass record with a 19-pound bass caught on a live eel in Lake Tarpon near his home.

The biggest bass caught recently was a 17-pound, 4-1/4-ounce fish pulled in by Billy M. O' Berry from a Polk County pit on July 6, 1986.

Authorities like Hannon believe that if any bass is ever caught that surpasses the George Perry record 22-pounds, 4-ounces, caught in Georgia, June 2, 1932, in Lake Montgomery, it will come from the "Bass Belt" in Central Florida. This is the area from Tampa through Gainesville where largemouth of giant size are still caught every year from the thousands of lakes and streams that cover the area.

Only two years ago, Harry Woods, of Mascotte, Florida, landed a 15-pound, 4-ounce bass on a cane pole while fishing for speckled perch in a citrus grove pond in Lake County. It was a record bass caught without benefit of a rod and reel.

If you dream of sometime catching the next world record largemouth bass, I believe your best chance is in Central Florida. There are still many almost pure streams unpolluted by man's intrusion and, despite heavy fishing pressure, there is sufficient cover for some old cannibalistic bass to live to a ripe old age of 12-15 years and reach monster proportions.

Here are a few of the best big bass places to fish in Central Florida:

Lake Tsala Apopka—In Citrus County, this chain stretches from Floral City to Hernando. It connects with the Withlacoochee River by canals. There are public ramps in Hernando County, south of the intersection of U.S. 41 and S.R. 200; another is located off S.R. 44 east of Inverness and still another is on S.R. 48 on the Duval Island Road, east of Floral City.

Moon Lake—Located six miles east of New Port Richey, this fish management area is promising. Ramps are on S.R. 587.

Withlacoochee River—Flowing through Sumter, Citrus, Marion and Levy counties, there are inviting stretches around Dunnellon and from Inglis to Yankeetown. Ramps are located at all of these towns and villages.

Crystal River—Fed by many springs, this short, clear river in Citrus County grows monster size bass. Good public access ramps are located at Crystal River off U.S. Highway 19.

Homosassa River—This nine-mile long river flows into the Gulf of Mexico from the deep spring at the Homosassa Attraction in Citrus County off U.S. Highway 19.

Lake Tarpon—Ramps are located on the lake three miles southeast of the town of Tarpon Springs on U.S. 19.

Fishing Up a Storm:
Foul Weather Provides Excellent Fishing

Veteran bass fishing guides and tournament professionals have long lauded overcast skies and stiff breezes as a better time to catch fish than blue-bird days when nature smiles on the land and the lakes. Few have gone so far as to say that the best time to catch bass is during rough fall and winter storms when most anglers are relaxing by a fire.

I guess I am an exception. Give me that stormy weather any time. I'll put more big bass in the boat then than I could ever catch on a so-called pretty day. I recall a memorable stormy day five years ago when the inclement weather was my choice time for catching wallmounts.

This 10-pound, 3-ounce trophy was caught in December 1989 in 40 degee weather

I remember many successful experiences when the weather turned foul and most avid anglers tied up their boats for the duration. But on the Tsala Apopka chain in Central Florida where I live, I watch for those ominous storm warnings when the cumulus clouds cruise across the sky. Gale-force winds sweep through the cypress tree tops. I know fantastic bassing times are approaching. I grab my foul-weather gear, bass tackle, a good life preserver and head my Ranger into the breakers. Waves roar across Little Lake Henderson at Cypress Lodge when the gales set in.

You must not forget to be careful when you fish those fall and winter storms. The waves often break across the gunnels of my big boat. I always keep the bilge pump going so water doesn't flood the deck. The sturdy Ranger won't sink even when it is full of water, but fishing is more comfortable if the boat is light and dry.

I will admit that there are times when I must surrender to the storm even when big bass are fighting to strike every lure tossed at them. Hurricane force winds, even when I am fishing close to shore are often entirely too severe to fish. Always, you must practice safety. No fish is worth getting dumped in the lake.

I'll never forget the cold, windy fall morning when Hurricane Helen swept in here from the Gulf of Mexico. Gale-force winds rolled up four-foot swells on the lake. For the first time in my life, I could see huge schools of bass in the curls of the breakers, even from the dock and the shoreline at Cypress Lodge.

My buddy, Jake Chastain, pulled his raincoat around his neck and walked out on the pier in the teeth of the storm. In disbelief, he turned to me with excited eyes. "Do you see what I see?"

I nodded and grinned. I knew what he was seeing. In the tops of those noisy breakers you could see spots of black. That tell-tale black was the tails of lunker largemouth bass that were caught up in the turmoil, the churning water. The storm had brought chaos to an otherwise serene fishing paradise. Bass instinctively know about storms and resulting atypical feeding conditions. Inclement weather alters behavioral patterns. Rather than scooting into deep holes in cover and staying put until a hurricane blows itself out, bass seem to grasp the gravity of the situation. They understand the storm and how it can momentarily change their lifestyles. Something tells them that it may be hard to catch a stomach full of forage fish for a day or two. They become super active, hyper, and scramble to fill their bellies. Frantically, they explode after food all over the surface. Forage fish sense the storm too, and they dash around in a frightened dither all over the open water.

Bass instinctively read the wind, storm and waves. It might be a week before such a bonanza of food again will be available. The bass are opportunists. They brave the weather to satisfy their hunger. I can recall my observations from that and many other storms that have roared across Central Florida during my guiding career.

Two lunkers caught in a gale

Ironically, these furious winds create a heyday for winter bass fishermen. It's unlike anything most anglers ever saw.

Donning my rain gear and with a quality life-preserver firmly tied around me, I jumped in my wave-rocked boat and motored off into the teeth of Hurricane Helen in mid-morning.

I didn't have to go far. I could see those black bass tails in the curls of the waves just a few yards from the hill. I ran right into the breakers, put my outboard in neutral and left it running. I knew it was no use trying to anchor. If the boat got sideways, I might need to move fast and head back into the waves to avoid swamping.

I had hooked a 1/2 ounce chrome Rat-L-Trap on my 12-pound test line before I untied my boat. I was glad I did because the water was so rough I had to hang on to the Ranger's gunnel railing with one hand while casting into the breakers with the other.

On the first cast I hooked a lunker. It was a struggle to get her to the boat. I finally did. She weighed 7 1/2 pounds, something I learned later at the dock. I just dropped her in the livewell and kept casting. Bass were fighting each other to get to the lure. Three times in an hour I doubled with two bass at a time on the same small crankbait with its treble hooks. Others chased hooked fish to the boat.

Finally, I was exhausted from reeling, casting and struggling to stay in the boat. I could still see the bass in the breakers. I decided to make one more cast. I underhanded the Rat-L-Trap about 30 feet into an on-rushing wave. I thrilled when I felt a hard hit. I set the hook. Even that was difficult in the melee. I grinned in the storm. The fish jumped twice and finally broke off the lure. She was gone! But I'm sure I lost my largest bass ever in that stormy, memorable moment. I previously landed a 15-pounder in this same spot, but that fish was even larger. I remember that unbelievable day with nostalgic chagrin. I was so excited I felt like minnows were flouncing in my veins.

Often that's the way it is in a storm. It is also true that on very cold days you may have the success story of your life in Florida. The bass turn on when the weather is bad, whether from wind or extreme cold.

Summarizing my adventure that day in the bowels of Hurricane Helen, I brought 28 bass to the dock. I kept them in my holding tank until the hurricane subsided, and released them. They all survived to thrill other anglers.

In addition to the first lunker that was a 7 1/2-pounder, I had eight fish that were even larger, one a 10-pound trophy. And then there is always the cherished memory of the giant that got away.

I remember the wind was even worse the next morning and sheets of rain blew across Little Lake Henderson so hard that the drops of water felt like sand was blasting my face. The bass were still gorging themselves. I caught 38 that day in the storm, four that topped 10-pounds.

The hurricane passed on. The bass apparently knew the chaotic bonanza was over. The wind stopped. You couldn't buy a bite. Bass went on a lockjaw strike. I believe that they ate so much those two days that they were not the least bit hungry for a week.

The days immediately after a storm are like those following a front. Bass won't strike and are inactive. I have witnessed several similar feeding frenzies of bass before and during high winds and extreme weather before cold fronts. I stick to my theory that bass consume enough food to hold them over for days. Like the biblical stories of Joseph in Egypt, it was a time of plenty followed by a famine. The bass seem to have read the weather reports, and reacted to survive the ordeal. It is an angler's dream, except for the discomfort of fishing from a boat that constantly bounces around and stands on its ends.

My recollection about the bass that got away in the storm is a classic. It's true—the big ones really do get away. They have the power, weight and experience to test and sometimes subdue the fisherman and his very best equipment. That big mama put a licking on me that stormy morning.

Don't Use Bad Weather As An Excuse for Getting Skunked

Extreme cold often gives even good bass fishermen an excuse for coming in skunked. But I have never been shirt-tailed when bass guiding or fishing in a tournament. I believe you can catch fish despite the cold weather, at times even better than you can when all the elements are stable and appear perfect.

I must be able to carry my clients out and catch bass when it is cold, and even when there are high winds. Many of them drive hundreds of miles to fish a few days. It may be their vacation time and the only chance they have to try to catch a Florida trophy bass.

Tournament professionals have to fish the inclement weather, too. Few events are cancelled because of wind, cold or rain. On the premise that the weather conditions are the same for everyone, they roar off from the starting point and do their best to catch bass despite the "bad" weather. It's important that those pros, and guides who assist winter tourists, know how to succeed in all kinds of conditions.

Successful fishing in the cold and wind in the South is always possible, even easy. You have to know something about the lifestyle of the Florida bass and how they react to temperatures below freezing. (We do have some 20-30 degree weather a few days in winter in Central Florida). The bass do what we humans do. They eat and stay comfortable. They look for places where they can loll around until the cold goes away and the weather breaks. They find those places and it is my job as a guide to find them. I can do it. And so can the better, experienced professional bassers.

I remember numerous successes catching lunkers when it was topcoat weather, rainy and often windy, too.

The limestone underground in much of Florida is like a heater. Spring water gushes out from the deep holes in the earth (headwaters for many short rivers). It flows through dense jungle rain forests. The water from the springs has a year 'round temperature between 68 and 72 degrees. As much as 7,000,000 gallons of this warm water spews out of these holes in the earth hourly, and every fish in the state would like to enjoy the comforts of living in that spring water.

When the inclement winter weather turns the fish off in the usual cover that I find them, I go to my honey hole spring runs. In Citrus County, just a few miles from where I live at Inverness, there are many such spring-fed rivers. Among the most productive is the Weeki Wachee, just off U.S. Highway 19 near Brooksville. This water is as clear as that from your bathroom tap. It's not easy to catch bass in such eutrophic rivers but there are always some tributaries, creeks and branches with slightly dingy water in deep holes. Big bass suspend in those holes in the coldest weather.

Other nearby spring-fed rivers are the eight-mile long Homosassa, the Crystal and Hall rivers within half an hour of my home base. The Withlacoochee River and Lake Rousseau are prolific waters and among my favorites for so-called bad weather winter fishing. This river and lake are wilderness areas where any outdoorsman would enjoy fishing if he didn't get a strike all day. But we catch fish in these desolate waters where bass love the comfort of the warm, moving water when other lakes have temperatures dipping down into the 50's and even the 40's.

Other great spots for cold weather bassing are the Chassahowitzka and Waccasassa rivers. I catch some of my finest trophies in these spring-run honey holes in the winter. The Rainbow River is another of my favorite cold weather spots.

At times, I travel as much as an hour or more to fish a particularly good spring run that I know is protected from the wind by dense shoreline cypress groves that make my fishing clients more comfortable.

Lake Kerr is another of the clear waters that I like to fish in the worst winter weather. It is relatively shallow and the bass have always been plentiful in Kerr. It's near Salt Springs and the St. Johns River, and has some excellent trophy bass holes.

The huge Harris chain of lakes in Lake County has many tributaries where water pours in through canals from the Clermont chain and other waterways. Often the bass fishing is fantastic where these runs have beaten out deep holes as they flow into Lake Harris. These are choice winter bassing locations

Co-Author Carter with wintertime Florida bass

where you can usually get some shoreline protection from the cold wind and rain.

Most of my modern-day record catch of trophy bass were caught using my dead-on-the-bottom and dead-on-the-surface techniques with a Culprit worm and a Rapala or other floater. All were on artificials, but a few were caught with other lures. In my wintertime successful jaunts, I still use those techniques. I seldom catch bass on a real cold day on top. My curly tail worm fished perfectly motionless on the bottom in the creeks and spring-runs gets a lot of strikes. I catch fish regardless of the temperature.

If you have confidence and some knowledge of where the spring-fed streams are located, you don't have to hang up your tackle when other anglers lean back and enjoy the fireplace. You bundle up with an extra pair of wool socks, tighten a heavy coat around your chest and pull the ear muffs from inside your cap. It's amazing how warm it gets in an open bass boat when a 10-pounder splashes on the surface and is scooped up in the net.

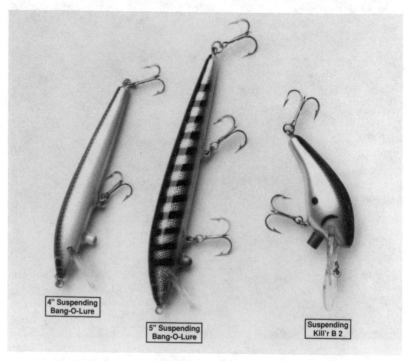

4" Suspending
Bang-O-Lure

5" Suspending
Bang-O-Lure

Suspending
Kill'r B 2

Many pros like Bang-O-Lures in bad weather

Recipe for Wee Hour Bassing
On the Tsala Apopka

A big plus for night fishing success on the 24,000 acre, six-lake chain of the Central Florida snake-like Tsala Apopka waters stretching from Floral City in the south to Hernando in the north, is knowing when to fish. At least that is my key.

Contrary to many conventional night bassers, I do not get up from the dinner table, step into my boat and go back on the water to fish. After all, fishing over 300 days a year in the sunshine with some demanding clients would exhaust most guides at 48 years of age. This New Jersey native often does his night fishing just for the fun of it. He enjoys the serenity and beauty of night on the Tsala Apopka even when he doesn't add to his impressive list of monster bass.

It's so pretty and calm with ideal temperatures most of the year, and I feel mighty close to God and nature when I'm out here on the lakes in the wee hours of the morning. And it is the wee hours that I prefer to fish at night. There are several reasons.

First, it gives me a little chance to rest after my daytime fishing. And I don't get much rest during the week when I fish five days in a row. I refuse to guide on Saturday and Sunday. Those are my days to stay in camp and the lakes are usually too full of water skiers and fishermen to do much guiding anyway. Monday is not a good day after the turmoil of the weekend, but I do fish Mondays.

Second, I like to get out on the lake about 2:00 to 3:00 A.M. because then the mosquitoes that are vicious in the early evening virtually disappear. The insects are not a problem and often these are the most windless hours of the day and night. That calmness helps me observe the shad rings that polka-dot the surface and when those signs of forage fish are present, I know the big bass predators are there, too. It's one of the best ways I have of locating big bass. Those circles on the surface indicate to me that bass are around.

A third reason in the summer months is the comfortable temperature. It may be near 100 degrees in the daytime, but always it is bearable, even desirable in the wee hours and you can cast without dripping wet with sweat. Even in summer, when showers are a harassment to bass fishing much of the day, there are very few mornings before dawn when rain is a problem.I am an Air Force veteran and I began my Florida fishing more than two decades ago when I was in the service and learned about the trophy bass population here. After returning to my lucrative Ford Motor Company position in New Jersey, my wife Kathy and I returned to Florida and bought Cypress Lodge in 1975. I began pursuing my cherished guiding career, a dream of a lifetime.

My corps of guiding assistants and I, who carry clients out for bass more than 750 fishing days a year, are moon watchers. Whether the angling is in the daytime or at night, we believe in fishing "the bright side of the moon."

From the new moon to the full moon is my choice for night fishing. Bass will not bite much the night of the full moon because it is so light they gorge themselves on the shad and minnows, and don't pay much attention to our artificial lures. The three days just before that full moon are ideal times for night fishing, and then a night or two after the full moon, the bass turn back on and we catch 'em pretty good.

Bass feel more secure at night. The boat traffic is not as disturbing to them and they can't see the fishermen on the surface very well. They may venture further from the deep water , however, under wee hour darkness, but always near enough to the holes to make a mad dash for the depths when they are hooked.

These are my lure preferences for wee hour bassing the Tsala Apopka:

My preference the first couple of hours when I am night fishing is a big, broken-back Jitterbug by Arbogast, and Rat-L-Trap's new Floater. You must know how to fish it, and that means learning how to move it and when to leave it alone. I believe that most people move their topwaters and their worm lures too much. I like to cast my lure and let it float, often for 15 minutes or more. The wee hour weather most often is calm, and that shadow on the surface looks easy and catchable to a big bass eyeballing it from below. She is more likely to hit it after it floats there awhile than when it plops down or when you twitch it. But there are no absolutes in bass fishing. Sometimes it seems the bass was just lying there waiting for the plug to hit and gulped it down before the ripples disappeared. But that 's not normal with me. As a professional, I have learned how and when to move that lure to entice strikes. I'm a slow, still fisherman.

It's usually small yearlings that hit a surface bait fast. The real lunkers are much slower to strike. They study the object, look it over and may then decide it's worth biting. I believe this is normally a hit from frustration or an invasion of the fish's territory rather than from hunger. If they think it is dead, the really big trophies may strike it. They know it isn't supposed to be there. I always fish slower at night.

The Jitterbug and Rat-L-Traps are not

Andrews' 4-Year-Old son John poses with Dad after trophy hit a topwater lure at night

the only good nighttime topwaters. Rebel and Rapala have big surface lures that work well, as do Storm, Bagley and Norman. I have just been spoiled with my success with the Jitterbug and it works for me. If there are some lights along the shoreline, the horizon, it helps silhouette a big plug. It makes it easier for the bass to see and to strike.

I have fished with some clients in the wee hours who believed a lure had to be jerked and bulldozed on the surface to attract attention. They would bury its nose in the water they retrieved it so fast. That's not my idea of how to night fish a topwater, but one man's trash is another man's treasure.

If I have fished patiently with my topwaters for a couple of hours and had little success, I shift to the old reliable Culprit plastic worm. When everything else sours, the worm will work, and I have caught 30 or 40 of my largest trophy bass with a worm,

51

fishing in the wee hours of morning. While I use the topwater during the prime time, often it is the poorer times that I have my success when I shift to the worm. Sometimes in the hot months of July and August, I'll actually fish the worm before I do the topwater. Floated on the surface, it is attractive to big bass, but they will also pick it up off the bottom when you fish it dead for several minutes. Again, I am unorthodox with my worm action. I am inclined to fish it slow like it was dead rather than giving it the conventional action.

As I have said, there are no real absolutes in night fishing. While I believe in slow movement and dead-in-the-water lures, there are times when buzzbaits will work, on top and moving. It's my commotion pattern. A number 11 or 13 gold Rapala sometimes will get big bass strikes by yanking and jerking it violently for a few seconds on top. Maybe it wakes up some of the old mamas that are not disturbed by the slower action lures that I prefer.

Where is the best place on a lake or a chain to night fish is a likely question that I am asked many times every year. Of course, it helps to know your fishing water to begin with. Where you catch fish in the daytime is likely to hold fish at night as well, but they may venture out further from their deepwater hiding places or into dense cover that protects them in the daylight. The big ones will always be close to the deep water or the cover or both.

I like to fish any concrete bridges or abutments that are in the lakes. I like to anchor some distance from the bridge supports and cast long—way back under the bridge where it is real quiet and still. The noise of the lure striking the surface echoes against the banks, and I think it gets the attention of the bass. They may wait awhile, but I believe they look it over and analyze what it is making such a disturbance.

If there are some good shallow points short distances away from a bridge, I'll stop there and fish awhile between 2:30 in the morning and safe light. Often the bass are on those points feeding and looking around before sunup. They will slink back to safer havens once it is good light. But they are night feeders off points.

In lakes like we have on the Tsala Apopka where there are numerous kicker trails through the grass and lily pads, I stop 30 yards short of the canal entrance and fish the opening intensely. Big bass often hang around this open water at night. If I get no

52

strikes in the mouth of the kicker canal, I'll slowly move up the path being as quiet and slow as I can. Sometimes the big fish may be way up the canal. These big fish are smart. You have to outfox them with your expertise in handling a lure in the canals or anywhere else that they are holding in shallow water.

I remember fishing a big silver Rebel topwater one morning about 3:00 when I just got too excited to be successful. A real giant largemouth popped out of the lilies along a canal path, and my lure disappeared. Instinctively, I yanked to set the hook, but I had forsaken one of my prime resolutions—always be patient. Before I could think, I had taken the lure right out of that big bass's mouth and she was gone. That fish mastered me that morning. She was smarter than I was and I'll not forget that soon. She was a real trophy bass.

In lakes where there are piers, big fish often hang around. Forage bait fish are plentiful around many piers, and the big predators stake out a claim there. They are more inclined to hang around the piers at night than in the daytime and are pretty easy to catch.

My pier theory has a lot of followers. A 16-year-old youngster fishing a private pier in the 2,200 acre Lake Sampson near Starke, Florida, in 1986 cast a worm a few yards from the pier and dragged out a 14-pound largemouth. In 1987 he did even better, catching a 16-pounder from the same pier. The big trophies certainly do like to hang out around the man-made structures, often where there is a lot of nearby aquatic growth. Some pier owners plant brush and cover around piers to entice the forage fish and the predators that follow. It helps to hold them.

Many of the piers on the Tsala Apopka and other lakes of Central Florida where there has been much shoreline development, have several big bass hiding out in those shadows. It's a good place to catch trophy size bass day or night. They get used to seeing people.

I like to fish these spots when I know there is some five or six foot water that the fish can find in the daytime. They just won't stay in water much shallower than that when it is a bluebird day. I've caught some nice fish in one foot of water, but it was only a few seconds away from much deeper spots with cover.

Wind is sometimes an asset to big bass fishing, particularly in the daytime when it can help to obscure an angler and his boat on the surface. At night, the calmer the water the better for me. I like it calm and quiet, and when you hang up with a big fish out there that you can't see for a minute or two, it's very exciting. Night fishing the wee hours turns me on, and I never make more noise than is necessary. But in the daytime, when the fishing is slow, I'll sometimes run my motor right into the cover and whirl it around a time or two. I wake the fish up. You don't do that kind of thing at night. You stay quiet. You know the fish are prowling, not just resting in the shade. I like a little wind in the daytime.

I know where most of the choice spots for big lunkers are here on Henderson, Spivey and Little Lake Spivey. I went to one of these spots often one summer and caught 12 trophy bass— one that weighed 11-pounds, 3-ounces. Of course, I released them all. I have only my three original trophies mounted. I have had several other big bass that died from being gut hooked. I hate for that to happen, but when it does, I have the bass mounted and hung in a school building. It's good for the children to see and talk about.

I don't believe in bed fishing the big bass. They need a chance to reproduce. While we fish the year around, we never purposely catch a mama bass on the bed. When we do, we release the fish, but we do not want to disturb bedding bass. Any fool can catch a big bass off the bed. It takes more expertise and experience to catch one not bedding. I like that challenge. And I can catch my share without breaking up a nest.

I am not a big believer in the various fish scent concoctions being used widely by the professionals and others today. I do douse my Culprit worms into some of the stuff in a plastic bag before I impale the bait on my custom-sharpened hook. I replace my worms after every strike or hang-up.

I put the fish scent on the worm more to get rid of the human smell than to attract bass to my worm. I think you can camouflage the worm smell by washing it down with this oily stuff.

Night fishing is a specialty of mine, but I am still learning. I have never been skunked in more than 15 years of guiding. I have more than half a hundred trophies in my den that attest to my professional tournament successes years ago. I do not mount bass any more. I release them.

54

New Pen Worm---
Sensationally Productive Bass Lure

My fifth and latest technique for catching largemouth bass was born late in 1989 when Culprit introduced the Pen Worm that I think tempts bass more than any other lure. I began fishing it, as did my guide associates at Cypress Lodge, late in October, and before 12 months passed, we documented total catches of more than 5,000 bass, all caught in Central Florida.

This fantastic success was enjoyed mostly in the Tsala Apopka Chain, but we used it in other waters within an hour or two of our home base at Inverness. We have found that it may not attract as many of the wallmounts, 10-pounds and above, but it is a great lure for the 4, 5 and 6-pounders with an occasional 8 and 9-pound bass gulping it down.

The first day I tried the Pen Worm with my clients, we dragged in 35 bass in about five hours. Doug Ellinghaus, a veteran guide who works with me, caught 40 bass with his clients the first day he tried the revolutionary technique, and Tom Guertin, another of my guides, has been catching from 240 to 275 every five days that he has guided. The three of us in 10 months have pulled in more than 5,000 bass over the gunnels. Of course, we have released virtually all of them, but the worm has certainly made bass fishing great fun for us and our customers in recent months.

This 6-inch worm comes with a rake tail. We bite off the tail to start with. We think that is one of the secrets to the worm's being so productive. We prefer the Tequila Shad color, and we hook it right through the midsection with a 4/0 hook. Using no weight at all, and with 8- or 10-pound test Triple Fish line, we flip it out from the boat where it almost floats for an instant. Then it very slowly filters down toward the bottom.

Hooked in this manner, the Pen Worm looks like a U-shaped worm that has fallen in the water and is sinking. Nothing could look more natural. A live night crawler will usually float down in this manner, and the artificial is a perfect mimic of the real thing.

We use a No. 10 swivel on a 10- to 12-inch leader. We double the test line. This gives us 16-pound strength when we are using 8-pound test line and 12-pounds when we are using

6-pound test. The swivel is the only weight we put on the line, and it is just right for slowly dragging the worm to the bottom. Bass simply cannot reject such a tempting mouthful, and that's why we have called it the "Temptation Rig." Culprit is now using that description of the Pen Worm rigged as we fish it.

The 4/0 hook stuck through the midsection leaves the point exposed and each end of the worm dangles and swings freely, much like a real worm would do that is washed into the water.

An earthworm doesn't swim like an eel. It curls up. The life-like effect of this rig with the short Pen Worm looks and acts differently from the other curly tail or paddle worms. It looks like a real earthworm in the water.

The small swivel between the line and the leader properly balances the rig, and I like to use a spinning reel on a 6-foot, medium-light action rod. Line size for maximum action with this worm should be either 6-, 8- or 10-pound test.

When I cast this Temptation Rig into a bass honey hole, I allow it to sink and stay put for about 10 seconds. Then I give it a twitch or two, and slowly retrieve it to the boat. It is a deadly lure as my guides, clients and I have proven since its introduction, as long as it is in the water

Another of its attributes is the way fish are hooked quickly and easily when they strike this U-shaped bait. Almost always they gulp it down in one quick strike. We seldom miss a strike. There is no waiting and wondering. As soon as you feel a tap, you set the hook. Most of the time you will come in with a largemouth that mistakes the Pen Worm for a real night crawler. You must have more brains than a bass has to tell the difference.

You can also use the Pen Worm as a swimming rig. Fished in this manner, I use a 2/0 hook on a 12-inch leader, and I stick the hook through the side of the worm's head about 1/4 inch from the end. I leave the hook point exposed, and I slip a 1/8-ounce black bullet sinker above the No. 10 swivel when I cast the swimmer into the grass and cover.

This rig is surprisingly weedless, generally swimming across lily pads and grass easily. It does not cause much line twist because of the swivel. I have my best success with the swimming rig by fishing it about six inches under the surface. It has a lot of action at that depth.

The third familiar way of fishing worms is the Texas Rig that all the professionals know about. I use a 4/0 hook threaded

Andrews (right) and Client with 12-pounder

into the head of the worm and brought out between 1/4 and 1/2 inch down. I pull the hook almost through the Pen Worm and turn it around so the point can be pushed back into the plastic. This makes it self-weedless, and when it is rigged properly, the worm will hang straight and you retrieve it straight.

A 1/8 ounce bullet sinker is ideal for the lightweight Pen Worm when being fished in this manner. You need the weight to make it sink quickly.

Pen Worms are only 6 inches long, and they are made in 8 colors, including solid, shad and fleck selections. They are packed in 20-count resealable bags, and special flavors built into the plastic tempt bass into more strikes. At least that's my belief about this worm that our experience seems to document.

I think this worm is the ultimate finesse lure because it is slender with a no-swim body. It has the ability to be rigged in dozens of different styles, and it is made in so many colors it is adaptable in all waters.

In 1989 when I landed my 324th trophy bass weighing 10-pounds or more, I made this U-shaped rigged bait the fifth of my techniques. The other systems include the dead-on-the-bottom worm that lunkers pick up after waiting a long time; the bumping worm that I twitch occasionally on the bottom; the topwater minnow-like lure by Rapala and Rat-L-Trap, among others; and my skip-jack technique of violently yanking these topwaters off the surface as soon as they hit, and letting them jump four or five feet before plopping down again.

It's these unique techniques that have made it possible for me to land so many wallmount-size largemouths in a relatively few years, and I know that others can catch these trophy-size fish, too, if they will use the patience that you must have and then perfect the presentations.

I enjoy devoting part of my time toward helping environmental groups and sharing my fishing acumen with civic clubs, government organizations, wildlife federations and especially young people who are interested in angling. I talk to these youngsters in the hope that it will broaden their education and excitement for the out-of-doors.

While fishing is my life and my livelihood, I continue my determination to couple successful angling with my ideals and good sportsmanship. I enjoy my seminars that I put on periodically at Valdosta State College in Georgia, and I strive to leave information in the minds of those students that while catching

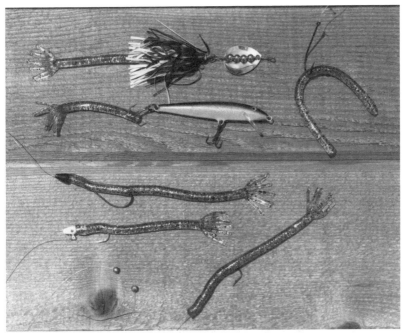

Pen Worm--- The ultimate finesse bait

fish is important, taking care of the environment and the species is paramount.

I have always loved to fish since my father began carrying me when I was a small boy in New Jersey. He impressed upon me the need for conservation, and as I have grown older, I realize many of the truths he taught me. He passed away when I was a teenager, but I'll never forget those great lessons that he taught me. I hope to pass some of those along to the youngsters who attend my seminars today.

Catching trophy bass was once much easier than it is today. There is a lot of public interest and fishing pressure now. I once averaged at least three big bass a month, but it took me a long time to go from number 323 to 324. Yet, with good equipment and techniques, patience, self-discipline, determination and conservation, there will always be some trophy large-mouths to catch.

I thank God every day for the bass we have to catch and for my love of fishing. I love to get up in the morning and head out across a beautiful lake or stream in search of another lunker. When I get up one morning,and I am not thankful for that opportunity, I'll quit fishing

Triple Fish
Line For Lunkers

There are many good monofilament lines today that will hold almost any trophy bass. They include DuPont's Stren and Prime, Berkley's Trilene, Bagley's Silver Thread, Courtland, Ande and others. But the line that the champion live bait trophy bass catcher endorses is the Triple Fish Cameo Escent. Distributed by Triple Fish, 321 Enterprise Drive, Ocoee, Fl. 34761, the Bass Professor, Doug Hannon, is explicit. "It is a great camouflaged plastic line that the fishermen can see yet it hides itself in the water," Hannon says. "Bass seldom see it."

I have now switched to this line too. When I started my great experiences with the relatively new Culprit Pen Worm, I began using the Triple Fish brown line, later changing to the camouflaged line that my friend Doug Hannon enthusiastically endorsed. I quickly found that this was a great line for aritificial bait bass fishermen, just as it is for the natural bait anglers like Hannon who now has caught more than 600 bass 10-pounds or heavier.

My guides and I now swear by this innovation in fishing line that I think has as much to do with catch success as the lure, tackle and expertise. Triple Fish is a breakthrough in plastic line that has rapidly built a name among trophy bass anglers everywhere

Andrews meets with Lowndes Middle School in Valdosta, Ga. They look over his Culprit Worm selection and instructor Lindy Evans points out his favorite worm

THE ORIGINAL RAT-L-TRAP®

Original
RAT-L-TRAP®

AMERICAS' #1 SELLING RATTLING BAIT

1/2 oz. Selected by a panel of experts as one of the all time top ten lures, the Rat-L-Trap has earned its place in history. It's great for bass, walleye, trout, salmon, stripers and many other fresh and saltwater species. The Rat-L-Trap...truely the most innovative and immitated lure on the market today.

MAG-TRAP™
3/4 oz.

MINI-TRAP®

1/4 oz. Most fishermen keep more than one size of a real producer. That's why this smaller version of the original Rat-L-Trap is perfect for the angler who likes to use lighter tackle.

The Mini-Trap will catch everything a Rat-L-Trap will, but it's extremely effective when fish are feeding on smaller forage.

Large lures catch large fish. That theory has proven itself time and time again. When a fisherman needs to go deeper, slow a lure down or just present a larger target, the 3/4 oz. Mag-Trap is perfect for all of these situations.

Home of Bill Lewis Lures

Assembly Plant

Made in USA really means something at Bill Lewis Lures. All of our lures are made in America and we don't stop there, we do our utmost to purchase only American made parts. We are located in Alexandria, Louisiana, and we employ over 350 people. Our plant has over 25,000 square feet of manufacturing facility and is equipped with the latest production technology.

Bill Lewis Lures   Made in USA   Page 3

JIG SPECIALISTS CATCH BASS TOO

I catch my big fish with dead-in-the-water worms on the bottom and topwaters on the surface but that doesn't mean you can't do well with other artificials once you learn how, where and when to use them. What catches lunkers for me, I think, will help you catch trophies too, but if some other lures have captured your confidence, then you can probably put fine fish in the boat with your preference.

In the same area that I fish, particularly in Orange and Lochloosa lakes, E. S. (Red) Phelps has dragged in big bass for more than 40 years. Long ago he retired from professional guiding but he still occasionally fishes for fun and still catches bass. His favorite artificial is a jig, and he knows how to fish that lure about as well as anyone.

Known affectionately as "Red" because of his thatch of red hair before he turned bald, this senior citizen didn't even let the slow fishing period around Dog Days stop him from bringing in big fish. As a matter of fact, he got to liking those hot, sultry August fishing days when most anglers stayed near a fan and cussed the fish for having lockjaw.

He loves the Cross Creek lakes and likes to tell about how he learned jig fishing secrets in Kentucky.

"When I started a memorable trip in Kentucky that introduced jig fishing for bass to me, it was 28 degrees with frost and ice all over the trees. A light fog hung over the rippling water at a place called 'Yamacraw' on Lake Cumberland. It was early in February 1950. We were out to catch walleyes and I had a supply of live creek chubs that I had caught. They were from one and a half inches to five inches long. I planned to fish these live natural baits off a sand bar that was behind my parked truck on the shoreline.

"I caught a few fish with my chubs and learned that the female walleye liked smaller live baits than the male. But I learned something far more important. There were a dozen veteran fishermen catching a lot of walleyes around me. They were fishing from the bank. Most of them were using jigs and their successful styles taught me how to fish that lure. It is something that has helped me put a lot of big bass in the boat for many years," Red reminisces today.

"Those fishermen were using open-face reels, six and seven foot rods and eight to 12-pound test line. They had a variety of jigs on the lines. I had heard about Thompson Doll Flies and Bill Upperman Bucktails, but had never seen either one of them. I was using a casting reel and thought that was the best tackle for me. I was wrong. The bank fishermen were using 1/4 ounce jigs on 2/0 hooks and the lead was about the size of a .32 caliber bullet. It was almost impossible to cast that lightweight lure on my casting tackle.

"I took note of everything. They were using a variety of colors but I concluded that the most successful jig was one with a red head and a yellow tail. I brought the observations of that jig fishing with me to Florida and I have been successful using it ever since," says Phelps.

With some variations, Red started flipping the jigs he brought from Kentucky in Orange Lake. He opted for a 3/8-ounce jig with a red head and yellow nylon tail. Fished in a variety of ways at different seasons of the year, it catches a lot of bass. It also catches crappies and mudfish.

"I am not a jig purist who will fish nothing else. I like to fish topwater lures and swimming worms on the surface. It's fun to feel a strike on a shad-like crankbait pulled through a school of bass. I like that jolt on the line when the bass hits and holds. But I know that there are times when these thrills are not available. Bass won't hit on top or from schools. It's those dry spells when I call on the old reliable jig to help me put fish in the boat. It's dependable the year 'round," he declares.

"There are four ways to fish a jig and catch bass. During the winter in Florida when the weather keeps the water temperature about 60° , I fish the jig in about 12 to 15 feet of water and I fish it slowly. It needs a little rod tip action, but never a fast retrieve. A little rod tip action is always better than a steady retrieve. I use a No. 2 elbow spinner rig attached to the jig in deep holes. The No. 2 blade may be either gold or silver but I prefer gold. I like the old Ambassadeur 5000 reel and a six foot medium stiff rod. I use 20-pound line for jig fishing and most other bass angling too.

"I never fish in one hole long. I move from one spot to another with the jig retrieved while the rod tip is twitched all the way back to the boat. If I catch a bass, I work that hole five or ten minutes. I know others may be there. If I get no more strikes, I move on.

"I believe the vibration of the spinner with these jigs is an important factor in success as I catch more fish in dingy-colored water than I do in spring-clear holes. I think the bass hear the vibration of the spinner. In the dark water the bass naturally depend more upon hearing than sight when they are feeding. Remember, I am talking about bass fishing at a time when the water is the coldest and the fish the most sluggish. You feel your

jig-spinner quit working when a bass inhales it and you must set the hook quickly and with gusto," this jig specialist says.

"The next best time to jig for bass is in the summer. Bass are bedding and spawning more than in the winter. Not all bass bed in early spring and summer but the majority do. I have caught bass spawning as late as September in Florida. But I am dealing with summer jigging here.

"I use a No. 3 or No. 4 Colorado spinner with gold blades. I fish it slowly around the lilies and grass. Most bass are caught at the tip ends of this cover where the water is from three to eight feet deep. If there is a slight breeze coming from the shore and blowing across the open water, the jig fishing along the cover line is the best. Sometimes I stray away from the jig on these cover points and cast an El Tango, a combination plastic worm and curved spoon that you seldom see on the tackle shop shelves any more. It is really effective in summer off these grassy points and I have put an 11 1/4-pounder in the boat on an El Tango. But I have a 12-pounder caught on a jig. Then I have a 13 1/2-and a 13-pounder caught on a purple Rebel crankbait. But I stick to jigs for the most dependable fishing. You never strike out jig fishing. Well, almost never.

"The other time that I use a jig is September and November. And you can see I fish it just about all year. But I fish it differently each season. The jig is most effective in these fall months if there has been a lot of low water in the summer. The days shorten, the nights get longer, the sun comes from a more southerly angle, the water starts rising, it turns cooler and that's bass jigging time in Dixie. Look for the bait fish. If you spot shiners, shad and small bluegills in the shallow areas where you see moss near the surface, you are on the bass. The outside of this moss where there is a drop-off in three to six feet of water is the honey hole. Mr. Bass will be prowling around. He is looking for food in the moss. I work the jig slowly on the outskirts of the cover where the bass is stalking a meal. I use a No. 4 or No. 5 gold blade and it gets action.

"The Dog Days of autumn, months when many bassers give up on catching anything, can be good jigging days. It's the one time of year when I feel the bass get the closest to shore, even when the water is very shallow. I like to be on the lake at dawn and fish cover along the bank before the sun gets more than a few degrees above the horizon. A light jig plopped a few inches from the shore, twitched a time or two and retrieved while the rod tip dips, will attract every bass in the territory if he doesn't see you before you see him. There are no bad times to jig fish," Red reveals his thinking.

He has a last bit of advice for jig-spinner fishermen. Keep the blade polished so it will pick up light that makes it more effective in clear and dingy water. Keep the hook sharp with a honing stone or file if you do not have one of the fancy hook sharpeners that are now available. Never forget to retie your line to the jig, snap or swivel before each fishing trip. Check the line carefully each time you land a pickerel, mudfish or bass. They put nicks in the monofilament that weakens it so you'll likely lose your next hookup if you do not replace a few feet of the line.

Red ends his advice to bass anglers with a bit of philosophy.

"A lure is no better than the fisherman who uses it. To catch bass consistently, you must know the lifestyles and and feeding habits of the fish, where they rest and hang out, and the times that they normally look for a meal. Be there when the bass are there with the right jig and if you handle it right, the odds are in your favor," he says.

Red calls his favorite artificial "that wonderful jig." He began using it in Central Florida when he moved from Kentucky in 1954. He was already a fisherman and that three-day camping/fishing adventure on Cumberland convinced him of the productiveness of jigs. He has never changed his mind. He has refined it and learned. To him the jig is big and always will be.

YEARLINGS SCHOOL ON SURFACE
WHILE GIANTS LURK UNDERNEATH

I reached a sleepy hand to the night stand and picked up the noisy telephone, which was ringing the sixth time so loud it seemed to rock in its cradle.

Half awake, I greeted the caller with, "Cypress Lodge," and "This is Bud Andrews."

"Bud, this is Doug Hannon at Odessa. You been wanting to fish in Lake Thonotosassa near my stomping ground north of Tarpon Springs. I got a little time tomorrow. If you are not busy, maybe we can fish that lake tomorrow and perhaps put you on trophy bass No. 321 that weighs 10-pounds or more," Hannon extended his invitation to me, knowing I had recorded 320 trophy bass on artificial lures in Florida public waters since 1975 when I started guiding.

I was immediately awake. Hannon is the "Bass Professor," famous for catching more than 400 trophy size bass caught on live shiners and I was proud to be compared to this prominent scholar with my 320 wallmount size, all landed on lures. The late Jack Nast, outdoor writer of *The Tampa Tribune*, once had said that when Hannon and I were together, it was the Bass Professor versus the Muhammad Ali of largemouth angling.

I joked a bit with Doug about the comparison and told him I sure was interested in fishing with him. I asked what time it was and he said "About 5:00. Can you meet me at 7:30?" Hannon asked. I came out from under the cover and assured him I would be there with bells on.

That started the eventful morning of February 9th, 1988 when I fished that lake for the first time, after Douglas patiently toured the entire lake, pointing out to me the best spots for hiding lunkers. I was honored that this nationally-known authority would not only invite me to fish one of his favorite lakes with him but was taking the time to acquaint me with the honey holes which he knew well from 20 years of fishing in this Suncoast section of Florida.

With the indoctrination session over, Douglas putt-

putted away in his boat and I climbed into my Ranger with my partners, Greg Conklin, of Chicago and his father. Greg is a 20-year-old airline pilot and I was guiding them while trying to land my 321st lunker.

Early that day I caught a nice 7 1/2-pounder in the first canal we fished. The lake looked promising. Then we worked hard for hours using my dead in the water surface lure system along grass lines with just a bump or two. I even tried out my newest gimmick, skip-jacking a topwater on the surface. That's been a real factor in my recent catch success when I cast close to the cover and twitch the lure four or five feet the instant it hits. It looks much like a live bait popping out of the water and running from some predator. Once the lure hits after the skip, I let it float perfectly still for several minutes. That's the heart of my topwater and bottom fishing, let the lure stay put so long that it irritates the giants of the territory and they strike it to get it out of their way.

With the sun high in the sky after I had cast many times along the shoreline where there were dozens of tiny circles, made by forage fish and insects, always a good indication that some largemouths are nearby, I shifted to my worm fishing technique that I have so much confidence in. I fish the worm on the bottom with great patience, often leaving it absolutely dead for 15 minutes or more. I may twitch it enough to make it wriggle but not enough to drag it away from its place on the bottom. I want it to stay put long enough to make the big bass in the territory curious and eventually disturbed enough to attack this intruder in their midst.

I started my worm fishing technique about a decade ago with what I then referred to as my bumping worm system. That was a technique of casting the worm along grass lines or where there was hydrilla growing on the bottom and flicking it every few seconds so that it would bump the weight enough to make the wiggler tail twitch slightly. I have watched this worm action in clear water many times and it entices bass because it has this crazy looking motion where a worm stands on its head, relaxes and lies flat for a moment, then up it comes on its head again. I later refined that bumping worm technique to my dead worm system. No self respecting trophy bass can stand this kind of activity right in her face. The big 'uns will investigate and at least occasionally pick up this mad worm and swim off with it. I use this system when the bass are aggressive. That's how I have

Andrews and Doug Hannon Get No. 321

caught many of my wallmount-size bass. But don't misunderstand me and think I have mounted all those trophies. I believe in releasing these big fish, and I have released all of my fish alive except a few that died. I have several mounted on my wall and have given some to children's hospitals. Only 12 out of 321 were mounted. I think it is a good idea to put some real nice bass on the walls at schools and children's hospitals so the kids can admire the fish and perhaps it will encourage them to be fishermen. At least, when I have a big fish that dies, it is better to have it mounted for the school children than filleted and thrown in a skillet.

Anyhow, that memorable day on Thonotosassa Lake I shifted to my favorite technique, picked up my Ryobi reel, five and a half foot Fenwick graphite rod and flicked a 7 1/2-inch Culprit black worm with a clear blue tail into a deep hole. The worm was impaled on a 4/0 Mustad hook with 1/8 oz. bullet black sinker, and I was using 10-pound test Royal Bonnyl monofilament line. That is one of my preferences of line because it is a brownish color that blends in with the tannic hue of many Central Florida lakes. I know that I lose some fish by using this 10-pound test line, but I also know that this light line gets far more strikes than heavier monofilament. I take my chances on losing some with parted lines and use the light weight mono. If you use your drag properly and patiently play a trophy bass, you'll save almost all of them once you get the fish out of dense cover, even if you are using light line. Patience is the key to landing these lunkers and a lot of self-discipline is also needed. I do use 17 or 20-pound test line when flipping .

It was 2:20 in the afternoon when I made the cast with that worm rigging that brought me my 321st trophy bass. The line moved off to my right after it had been still for several minutes on the bottom. I lowered my rod tip, took up all the slack in the line, locked the reel, and after about three seconds of watching the line play out, I set the hook with enough gusto to stick the fish but not hard enough to snap the line, something that novices often do when they have giant size bass on the line. The fish jumped and danced on the surface and we all knew this was another trophy fish. I held on and a minute or two later the fish rolled over on its side just a foot or two from the boat. I lipped the big bass and put her in the boat. She weighed 10-pounds, 3 - ounces and I was all smiles.

My 321st 10-pounder or over also substantiated another

of my strong beliefs. I catch most of my trophy size bass in the middle of the day, not early and not late. Some say I catch them during banker's hours from about 10:00 A.M. until about 3:00 P.M. I catch some early and late but usually these are yearling or schooling bass, not the kind that I go after with my customers who almost always come to Florida searching for a fish of wall mount size. I do catch some big bass in the wee hours of the morning and from about 2:30 A.M. until dawn on the Tsala Apopka chain of lakes where Cypress Lodge is located on Lake Henderson. This 24-mile chain of lakes from Floral City to Hernando is excellent big bass territory and early morning hours are often productive. Mosquitoes are not biting much those hours either, and it is a beautiful time of day. I like to fish then, particularly in the summer months in the open water where the fish are schooling but when I am daytime casting for bass, I do better in the middle hours of the day. Incidentally, my guide, Doug Hannon on Lake Thonotosassa also is a great believer in middle of the day success when going after monster size bass.

I slipped my big bass in the livewell after treating the water with some Catch and Release chemicals, and we cranked the motor and headed for the dock. Hannon was shivering on the dock from the cold north wind and had his jacket collar turned up around his neck.

"You have any luck?" he asked as the boat glided to a stop.

I told him we had struck out and asked how he had done.

"I caught a few little ones but nothing sensational," Hannon said. "It's too cold to fish."

Then I opened the live well and showed him the 7 1/2-pounder I had caught in the first canal that morning. It got his attention. Then I pulled out the 10-pounder and he was all smiles.

"Yeah, you got your 321st. That's good, " he said with enthusiasm. Obviously he was pulling for me.

We admired the big bass a few moments, then found a warm spot and talked bass fishing for awhile. One of the facts we had both considered for a long time was the association of yearling size largemouth with giants of the species. I had noted for years that often when dozens of schooling yearlings are tearing up the surface, the real trophies are close by. Those that you catch when they are schooling are usually from about one pound to perhaps as much as three pounds or more. I have learned from my experience as a guide in Florida that often there are several trophy size bass suspended under the yearlings and a few feet off the bottom. Lay bass fishermen can profit from this observation. When you want to go after a big bass, not the schoolies on top, use weight to let your lure fall through the small fish and down to where the larger ones may be stalking food. They were forced to flee from the chaotic frenzy above them. A bright colored Rat-L-Trap and deep-diving Bagley or Rebel crankbait will often stir the big 'uns into action if you can locate the schooling little fellows and then put your artificial right in the face of the lunkers. A weighted 7 1/2-inch or longer worm sometimes will catch big bass under the schoolies.

Another thing Hannon and I agreed upon was the need for avoiding all forms of bass bed fishing, whether with live baits or artificials. We know that these big spawning mamas deserve a chance to lay and raise a family. Big bass genetics are proven. They had to be smart bass to reach weights of 10-pounds or more, often requiring a lifespan of ten years or more. Smaller bass may not have the instinct and know-how to reach such sizes. Big bass are cannibals, often eating yearlings of their own species. It makes them grow to giant size. Most tourist bass fishermen who come to Florida are looking for a big fish and that's why they hire guides. There's nothing wrong with that, but we do need to protect the spawns and thus protect the strain of Florida bass that has proven its genetic ability to escape predation and grow to trophy size. You can still catch plenty of big bass throughout Central Florida in summer and winter without stooping to raiding the nests of the spawners. It's bass murder and your own fishing suicide to go after spawning lunkers.

I have learned over the years that in bass fishing you have to establish a defense to get on the offense, as you often hear athletes in competitive sports say. What is offense? In fishing, it may be a cold front. These fronts often create difficult times to catch bass. That's when I concentrate first on my defense. What is defense? That's the presentation of your artificial lure with proven technique. Present your artificial bait in the most natural fashion possible. The presentation is one of the utmost importance if you want to meet the cold front head on and challenge the weather conditions. Once you master a technique, like my dead in the water worm or topwater with my skipjacking, you'll learn that you can catch fish regardless of the cold front conditions.

When I fish during a moving front, I find that most of my

fish are active regardless of the cold temperature and wind conditions. It's after the front moves through that I find it more difficult to get strikes. That's the lockjaw time frame of mind.

During the active period fishing ahead of a front before it has arrived, I use my bumping worm technique. The bass activity is documented when you see bait fish dashing around and jumping trying to avoid predators. Often you can also detect this activity by seeing movements in the aquatic vegetation. Bass moving through buggy whips, cattails, bulrushes, lily pads, peppergrass, hydrilla and milfoil leave tell-tale signs of feeding when they bump and shake the weeds. My bumping worm is Texas rigged on a light line with a 1/16th or 1/8th ounce bullet slip sinker. Fishing in 12 feet or more of water, I cast about 50 feet and let the worm slowly drop to the bottom. Then it stays there motionless for several minutes. The cold front may have made the bass dormant, but if that worm stays there awhile, they'll analyze it and hopefully strike. Natural currents may move the worm a little but you'll do better if you have nothing to do with that movement. You see, the bait is acting dead or dormant like the fish you are stalking see it. Bass observe it as a natural action. It has a naturalness that even the smartest bass will not perceive as a trap. The no-motion worm is a challenge and enticement to bass that has no appearance of danger.

This dead bait fishing requires patience and self-discipline. It separates the men from the boys. Those who learn the system will catch fish before, during and after a cold front, as well as the better times. Those who are not willing to wait and wait, won't have as much to write home about. Patience here is a real virtue.

I have a bit of advice to pass along to bass fishermen when they succeed in getting the strike of their dreams and finally have the trophy at boatside. Take pains to remove the hooks reasonably quickly and as gently as possible. Don't squeeze the fish and don't use a net if you are an experienced angler and if you can avoid it. You must be careful in lipping a fish with hooks in her mouth. Nets rub off slime and require more handling than just picking up your fish with a thumb and forefinger clamped on the lower jaw. But I do not recommend that youngsters try to handle a fish with a lure in its mouth. That is too dangerous. Once you have taken a picture or two and smiled over your good fortune, release the fish gently. Don't toss it back carelessly. Place it softly in the water and let it swim away. The feeling you get from catching a monster sized fish, fooling the bass into striking a man-made object, thus making a mistake, you'll have a thrill to remember. That thrill will be even more etched in your memory if you properly release your catch and see it swim away healthy and capable of thrilling some other angler on another day. Also the only way I know of continuing to catch trophy bass is to release as many yearlings as possible.

I parted company with Hannon on the shores of Lake Thonotosassa and returned to Cypress Lodge at Inverness. I gently lifted my big bass out of the livewell, snapped a couple of pictures, eased it in the clear water of Lake Henderson and it calmly fluttered away from the dock and downward in to the safety of the tree-lined shore.

It had been another great day for me. I had another notch on my rod handle for my latest lunker landing. I had learned some lessons from the Bass Professor and he had acquainted me with some of the honey holes of Lake Thonotosassa. I had boated another fine largemouth and handled it carefully enough that it might well thrill my 2 1/2-year old son in the years ahead. Like the TV commercial says, "Boys, it just doesn't get any better than this."

I'll guide more than 200 days in Central Florida this year and hopefully for many years after that. I just hope the big bass population is maintained so that most of the clients who spend their money with me and my associates go home with smiles on their faces.

BOGGS' BIG ONES THAT GOT AWAY

Wade Boggs is not only the baseball hitting champion who plays third base for the Boston Red Sox, he is also the owner of the Fin-Way Fish Camp on Highway 301 south of Hawthorne, Florida, on Lake Lochloosa. Wade's personable father, Winn, says Wade's great love, after baseball, is fishing. "He will fish anywhere that there's water."

He tells the story about an experience Wade had on Silver Lake in Florida when he cast near the shoreline and a big mama bass inhaled his lure. He carefully played the fish and brought her to the boat. Moments later, he cast to the opposite shoreline and hooked another lunker. They were flouncing in the boat at the same time and were identical twins. Proudly Wade weighed them and they were exactly 9-pounders. The fish were such trophies and the same size that Boggs decided to have the pair mounted together.

He returned home to Tampa and put the wallmount bass in the sink, ran a little water over them and left for an appointment he had downtown. Returning home a few hours later, his fish were not in the sink. You guessed it! His grandmother came along, thinking the fish were for dinner. She dressed them both. So much for the twin wallmount trophies.

Wade has not been able to catch two such trophies since, but he did continue to lead the American League in hits year after year.

SPAWNED BASS LOST THE LAKE RECORD

When Rodney Cox, of Pasadena, Texas, caught a 10.29-pound bass in the Fourth Annual McDonald's Big McBass Classic on Sam Rayburn Lake, it was big enough to win him over $40,000. The bass was a 29-inch female and a biologist with the Texas Parks and Wildlife Department said the fish had spawned and would have weighed about 13- pounds if she still had her eggs. That would have been a new lake record.

RAT-L-TRAPS ARE MONEY LURES

Bill Lewis' Rat-L-Trap lure is the favorite of many veteran bass anglers who call it the "money" lure because of its consistency in catching nice largemouths. This lure, particularly the chrome with a blue back, is popular from Florida to California and it has grown in popularity all during the '80's. Made primarily by hand by the biggest little company in the country, the Rat-L-Traps is hot. It may be the most-used minnow-like lure in the country in the spring and second only to the plastic worm on a year 'round basis.

The noisy lure that comes in three sizes and more than 100 colors is a hit all over the country. Bass anglers swear by this rattler. That's because it catches fish.

LADY BASSER'S LUNKER ON RAT-L-TRAP

Marie Brodnax, of Pineville, Texas ranked tenth in the first round of the Lady Bass Texas Invitational Tournament in Sam Rayburn Reservoir in 1988 with a weigh-in of 10.6-pounds. Fishing a practice day on Monday prior to the tourney opening Wednesday, she landed an 11.16-pound giant, more weight than her five-fish limit in the tournament.

It was the largest bass Professional Brodnax had ever landed. She caught it on one of her sponsor's lures, the Bill Lewis MagTrap.

SKIP-JACKING FOR YEARLINGS

Sometimes when the trophy fish all seem to have lockjaw and won't hit a thing you toss at 'em, you still have to catch some bass or come in mighty disappointed. If you are a guide, as I have been for the past 14 years, you'll have your bread and butter endangered if your clients don't catch something. They are looking for a return on their money and that makes me constantly on the lookout for ways to catch bass when my proven big fish methods fail.

In 1987 I came up with a simple addition to my fishing techniques that has been a god-send when patience and dead-in-the-water worms and topwaters attract no attention. I call the newest gimmick in my repertoire "skip-jacking" and it sometimes works when all other efforts are useless.

I use this skip-jacking around aquatic cover generally and in fairly shallow water where yearling bass may be schooling and feeding on shiners, bream, minnows and other small forage fish. I like to make fairly long casts with an open-faced reel on a 6 or 6 1/2-foot limber rod with eight or 10-pound test Stren line.

Bang-O-Lure topwaters are good for this kind of fishing as are Rapalas and Devilhorses and several others as long as they are heavy enough that you can get them 100 feet or so away from the boat. You must be accurate enough to place it within a few feet of the grass line or other cover where the bass are holding. Often you can observe these smaller bass thrashing in the grass or breaking the surface after a lively bait. You know they are after food and you want to entice them into making a mistake. And that's what every fish does that is caught on a lure. He makes a mistake and thinks he is getting a nutritious meal when actually he is challenging a piece of wood or plastic.

Often I have been casting along a grass line and observed tiny fish humpbacking in and out of the water, obviously trying to escape from a bass or other predator that is in hot pursuit. This skipping on the surface, in and out of the water, is what prompted my discovery of skip-jacking. I reasoned that if natural baits jumped out of the water when a bass was around and giving chase, an artificial performing in like manner should appear to be the real thing to a predator. With that premise, I started skip-jacking.

I cast my topwater as near to the grass line as I can, then just as it hits the surface, I twitch my rod tip vigorously. I snap it overhead hard enough to yank the lure out of the water and then it dives down five or six feet away, hopefully still near the cover. It gives the lure the appearance of an escaping fish and I have been pleasantly surprised with the productiveness of this simple movement.

Some yearlings have jumped on the lure just as I twitched it trying to make it jump, but most of the strikes have come when the bait plopped down the second time. It appears that the fish are upset when they miss it on the first landing and make a headlong dive to catch it on the second splashdown before it really makes a clean get-away.

While I have not caught any trophy bass with my skip-jacking, the viciousness of strikes from the 3 and 4-pounders has been thrilling. They seem to challenge my tackle more than when they gulp down worms and other artificials that are not as active on the surface as a skip-jacked lure.

In Florida where schools of bass from 1 to 5-pounds often cover half an acre in September and October, the fish feeding in a frenzy on millions of tiny shad, skip-jacking seems to be a highly productive technique. A topwater cast into the melee and then skipped a few feet to another splashdown, turns the schoolers on. It gets strikes when the normal cast and retrieve is ignored. Apparently the lively naturals are skipping on top and an artificial looks much the same when the bass are blindly chasing and gulping down everything in the neighborhood.

I have always fished these schools by giving my topwater or crankbaits a lot of action. The schoolers seem to go after them much better when they are jumping and bouncing rather than simply retrieved and cast again. Skip-jacking seems to be the best of the methods we have tried to date on schooling bass in Florida lakes and streams. But it hasn't added anything to my trophy bass statistics.

WHEN ALL ELSE FAILS

Bill Ignizio is an Ohio free lance outdoor magazine writer who came South and fished with me in 1987. He was impressed with my bass fishing techniques and subsequently wrote a story for Field and Stream about the experience and other systems. The story follows:

By Bill Ignizio

There's an old adage (or at least there should be) which states that "half the game is knowing when to break the rules." It's advice more bass fishermen should heed. Though the rules that tell fishermen how, where and when to fish work most of the time, there are days– and we've all had more than our fair share– when the fish simply don't respond. On those days when all else fails, the angler willing to break the rules will catch fish while his by-the-book compatriot will only simmer in frustration. These unorthodox approaches include, but are not limited to, altering the way a standard lure is retrieved, investigating "non-productive" locations, and using offbeat tackle.

For example, standard operating procedures state that a topwater lure should be allowed to sit motionless until the ripples caused by its landing have dissipated. Only then should you begin a twitching retrieve.

That's sound advice, and the tactic has produced well enough over the years to become set in stone. But a "dead lure" method also works. I learned this tactic from guide Bud Andrews, who should know– he's taken well over 300 10-pound-plus largemouths from Florida's public waters.

"When fishing gets tough," he says, "you can sometimes get bass to hit a topwater lure by just letting the lure sit still. I do the same thing with an artificial worm. Bass see it drop down. You don't have to hop, skip, or drag the bait to get a hit. You have to watch the line very carefully, though, or you're going to miss the pick-up."

Fishing a deep-diving plug in the shallows can be effective–

if you do it properly. Cast the plug near shore, keep the rod tip high and slowly reel in line. If you feel the lure beginning to hang up, reel in even slower or stop cranking altogether. A buoyant plug usually pops to the surface as soon as you halt the retrieve; at that point begin reeling in again at a slightly faster pace.

Deep-diving crankbaits also can be fished in unorthodox ways. Despite the double set of treble hooks found on most of these lures, it is possible to work them successfully along thick weed edges and humps. Occasionally the lure snags, as you might expect, but it usually travels only a short distance before a bass takes it. A guide I know routinely trolls these plugs through areas thick with fallen trees and stumps. By removing the belly trebles and snipping off the forward hook of the rear set, he hangs up far less than you would think.

Another rule-breaking tactic is to work a deep diving crankbait as a topwater plug. Toss the lure out near docks, stumps, lily pads or other types of cover and twitch it as you might a popper or stickbait. After twitching the bait several times, you can retrieve it in the conventional manner.

You can also induce strikes by swimming a jig (retrieving it as if it were a spinnerbait), and on hot summer days, working a spinnerbait on the bottom like a jig can be just the ticket for lethargic warm-water bass.

The popper is another lure that can be fished unconventionally. Instead of retrieving the lure as you normally would– creating a pop or gurgle– try twitching it slightly. Long-bodied poppers and chuggers can be "walked" back to the boat, and a steady jerk (either upward or downward) of the rod tip causes the elongated popper to mosey back in a zigzag pattern that can really turn on bass.

One seemingly cast-in-concrete rule is that it pays to fish remote stretches of water. Anglers always seem to blast off from wherever they put in, searching for untouched waters. There's nothing wrong with the concept, but anglers who make long runs to "virgin" waters often pass prime cover.

A favorite Canadian lake of mine holds huge expanses of weedy bays. For years, I motored by a particularly good-looking bay on my way to distant fishing grounds. I had been told by anglers "in the know" that this spot simply didn't hold many good bass. One year as I was routinely passing the bay, my companion– a newcomer to the lake– remarked that the spot looked great.

I stopped the boat only to humor my friend, but the joke was on me. We caught several fish in the 2 to 3-pound class– all from a bay miles closer than many of my other top bass spots.

Many anglers routinely ignore built-up sections of a lake while searching for pristine areas. Yet some anglers have discovered that bass can be taken from heavily populated waters. The seawalls homeowners build to prevent erosion often hold good bass, as do boat and swimming docks. In fact, some of the best holding spots can be moored boats. Boathouses are other potential bass-holders.

Because the features on these "civilized" waters are so heavily used by the natives, you will have to work harder for fish than you might on a wilderness lake. Instead of swimming a spinnerbait by a dock once or twice, for example, you may have to make a half-dozen or more casts. If no fish shows an interest, switch to a different bait and continue working the cover. It's not that unusual to make a dozen or more casts before getting a fish to strike. If a spot is worth hitting once or twice, it may well be worth one or two *dozen* casts.

Many bass fishermen not only refuse to work an area that completely, but they also balk at fishing so-called "used water," an area another angler has just worked. But the fact that the guy before you has scoured a series of docks with a spinnerbait and come up empty doesn't necessarily mean no bass are there. By switching lures or changing tactics, you may be able to move into the same cover and catch bass.

Lakes rocked by power boaters and water skiers can also be productive. A friend long ago laid claim to a wild-and-woolly lake ruled by hordes of pleasure boaters. Fishermen naturally avoided the impoundment, but as skiers and speed merchants tore by, my friend quietly and consistently plucked out fine bass from the churning waters. He claims that these fast-lane bass long ago became accustomed to the frenzied lifestyle of the boaters on their lake and so were as catchable as any other fish.

I've tried to outline just a few of the ways anglers can break the rules and catch fish. Always begin with tried-and-true tactics; after all, they're tried and true precisely because they work– at least most of the time. But don't be afraid to deviate from the norm when standard approaches fail. Actually the only unshakable rule is that there are no rules, only what works on any given day.

MY FAVORITE BASS TACKLE

While I place more emphasis upon knowing where to find big bass and how to entice them to bite than I do on rods, reels, hooks, lines and sinkers, tackle is important. I am frequently asked what tackle I used to catch my 321 trophy fish 10-pounds and above. Here is what I have generally used for the past 12 years:

Ryobi and Fenwick rods, Ryobi and Quantum reels, Garcia's Royal Bonnyl II and Stren line, Mustad and TruTurn hooks No. 4/0, 5/0 and 6/0. I use the 4/0 when fishing my dead worm and bumping worm on the bottom and 5/0 and 6/0 when flipping.

I never use a line that glows. I don't think that is natural and it might spook big bass.

Occasionally, when I am flipping in heavy cover, I use 17 and 20-pound test line. All other times I use 8, 10, or 12-pound test.

I fish from a Ranger boat.

WHERE TO FISH
UNDER THE LILY PADS   OR   BETWEEN
THE EARS?

The mental aspect of fishing is of primary importance not only for the tournament fisherman but also for the weekend bass buster. I believe that fishing is something that can be done between the ears, before we even get to the water. We have seen many fine athletes with great form and style, but who have a poor mental approach, and they fail. Yet, another athlete with poor posture and equipment but a positive mental outlook and attitude may become a champion. When you are a fisherman with the proper equipment, the mechanically sound technique and the positive mental approach, you can become a champion fisherman.

Concentration is the ability to direct one's attention toward the task at hand and to think only about that particular goal. It means being able to mentally block out all distractions. A good tournament bass fisherman must learn to live in a vacuum, not to be distracted by noise or movement. He must have the complete feeling that he is out there alone against the fish. Complete attention must be directed to what you are doing; constantly checking your line, looking for movements of fish, watching your depth finder, sticking to your pattern, knowing exactly what your next move is going to be and doing it all instinctively. You maintain intensity.

Concentration also means keeping an eye on your fellow competitor to see his reactions to fish, why he loses a fish or misses a strike. You can capitalize on his mistakes. Concentrate on past experiences at the same lake.   Watch for weather changes. You must continually keep feeding the brain positive information to determine the next logical and intelligent move. The mind cannot wander or you will make mistakes.

Tournament fishing is an individual sport, but it is a team effort in a boat. As a true sportsman you can encourage your fellow competitor if he is a rookie. It is not an absolute necessity that boat members like each other personally, but it is necessary that they encourage each other to do well. Show interest in the performance of your partner. Personalities must be left out of the boat, and the importance of safety and good sportsmanship must prevail.

Convince yourself that you will succeed with the least possible margin for error. This position is brought about by strategy and positive planning. Now is not the time to hope for miracles. Tournament fishermen who are consistent winners are the ones who plan three months in advance and not the ones who plan the morning of the tournament. Weekend bass busters who want to catch fish must plan prior to launching their rigs. Don't plan after the motor is started. It could be too late. This is true especially in changing weather conditions.

Be mentally prepared to fish in wind and rain. Remember, everyone else is under the same condition. A good cast and a good hookset will prevail, success will follow. Fish with *CONFIDENCE*. Guard against negativism in the form of overemphasis on minor problems. The good and the bad casts will eventually even themselves out. You will land many large fish but you will also lose many large fish, either during a tournament or on the weekend. Those who are thoroughly prepared with positive mental attitudes will always finish on top.

The tournament fisherman and the weekend bass buster are really the same type of individual with similar objectives.

KIDS SHOULD NOT LIP LAND BASS

While experienced bass fishermen often lift their trophy bass over the gunnels by clamping their thumb and forefinger tightly on the fish's lower lip, I caution youngsters not to land their fish in this manner when there's a lure in its mouth. It takes a lot of experience to master this technique without suffering painful injury from hooks in the lure that end up in the hand or arm of the fisherman. A hook in your hand with a live, flouncing bass still attached can do a lot of damage and ruin a fishing adventure.

Lip landing a bass is good for the fish. It doesn't rub off any of the protective slime coating, but it is dangerous for the novice who doesn't think about the sharp hooks in the lure. It's better to handle the lure with a pair of pliers and avoid the antics of the bass when a violent head shake can impale treble hooks in sensitive flesh.

WEEDLESS TOPWATER LURES ADD NEW DIMENSION TO BASS FISHING

Smoothly underhanding a 35-foot cast into a washtub size hole in a sea of lily pads that sheltered the bass of Lake Lochloosa from the light and heat of the summer sun that bears down in Central Florida, Terry Nash, a transplanted Kentuckian who guides year 'round, grinned a little when the water exploded and he felt resistance on his reel as another lunker surged and jumped. Again he was experiencing success with topwater bass catchers that he wouldn't have dared risk in such heavy cover a few years ago. Now weedless for the first time, he had confidence in saving his new-fangled lure and the bass that struck it, whether cast into lilies, grass, weeds or brushpile stickups that often provide hangouts for largemouths stalking forage fish in the protective habitat normally considered no-man's land for most artificials.

Topwater bass fishing has undergone a revolution and Nash is thankful for the innovations that make his catch record more attractive from April through September, hot months that are not his favorites for shiner floating that he pursues for his clients when the weather and water are cold.

Changes in topwater bass fishing began at 3:00 A.M. August 21, 1984, when Bing McClellan, of Burke Lures, Traverse City, Michigan, awoke from a troubled sleep, sat straight up in bed and realized he had brain-stormed an idea that would forever alter the technique of bass fishing on the surface. If his idea worked, bassers would no longer have to cast along the open water adjacent to the weeds and shoreline, they could cast right into the face of the bass hiding in the thickets. If no strike thrilled the angler in that spot, he could easily retrieve his lure and cast again into habitat that most certainly held the lunkers that the devout amateur and successful professional sought. No self-respecting bass would endure the temptation of a lure that so closely mimicked a real morsel flitting right in her face. She might have ignored it yards away in the open, but not when it dared invade her sheltered domain where topwater artificials had always feared to tread. McClellan's invention of a weedless topwater series with a variety of actions has changed all that.

The Burke lures had soft, pliable bodies before McClellan's innovation was revealed in his dream. He simply added two stainless steel trapeze wire guards, that look like short old-fashioned hat pins. Stuck into the soft foam body of the plug and allowed to extend over the 5/0 double hook, the new concept lets the lure glide over logs, pads, moss and hydrilla and yet it trips with the slightest pressure and sinks into the jaws of bass and other predators stalking in the shade and apparent safety of heavy cover.

A year later, McClellan refined that invention and today those topwaters that he calls the Pop Top, Bassassin and Top Dog have, tiny "frog-feet" plastic extrusions that seem to naturally hang from the lure body to cover the hook points and these artificials are even more foolproof and productive than ever. They are naturals that even bass with graduate degrees can't guess are phony.

Nash likes the new topwaters that he says entice bass strikes in areas once believed out of bounds. You can cast the Pop Top right into branches and limbs and get it back. The Bassassin is ideal for milfoil and hydrilla where you can stop it in holes where bass lie in ambush. The Top Dog is so named because it is like walking your dog. You can "walk" it right over the cover and thrill to a lunker jumping on it as it "steps" into a clearing in the pads or weeds. These lures are unlike weedless spoons that you must retrieve rapidly as soon as they hit the water; these flex plugs float and can be worked and twitched in place, performing a deadly dance never possible before.

Some people, like Nash, refer to this new topwater fishing as "cardiac casting" because you can now watch the water boil and explode by fishing what once were impossible places. They are weedless wonders that work. Guides and lay bassers are reaping the benefits of this new breakthrough during all the warm months everywhere.

Another innovation that Terry Nash has found unusual and productive is the Snakebait, a realistic small topwater that is the exact replica of a real serpent that Burke now markets. The heads of this new topwater were sculpted by Lynn Hannon, wife of the prominent Douglas Hannon, the "Bass Professor" of Odessa, Florida. Lynn is a nationally known wildlife sculptor and her life-like soaring bald eagle with a 75 inch wingspread has drawn praise from all over the nation. The heads are exact likenesses of a moccasin, green snake, rattler and copperhead. Curly, seven inch flip tail worms fasten to the heads by a hook on a line that slips through the snake's mouth. These topwaters are also weedless and dynamite in most Southern lakes where snakes have long been an important part of the bass diet.

The hookup on this snake-like bait is somewhat like the Texas style with a Wright and McGill 2/0 No. 44F hook that Hannon believes is the best for this particular type lure.

Nash believes it is important to hook up the Snakebait so that the curled tail is parallel to the water. The hook and head should be so aligned that the hook looks like a boat's keel. The Snakebait then weaves along over cover like the real thing. The retrieve brings it through broken lily pads and grass patches so that few self-respecting bass can stand the enticing meal on the surface. It brings boiling swirls and fish to the boat in areas impossible to fish before.

This new weedless topwater was designed by Hannon after he found numerous small snakes in the largemouths he caught. He didn't have to kill the bass to find this out. He releases everything. Several times he found live water snakes in his livewell after he caught a lunker and put the fish in the box to give her time to catch her breath before releasing. At first, he thought the little snakes came through the drain hole in the livewell but once when he had his bass recuperating in a 48 quart aerated cooler, he found a live snake. He knew then that it had emerged from the snake's mouth like Jonah from the whale and is sure that these snakes are delicacies that largemouths stalk.

Nash flipped the Snakebait around a cypress knee along the shoreline. A splash broke the silence of the early morning. He set the hook with gusto while his heartbeat picked up and his eyes sparkled. Moments later he lifted an 8-pound bass over the gunnels. He reached to unhook the fish and was almost frightened as that lifelike snake head peeked at him. It fooled the bass and it is so real it can fool the fisherman for a moment when it stares back from a fish's mouth.

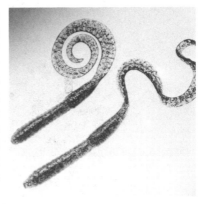

Hibdon Lands Real Lunker

CATCHING BASS OFF BREAM BEDS

Most of the largemouth bass scholars oppose catching spawning mamas off their beds on conservation grounds, although realizing it is the time of the year when many of the giants of this species can be taken with either live baits in the nest or a variety of artificials cast in the vicinity. If you have some ability to find bluegill and shell cracker spawning areas, you can pass up the bass nests, remaining loyal to your ideals, and catch even more largemouths by fishing water where these bream have concentrated their hatchery.

While most students are aware that the bream becomes a predator and attacks the eggs and fry of largemouths when the bigger species is guarding a nest, particularly when the bluegill noses down toward the hatching fry, few scholars of sunfish have had much to say about catching lunkers preying on the food supply around the bream beds. But this is one of the finest times and places to catch a limit of largemouths. They feast over bream beds when gambusia minnows swarm into the hatchery, gulp down mouthful after mouthful of the panfish eggs, and turn blood-red in the process. The change of color reduces the camouflage of the minnows and every largemouth in the territory will congregate in the bedding area to gorge himself on the easy-to-catch host of three inch forage fish that sometimes literally covers many square yards of bream beds, far too many in number for the guarding bream to successfully chase away.

If you can use your senses after some years of experience to locate the bedding bream, you will have found at the same time one of the very best places to catch a livebox full of largemouths. Not every bass angler can find the bream beds. Here are some clues that will help:

Use your nose to smell the beds. It's a strange odor and impossible to explain to anyone unfamiliar with the scent. Almost everyone describes the scent differently. I say it smells like a musty cellar, a basement under a house in a warm part of the country. Others describe it as a watermelony odor and some simply say it smells a little different in an area from the normal.

Assume you are near a bream bed and start looking in the grass, the lilies, the brush or wherever there is nearby cover. If it's the bream spawning season, usually one of the first three warmer months of the year, although in some Southern States these panfish nest right on into September, you may have visible signs that will pinpoint the bream beds.

If the bream are present in consequential numbers, and often there are literally hundreds of beds packed close together, there will be so many guardians of the hatch that their vicious rushes at invading minnow predators will keep the aquatic growth that protrudes above the surface shaking. The bump of a charging adult panfish makes the grass and the lily stalks tremble, almost as if a human hand shook them from near the roots. It's easily distinguishable from wind movement. When bass are gulping down red minnows on these beds, there are times when many tell-tale bumps can be seen at once throughout an area a dozen yards square. Bass bumps come from chasing the minnows and the bream create a slightly less vigorous shake as they tirelessly circle their saucer-shaped indentation in the sand that houses their eggs and offspring.

Other visible signs of bream spawning are often possible by observation of what is floating on the surface. In areas where there are water lilies and sawgrass, bream will often nose up large quantities of hair-like white roots from the bottom. These will float to the surface and often cover holes in the aquatic growth. Where the growth is dense, the roots cannot easily blow out of the area and may mark a bream bedding area as distinctly as a channel buoy directs shipping traffic. IF THESE ROOTS ARE WHITE, your bream are still there. If they have turned brown, you may be a few days too late. The brown roots indicate they have been floating several days, maybe a week, and the spot you are seeking where bedding is active, may not be present at that moment.

You can also use your ears to good advantage. Panfish bedding in shallow water frequently will splash and chum the surface when they go after an invader. They may also create some noise by striking a floating insect, a grass shrimp that may swim too close to the bed, or even a minnow that is not too large for the small mouths of bream to swallow. A full grown bream may even try to fight off a yearling largemouth foraging in her nest and in the shallows, splash and create waves, discernable and giving you a fix on a spawning ground that you are looking for.

90

With your bream beds located, you can catch more bass than you ever thought possible. It is a happy hunting ground for largemouths, a feast spread before them, and in that they are here to eat, you have an excellent opportunity to take advantage of the appetite in an area where the bass are congregated. They are not too choosy about what morsel they gulp down, although to be sure, they are more likely to strike those attractive red minnows that they are stalking than anything else.

I once fished alongside a man, his wife and 12 year old boy in Lake Griffin, at Leesburg, Florida, for three days around the full moon in June, perhaps the best month in the Sunshine State for panfishing on the beds. I was after bluegill and shellcrackers and fishing with grey crickets in an era before this live bait was easily available at Leesburg. I was having reasonably good luck but relative to the way this family adjacent to my position was catching bass, I was a real loser. Fishing only three hours in the afternoon the first day, this bassing family anchored on the bream bed and began dropping red minnows in the holes in the lilies, they pulled 34 bass over the gunnels. They weighed from 1 to 4-pounds and they lost some giants that became unbuttoned from their No. 4 Eagle Claw hooks or else broke their light lines in the heavy cover. They were using small hooks, stiff cane poles or long spinning rods, and simply dropping the bait in the holes within reaching distance of the boat. They used a tiny bobber on top and a single lead shot a few inches above the hook. They had no room for casting, it was more of a flipping technique. Every fish they hooked was a challenge to land but they were boating most of their strikes.

It was the first time I ever saw this red minnow bass fishing on bream beds but the very next day the Leesburg native and his wife and son anchored at the same spot as the day before. With 34 fish pulled from there the previous day, I couldn't believe they would be successful again. Believe it or not, they hauled up 56 bass that second afternoon, again nice fish up to 4 and 5-pounds. And they lost several bigger than that.

To complete the story, they fished the third consecutive day on that bream bed and this time they filled a cooler with 74 bass. You wonder what they would do with so many fish? It was an era when bass in Lake Griffin were obviously plentiful and before the day of catch and release. The catcher of those bass carried all of them home. He said he was in the citrus fertilizer distribution business and that he was dressing all those bass and giving them to his older customers who were no longer able to catch fish for the table themselves. It sounded like a reasonable use of the resource and to be sure, the bass were plentiful enough to stand even that wholesale slaughter.

In the days following that memorable experience and for years thereafter until pollution ended the largemouth bonanza in Griffin, I adapted my bass fishing to the success of that fertilizer salesman. It worked! My fishing buddies and I caught many fine stringers of largemouths on the bream beds in the lily-covered shallows of that big lake. I don't think we ever had any three day success story like he had, but it was not unusual to catch 15 or 20 yearlings in a couple of hours after you pinpointed the beds of the panfish. We almost always caught all the bass we needed to eat and shared them with friends and neighbors.

The first thing we had to learn after observing the fertilizer fisherman's success, was how to find and catch the red minnows. They are never red except when they are on the bream nests and after they have swallowed a belly full of eggs. Often you knew where to catch the little red minnows when a half dozen or more regular grayish minnows circled crazily just inches below the surface in the bedding area. The minnows acted somewhat crazy, almost as if they were doped or injured. Directly on the bottom underneath these circling forage fish, the red minnows were almost always congregated literally by the thousands. You could dip up these circling regular colored minnows easily with any kind of small mesh dip net. We impaled one of those through the lips and then dropped him in the bream beds, usually in water about three or four feet deep. When the bass were thick, they would often swallow this normal minnow, but not nearly as quickly as they would the red ones. But while you are in the process of catching the real red things, you can fish with the natural gambusia.

I have never seen a commercially manufactured trap that would successfully catch the red gambusia or any of the other popeyed minnows that change colors on the bream beds. I carefully inspected what kind of rig the fertilizer fisherman used to trap his red baits. It was a piece of ordinary metal screen wire about a yard wide. He fastened a lead weight in the center and tied a masonry cord to each of the four corners. With the corner lines tied and attached to a center pull string, he lowered the homemade gadget right into a bream bed on the bottom and left it there for five minutes or so. It was not baited in any manner.

It was simply in the bed where the minnows had been feeding on the bream eggs and tiny offspring. Then he quickly yanked the wire seine to the surface. It was not unusual to catch dozens of red minnows at a single retrieve and almost always there were a few large enough to bait the hook while the trap was submerged again in quest of more red baits.

These minnows cannot be kept from one day to the next. As soon as they are snatched off the bottom and put in your minnow bucket, they start losing their red hue. Within an hour they are only speckled red and in a few hours they are back to their normal, natural color. But if you keep your trap out at the right place,you replenish your bait supply as fast as you use it and keep the best possible offering in the face of the bass you are after.

Is this kind of bass fishing too simple for today's sophisticated anglers? Maybe so for some. Is this kind of bass fishing unethical and unacceptable to the purists? Maybe so for some. In that case, you can still take advantage of knowing how bass feed on the panfish nests. Just knowing that the largemouths are here gives the astute bassman an opportunity to use his own expertise, his own ability to put more largemouths in the boat. If he doesn't approve of live bait fishing of any kind, he may still catch some fine fish his way.

Using the new Burke Lures Skitterbuzz baits, a topwater with some red and natural colors and a spinner in front, bass anglers are catching many yearlings when retrieving this nearweedless artificial across the grass and lilies around the bream beds. It's natural enough to bring some of the charging bass to the surface.

Likewise, the new Burke Snakebait, a near perfect lookalike of small snakes, is catching bass over bream beds when slowly skittered across holes in the cover. Snakes are predators of bream adults and fry, as are the bass, and presumably it is a natural sight to find a snake in the bream bedding area. It gives a hungry bass something else to go after.

A short, bright red plastic worm allowed to fall to the bottom without any weight on a light monofilament line is attractive to bass stalking the colorful gambusia. Whether the bass mistakes the worm for a minnow is anybody's guess but for sure, it will attract strikes. Often it's a struggle to get the fish aboard from heavy cover but it is a thrilling adventure to hang one bass after another in bream beds where lilies, brush and grass often make it near impossible to get the fish to the surface.

Another good bream bed bait for largemouths is a tiny jig, like the Hal-Fly or Super-Jig. These come in a variety of colors, weights and sizes, some super-Jigs now are fluorescent red. It may help some to impale a small minnow through the eyes on this jig when fishing in the bream beds, but you can catch some fish just with the lure dropped to the bottom. The Super-Jig has many tiny, colorful tentacles that sway in the water, giving a realistic look of life. It is most successful held still on a light line, not twitched as you would a No-Alibi or some other similar artificial. It should be held just inches off the bottom. If there's any current, it gives it added realism.

Catching bass off the bream beds may be old fashioned to some. It may be a novel approach to others. It may even be doubted by today's modernists. But make no mistake. Largemouths love to live off the eggs and offspring of the other sunfish. While much has been written about the predation of bullheads, shiners, catfish, garfish and bowfin that gorge themselves on the young of other species, no other family of fish feed more actively around the bream hatchery than bass. Knowing this and then learning how to find those bream nests may open up a new frontier for catchin' bass when you go after them during the summer and fall months, sometimes when you can't find them feeding anywhere else.

TROPHY WON LEESBURG TOURNAMENT

Fishing with professional bass angler Shaw Grigsby, of Gainesville, Florida, in the Harris chain of lakes at Leesburg in 1986, I landed a 10-pound, 2-ounce largemouth on a six-inch blue Letts worm in the cattails. It was the largest fish caught in the Florida State Pro Boat Bass Tournament. The fish broke the tournament record by 11-ounces.

That day Grigsby and I brought in six fish that weighed 25-pounds, 11-ounces and the team placed sixth out of 140 contestants. Our fish averaged over 4-pounds.

The previous year, I boated the big fish and got the prize in the Florida Military Bass Association's State Championship.

I have always had a knack for catching big bass.

HOW TO CATCH BASS OFF THE BEDS

Here in Florida, as early as November and December in the southern portion of the state, bass begin their spawning cycle. In Central and Northern Florida, the bedding can take place as late as May. Therefore, it is safe to say that bedding takes place for six months of each year in all three zones. For this reason, fishermen, we should all get on the catch and release program.

We have dozens of tournaments every weekend plus thousands of regular anglers who are after a trophy bass. During this vulnerable time in their lives, the big spawning bass are easily caught. Just when the reproduction cycle starts, an army of trophy seekers puts pressure on a very important renewable resource. There are no set guidelines or laws to prevent the rape of the bass beds.

As far as I'm concerned, a professional guide or tournament fishermen should not try to catch the bass off the beds. We should set an example for future generations to follow. This applies to land developers as well as sportsmen. I hate to watch a nationally televised fishing show that depicts a so-called professional teaching viewers how to catch bass on the beds.

We are all aware of the steady decline in bass populations. I understand that in the last five years many of our lakes have gone from 400 bass per acre to less than a dozen. Remember, tournament fishermen, that when you go through the weigh-in process you can kiss that bass and bed goodbye. I know some anglers who catch the small males that are guarding the bed first, then concentrate on the female on the bed. This practice is disastrous.

My guides are not allowed to catch or keep bass caught off the beds. If I find out differently, they are immediately terminated. I pray that other guide services pick up on this type of preservation. Like it or not, we all have to start taking a serious interest in this matter.

We're not just hurting ourselves, but also the future of bass fishing for children and grandchildren. I cannot over emphasize the importance of catch and release.

Catching bass **off** the beds is very simple. All it takes is a lot of patience and self-discipline. Present your artificial baits in the proper natural fashion. The first step is using a top quality light line. Line in the 8 to 10 pound class, preferably the non-glow type. I believe a glowing line will spook a fish in shallow water. I recommend the lightest possible bullet weights. Black works best for me. Hooks no larger than 4/0 in either black, blue or brown. Silver and gold do not work as well for the plastic worm rigs. Plastic worms in the crawdad color and covered with a quality scent get you ready for action. The scents are controversial, but I use them if for no reason other than to remove the human odor from my hands that have been handling other fish, candy and snacks. What I prefer during the bedding cycles are canals, coves and the north end of lakes. The north end catches the sun first and maintains a steadier temperature. Bass will start to make their move back to the bedding areas as soon as the water temperature reaches the 60's in the spring.

The mouths of the coves or the entrances to the canals are good places to catch the moving fish. In many cases they are in a feeding frenzy before going on their beds. When I see an area being "fanned" I back off to the nearest cover or dropoff. A seven-to-ten foot dropoff will hold good fish. This is where I use my dead worm techniques. When the fish are quiet, I use my dead worm cast. Just let the worm sit until the tight jawed lunker is agitated into inhaling it. Be patient. It may take several minutes to get the hit. If the bass are feeding, the raising and dropping of the worms gets savage strikes. Bump the worm along the bottom and greyhound it through the thermoclime. You'll be catching enough fish to make your trip worthwhile.

In the Thursday, March 31, 1988, copy of the *Orlando Sentinel* , The Associated Press released a photo showing Bill Johnson, of the Florida Game and Fresh Water Fish Commission netting dead bass in an inlet off the Dora Canal just south of Tavares. John Benton, of the Commission, said 217 bass were picked up and that another 100 were floating in the canal. Biologists say the bass died after they were released in oxygen depleted water. The bass had been caught during the weekend in three tournaments and released. This is proof positive that something must be done to save one of our most valuable natural resources, the largemouth bass, that is not always handled intelligently at small tournament weigh-ins.

FOR TROPHY BASS....
DOUG HANNON LIKES SPINNERS AND PLASTIC WORMS

(Hannon is a recognized authority on bass fishing and the authors are happy to include his big bass lure advice in this book.)

By Doug Hannon

Trophy bass are the most evolved and adapted to environmental pressures for two reasons: (1) They have been exposed to the environment for the longest period of time or they wouldn't be so large, and (2) They have proven by their superior growth rate that they have developed an efficient feeding and behavioral pattern.

Important environmental factors are a bass' ability to reproduce, feed efficiently, survive and prosper during extreme seasonal changes and achieve fast growth rates by dominating the water in warmer parts of the lake during the winter seasons. The influence that fishermen have on the bass survival cannot be minimized, even if some biologists disagree. It's a major factor.

Fishing pressure is relevant because it is usually selective and it is an intelligent pressure directed at big bass, which are best adapted to survival. I believe that sophisticated, heavy fishing pressure and a huge harvest of the lunker bass population can and will harm the future of the species. This is particularly true of largemouth bass that may, on occasion, live to the age of 18 and still pass on genes to their offspring each year that they reproduce.

Lamenting the passing of big bass is not an indictment or criticism of bass fishermen. Expert anglers with catches of 321 like Bud Andrews, who releases all his bass, are not doing a great deal of damage to the lunker survival.

My remarks here are designed to help the big bass angler succeed in catching these rare giants. But the fisherman must face reality. A simple grasp of the basic environmental requirements of big bass no longer ensures success. You must acknowledge and overcome the significant, new environmental factor affecting these large bass—that's the human predator element.

Obviously, pressure selectively reduces the big bass populations. We can't stop all of the slob fishermen or fish hogs. But true conservationists can hunt these trophy fish and preserve the species by releasing them and protecting them wherever possible. My task here is to help you intelligently hone your techniques and knowledge of the big bass so that you can catch some of these monster largemouths responsibly in waters where a few of them continue to survive.

Three pitfalls fishermen must overcome in order to catch a lunker bass are: (1) Lack of knowledge of the bass lifestyle, (2) basic misconceptions about big bass and successful techniques, and (3) the tendency of fishermen to react to failure and frustration by over-complication rather than simplification of technique. These fundamentals are the backbone of your approach to lunker bass success. Use your knowledge, then blend it with hard work and your personal experiences in pursuit of the giants.

Only one to two percent of the bass population have proven their superiority and reached weights of 10-pounds or more. To catch one of these scarce trophies, you must understand their basic needs. Big bass live in the same world as their smaller relatives and they are more dominant and aggressive than the smaller fish. They eat the most and they are the first to strike when there is a feeding opportunity.

Some anglers call this aggressive nature "anti-survival" and "dumb." Many fishermen think the big bass is a recluse, cagey, picky and seldom aggressive. That's simply not true. They would never have reached the monster size had the lunker not been out-competing, out-eating and out-growing the rest of the species in his territory.

Big bass are elusive and hard to catch simply because there are not many of them. They are no more intelligent than the younger, smaller fish.

In terms of surviving mankind's fishing pressure, they are not as intelligent as the smaller bass. The number of big fish in heavily fished versus unfished waters proves it. Big bass do have one noteworthy survival instinct that shows up in my extensive tagging experiments. The big bass are very territorial wherever they are released. Some of them I have caught as many as six times and their dominance and knowledge of a particular area of a lake fulfills all their needs and thus limits their movements. This tends to make them exposed to fishermen who understand this trait.

Many lunkers are vulnerable and catchable only when they move out to the shallows in the spring to nest. Most of the territories with the good elements are obvious to the experienced angler and many have already been fished out. Thus, a good fishing spot must not only have the key survival elements, it must also be difficult for fishermen to recognize or reach with a lure.

There is no evidence that the big bass is so astute that she can pick a discreet territory. I call these places "smart territories." Since I began tagging big bass more than a dozen years ago, I have moved lunker bass from one lake to another several times. I found this to be a death sentence. They didn't die from disease or injury. But within a few weeks fishermen call me (my phone number is on the tags) to report they have caught the 10-pounder I released.

It's uncanny that the tagged fish lived maybe ten years or more and was not caught and then a month or so after being placed in a new territory, she was suckered by a fisherman and caught again. She is usually caught this second time after being transplanted in a "smart territory" in her new lake that is a likely-looking place to the experienced bass angler. It's usually a place close to where she was released and a spot that was undoubtedly a big bass territory years ago. You get the picture? I now do not move my tagged fish out of their home lakes. I want them to go back to the territory they know best where they escaped predation for a long lifetime.

A few elements make up a "smart territory." These elements are well known to most veteran bass anglers. They include a productive feeding flat. The flat ideally will be heavily weeded. It needs various types of aquatic growth with plenty of pockets in four to eight feet of water. Trees, stumps, bushes and ledges are also beneficial.

It would also be nice if there were some deeper water, 17 feet or more, as nearby her home territory as possible or better yet, if there were a source of inflowing water, like a creek, to moderate the effects of seasonal changes. We need nearby firm spawning bottom sand, gravel, rock or clay and perhaps some cow lilies in about four feet of water or less. This area needs to be calm and protected from north winds.

Then it is important that this spot be hard for fishermen to find. The presence of big fish is often the most obvious indication that these environmental factors are present. You need to study the features of the territory to determine if it is potentially consistent to support super bass throughout the year.

I have a few hints that will increase your chances of finding a "smart territory" and catching a giant mama bass. Treat these territories with respect like their scarcity deserves. If you don't, you'll over-harvest the fish and everyone loses.

The limitless imagination of fishermen often gives us a bum steer. Man is the only living thing that will wander and die in a desert chasing mirages rather than using the sun and stars as a compass to find his way out. This kind of thinking makes anglers imagine huge populations of big bass lurking in the mysterious crevices of the deepest water in the lake. Any analysis of the basic environmental elements necessary for big bass survival, clearly indicates they are not present in the recesses of deep water in the lakes.

Simplicity is the key. You can name several common environmental elements necessary for sustaining big fish populations. But the one element paramount for sustaining life of the really big trophy bass has to be a better-than-average supply of food. My catch records of bass over 5-pounds include hundreds of fish. They indicate that big bass primarily feed in water from three to 13 feet deep.

I center my search for a large bass on an eight-foot contour line and look for the following: (1) Submerged weed or moss beds, (2) trees, brush or stumps, and (3) rock or other natural ledges or structures. I start this search in the north or northwest portion of the lake because of what I call "Hannon's Northwest Factor." I also begin by fishing the south sides of bars, points, flats and any other unique features.

There's another misconception that big bass only feed at night or at dawn or dusk. This isn't true. You are likely to find big bass feeding in the middle of the day. These lunker bass can only get bigger by feeding more often and longer than smaller cousins. They are more in step with the ecosystem and are thus first in line. The giants are the first to respond to cloud cover before an approaching storm, the migration of shad to and from open water, and even the daily and monthly effects of the moon. The shad movement is usually greater about mid-morning or mid-afternoon.

Sloppy technique is more likely to show up in the light of day. Then fish are harder to catch in daylight, not because they are shy and spooky, but because they are brave enough and curious enough to swim right up to you to see what you are.

When you decide what areas you want to fish, fish carefully and make sure you are at those spots during all times of the day. Be sure to fish during the prime moon periods. If you do not have the stamina, determination, time and patience to do this, you'll never catch dozens of the big bruisers. Keep your objective in perspective. Most fishermen would be happy to catch one or two huge bass in a season. You can probably accomplish that by fishing hard and smart on a few weekends.

Fishermen often respond to failure and frustration by over-complicating angling theory and their techniques. As much as

The Bass Of A Lifetime

101

it helps our egos to regard a difficult task as complex, this thinking is often the biggest obstacle in the path of success. When you accept two characteristics of big bass, namely: (1) The simplicity of their lifestyles, and (2) their rarity, you know it takes a special breed of fishermen with simple techniques to consistently catch big bass.

Adopt a basic approach. Turn the odds in your favor by separating your lures into two categories: (1) Those which attract attention, and (2) those that trigger strikes. Characteristics that might attract attention include bright colors, like chartreuse and yellow, extra-large plugs, or lures with noise-makers or rattles. Triggering characteristics include natural, subtle colors and paint schemes; long, slim, worm-like shapes; small or moderate sizes; and lures that are quiet when being retrieved.

Confine your lure selection to the natural triggering characteristics inherent in plastic worms and minnow baits like Rapalas and jigs. To catch big bass, use repeated presentation and slow retrieves instead of trying to catch a fish's attention with gaudy contrivances.

You may not realize that spinner baits are one of the quietest lures you can pull through the water. That's because the blade runs in harmony with the flow of the water, never changing directions. The off-center turning of the weight, like an out-of-balance wheel, imparts vibrations to the soft skirt or jig. This causes a wiggle, and it transmits much less disturbance in the water than many other types of lures.

Fish see and strike, generally, only the swimming body of a spinner. If you are missing a lot of strikes on a spinner bait and think maybe the bass are hitting only the blade, tie on a lighter color with a more visible body to draw attention away from the blade. Spinner baits are great for big bass.

To consistently catch big bass, you must make your approach and presence blend into your surroundings. Use a dark-colored boat with low seats. Don't fish standing up and don't wear bright clothing during middle of the day fishing. Avoid fluorescent lines. Pale green line is my preference. Disregard the high-tech, fast-paced pattern of today's fishing. Settle down with natural elements around you and you'll be amazed at the results.

You never forget the excitement, the exhilaration and awe you experience when you get that first glimpse of a giant bass on the line.

A voyage in search of knowledge need never abandon the spirit of adventure.

THE KAHLE CONNECTION—
NEW TWIST IN WORM FISHING

Originally fishermen enticed bass to bite the real thing, a giant night crawler dangled in the cover where largemouths lurked, waited and attacked almost anything alive that they could swallow. They caught bass on the bottom and the top with these live wriggly morsels that were irresistible to a hungry fish. Along came the plastic worm a couple of decades ago and it has been far and away the most successful artificial lure ever devised and fills tackle shop shelves in hundreds of sizes, colors and designs. Few astute bass anglers would dare not have a variety of these bass catchers in their tackle boxes to flip in front of stubborn bass when everything else has failed. Over the years it has been refined, sophisticated, tested and proven successful but every now and then a tiny variation, an innovation of style and procedure, has been introduced by some knowledgeable basser that revitalizes interest in worm fishing and now even greater production than ever looms.

Such a change was introduced in Central Florida by Bill Darby, of Gainesville, and the late Curt Layser of Cross Creek. Darby used the "Kahle Connection" years ago but only recently did he and Layser make it popular in Central Florida. It has been sensationally productive from spring to winter and these two veteran bass anglers are sharing their breakthrough. It's simple but it works.

Call it the "Kahle Connection" because they swear by this strong hook with the "dumb bend" as they put it. It does have the wide open bend that makes it look like it is deformed, damaged in manufacturing or somehow unorthodox enough to attract attention.

Curt, before his death, used this Kahle in 3/0 size and Bill prefers the 4/0 size. Curt prefered a casting reel while Bill sticks to a spinning gear. But the system is the same from there on as these old-timers stick a hard, purple, eight inch worm with white spots through the head, never more than 1/4 inch from the end. It is not weedless. It is not weighted. It is so simple that it

103

seems impossible that it works. You do not weave the hook around and stick it back in the plastic. It remains naked, protruding right through the spotted worm's head. Its action is fantastic, better than the Texas rig.

With this kind of impaled worm, Curt and Bill use their accuracy in casting to keep from being constantly hung up. They do not fish lily pads much as this open hook will grab at every lily stalk in the neighborhood. They toss it in holes in the lilies. Grass is not quite as hazardous. The open hook in the head of the worm will skim over grass normally. When they can't fish inside the aquatic growth, they simply cast it near the cover. That's usually all it takes as this Kahle Connection worm draws the largemouths out of cover when other lures seem to be ignored.

"Hooks with weed guards sometimes snap open when a bass strikes and you miss the fish," Layser said.

"We never let the bait go to the bottom. In the first place it has no lead head, no weight at all, and it is a floater. We just cast it as close to the cover as possible and start reeling and twitching it back to the boat. It's a funny looking lure. The white spots on the worm make it look all white as it comes through the water. I don't know what the bass think it is on top but I know it brings them a' running. They will hit it on the top when reeled in rapidly or five or six inches under the surface when we twitch it slowly toward the boat and it looks yellow or gold colored, like natural golden shiners. The bass mistake it for a live shiner. We have caught bass with it like you wouldn't believe," Layser revealed.

These bassers with expertise with the innovation point out that to catch fish with this kind of hookup, you must be a line watcher. When the worm is slightly under the surface, often you will not feel a thing even when a big lunker gulps it down. The line will just suddenly start moving off from its course toward the boat. There may be no bump-bump or tap-tap at all, just the line moving and you'll suddenly feel a pull like a wet blanket on the hook. The bass already has it then and there's not much need for hook setting. The sharp, open hook sinks easily with just a little yank and then you have the thrill of bringing the fish to the boat.

"The Kahle Connection worm hook up is a fine open water lure when you find schooling bass feeding. They really go after it," Darby says.

"We release all the bass we catch that weigh over 5-pounds and some that weigh less. Let me tell you we put a lot of fish back in the water over the past few years," Layser said.

"We use 12 and 14 pound test line. You can throw the light bait better with a line no heavier than this but we hesitate to use a weaker test because of the big fish we hang with this Kahle rig," Curt said. "Darby landed one in '86 over 10-pounds and many in the 8 and 9-pound range."

In Central Florida where the hydrilla curse has been prevalent for several years, the Kahle worm has been successful as it will skim over the weeds on the surface and it is equally productive flipped around the outskirts of hydrilla islands where trophy bass have been found frequently the past decade.

There are some other bassers using the Kahle system with weaker hooks, like the 2/0 gold speckled perch catcher in Florida. This hook bends easily and is extremely light weight. In the Rodman Reservoir where hydrilla is still as thick as a meadow in some places, this spotted worm on the speck hook can be skimmed over the surface and is deadly for hiding bass in that cover. It has the disadvantage of not being strong enough to hold a real lunker when you use much gusto. You simply have to let the fish do the fighting and patiently hope your hook will hold until the fish tires and you get your fingers clamped on the lower jaw. While some disciples of the Darby-Layser discovery are successful with the weaker, gold speck hook, the duo prefers the hook with the "dumb bend" that is much stronger and won't succumb when horsed to the boat.

Oddly enough, this dynamic duo declares that you can not catch nearly as many bass if you are using any other color worm or if you impale one with a curly tail or that is soft and pliable. Only the hardish worm that is straight and unsophisticated with the leopard spotting over its body pays off.

"We have had trouble finding these worms. For a time we got them from Indiana but then that source dried up. We searched tackle shops around Central Florida and finally we found a big batch of them at Gates Distributing in Ocala, Florida. The manager there said he had to buy 29,000 of these worms, one shift's production, to get them but he had gladly done that as it was a proven success." Layser and Darby bought 10 pounds of spotted worms.

Darby has used the spotted worm for about 20 years and even The Kahle Connection system is not new to him. He introduced it to Layser and the partners in a bass boat made it popular in Central Florida. Both bassers emphasize that the success of the system is sharply reduced if you hook the worm more than 1/4 inch from the head. It does not have enough action to entice the predators.

The Kahle Connection rigging seems to work both early and late but it is not as productive in mid-day when topwaters of any kind are usually rejected by bass. They haven't tried it at night, but believe it would be a good nocturnal lure.

Neither Layser nor Darby is a live bait fisherman. They are the purists who go after bass with only artificials, but they know some other astute anglers who use the Kahle hook with shiners, especially some friends in Alabama, who swear by this "dumb hook" under the shiner dorsal or anal fin.

With a new supply of spotted purple worms, Darby fishes several times a week on some Central Florida lake or river and it's an exception when he does not come in with some stories of success, even if he releases his fish and comes in with nothing. Darby's 22/30 Zebco equipment with these leopard spotted worms on Kahle hooks establishes a new twist to worm fishing and he keeps sharing his discovery with everyone interested.

"Remember," Darby says, "It is a bait that attracts the predators and that means muds, gars and pickerel as well as largemouth bass. Anything that likes a live bait will go after this lure when you skim it over the surface or twitch it a few inches under the water. It's a real go getter."

Doug Hannon and Andrews with Nice Bass

THONOTOSASSA BASS FISHING GOOD

One of my trophy fish was caught in Lake Thonotosassa in the Tarpon Springs section of Central Florida. It, along with Lake Tarpon, are great bass lakes today that any artificial lure angler will enjoy fishing.

Phil Chapman, biologist with the Florida Game and Fresh Water Fish Commission, credits much of Thonotosassa's big bass success today to a program of planting bulrushes in the lake six years ago. They have spread widely and created excellent bass habitat and the 'rushes have helped to firm up the otherwise mucky bottom.

Thonotosassa is one of those lakes where astute bass anglers can locate feeding fish by watching for surfacing shad. They make little dimples on the surface that I refer to as "circles." Sometimes these shad create a shower as dozens leap above the surface together when trying to avoid a big bass or other predator.

Doug Bass operates Reece's Fish Camp on this largest lake in Hillsborough County. The camp is located off I-4 exit 8 on Thonotosassa Road that branches off Skewlee and Taylor Road north. The phone number is (813) 986-9806.

I caught one of my 321 trophy bass there the first time I tried the lake and it was in a slough bordered with bulrushes. The big fish hit a topwater that I had left dead in the water for several minutes, my normal practice.

This is a good lake for anglers to go after wallmounts

HOW I FEEL ABOUT TOPWATERS

I believe that topwater lures like the Rapala, Rebel, Bang-O-Lure, and others, can coax bass into striking when other baits fail. I have seen times during cold weather when all of the usual lures failed and bass seemed turned off of everything. Then I would put a topwater near some cover and let it stay motionless for a long period. A lunker would attack it.

108

CRANKBAITS—REALISM IN LURES THAT CATCH LARGE AND SMALLMOUTHS

Fishing with Betty Haire, of Charlotte, North Carolina in the second annual Lady Bass Classic on the 35,400 acre Lake Chickamauga near Chattanooga, Tennessee, the press observer was having difficulty finding an open hole in the milfoil to plop a bait when she chose to resort to flippin' a plastic worm for the elusive keeper-size largemouths she was stalking for the weigh-in. When she was 40-50 feet off this weedline, there was plenty of casting room but when she eased the boat into the middle of these weedy jungles, she had to either put her tackle in the boat or change tactics. It made the double treble hook Little Ticker that Lee Sisson made impossible to crank to the gunnels without dragging massive loads of the recently-poisoned aquatic junk and then tediously cleaning prior to another cast. Suddenly, it occurred to the observer that while he had no flippin' stick or worms, why wouldn't these bass in the weeds hit a crankbait that floated down in any of these holes, tempting and enticing the fish to strike? Maybe it didn't have to be cast and retrieved the way he had always fished a crankbait.

Fortunately, the Little Ticker that dives up to seven feet deep when retrieved,will sink tail-first, slowly and invitingly for any predator hungry enough to make a mistake and gulp it down if you wedge a shot between the tail treble hooks. Yet, when you give the rod tip even the slightest twitch, the lure jumps upward and forward and for a moment its head is down, the most desirable position for a lure to attract bass strikes. He watched the action of the lure when tested in a hole four feet off the stern of Betty's Ranger. He couldn't get any further out than that with a six foot Fenwick rod and ProStaff Zebco closed-faced reel without fouling in the milfoil. But there was a washtub size clearing within reach. He reasoned it would be more fun to vertically jig a crankbait in that hole than wait for Betty to leave this cover where he could fish the lure in the conventional manner.

Nonchalantly and with little confidence, he watched the small crankbait descend three or four feet in the clear water and then disappear in the milfoil. The flasher indicated they were hovered over about 11 feet of water. It touched bottom, the line wrinkled and the observer reeled it up a foot or so, twitched the rod tip. He could feel the lure dart upward and forward, then relax as it slowly went downward again. He picked up an apple from the lunch bag and took a bite, holding on carelessly to the rod butt with one hand. Bingo! Something crashed into the Little Ticker like a locomotive that Chattanooga is so traditionally associated with. He dropped the apple, grabbed the reel handle and began turning and at the same time yanked the rod overhead. In that deep water, it was only a moment until a yearling bass was airborne and soon lay flopping on the deck at his feet.

Betty turned around somewhat perplexed. Like the observer, she had never before seen anyone flip with a crankbait in heavy cover. But obviously it worked and the bass were attracted to it underneath the milfoil just like they were when they were casting and retrieving on the outskirts of the cover. Suffice it to say, that time after successful time since that revelation at the Lady Bass Classic, the observer has caught fine bass with a sinking, small crankbait around cover, especially holes in the lily pads and around logs where there is not as much chance of a hang-up that will cost you another lure. The treble hooks make it difficult to flip where the cover is heavy but if you can pick out a few holes with enough structure to hold fish, it works even when fished vertically and almost under the boat.

Crankbaits are the favorite artificials of many professional and novice bassers around the nation. It's easy to hang a fish on a crankbait with its hook assortment and doesn't require the intensity and hook-setting so essentialwhen you are fishing a plastic worm and feel a tap-tap ever so lightly that gives you only fractional seconds to react and set the hook. Not so with most crankbaits. The bass hit them with a vengeance and often hang themselves, whether you are casting and retrieving or flippin' vertically.

It makes sense that the crankbait is a productive bass lure. Only the plastic worm has the characteristics of the natural food as realistic as a minnow-like artificial. Fish have to make a mistake when they are caught on artificials and rationally it would be easier to mistake a phony crankbait than a spinner, jig, pork rind or even a topwater lure. How many times have you seen a shiner swimming on top of the water? Topwaters catch fish but something the same shape and size of a minnow under the surface where the bass lives realistically should attract more strikes.

Everyone has had some strange experiences with a crankbait if he has fished a few years. I recall an incident in Hanes Creek near Leesburg, Florida, some years ago when I was fishing a Rebel Deep Wee R along a jungle-like shoreline. I had caught two or three bass and decided to take a break and drink a Coke. The sun was high in the sky. It was a real bluebird morning. I laid the rod down across my lap, carelessly letting the lure drag outside the boat. The current was moving me along fast enough to force the little lure to submerge, and it jiggled, dived and darted a foot or so under the water. I was startled and almost fell out of the boat by the time I swallowed the first mouthful of Coke. The rod butt hit me in the face and headed for the bright blue yonder before I could grab it. I never saw that bass but after half an hour of dragging the bottom, I caught the line and retrieved my fishing tackle, minus the crankbait. The big lunker had snarled the monofilament around the bushes on the bottom and broke off the lure. It was a case of pure carelessness, but it did prove to me that the bass will strike close to the boat and the crankbait is productive when you are after largemouth bass anywhere.

But it works for other species too. Recently I was after smallmouth bass in the downriver sloughs of Center Hill Lake near Rock Island, Tennessee. Great, steep, rocky cliffs rose 100 feet along both shorelines and rocks and fallen trees were half-submerged in beautifully clear water everywhere you looked. I tied on a Bagley four inch crankbait and bounced it off the cliff. It splattered water on the surface, and I twitched it a time or two, then reeled slowly and steadily. The crankbait eased past a big boulder and I thought it hung on the bottom. I yanked the rod overhead hoping to dislodge it. It came loose and almost circled the rock. There was a fish on and it took me several minutes to get that critter to back track and come toward the boat. It was a 3-pound, 8-ounce smallmouth, the largest bronzeback I have ever put in the boat. The old reliable crankbait had done its job again.

Crankbaits are the nearest thing to natural forage fish and they will catch all species of bass, other fish too, when flipped close to a hungry critter.

MY BASS SEMINARS

For over a year I have been holding a kind of bass school or seminar at Cypress Lodge for people interested in learning how to catch big bass in Central Florida. The reception has been extremely exciting with both men and women coming from great distances to hear me share what I know about successful bass fishing.

I talk about successful baits, techniques and more importantly, how to find bass. Some of my students in these classes have returned time after time to increase their know-how and it has been gratifying to hear many of them share their experiences of successfully landing a nice bass and then releasing it.

Success in bass fishing always goes back to confidence, patience and desire to learn the lifestyle of the fish and then adapting to methods that have proven productive by guides, lay veterans and professionals down through the years.

Teaching this class and the attentive faces that I see has made it one of the most gratifying experiences of my life.

HOW TO CATCH A TROPHY BASS OUT OF SCHOOLING FISH

During the lockjaw period, my dead bait technique pays off. After the bedding cycle is over, the fish start to leave their shallow water (usually around three to five feet in depth), and head out to open water of seven to 12 feet in depth. They prefer open water that offers underwater vegetation such as hydrilla, coon-tail, and pepper grass. What's happening is very simple. Shad (bait fish) are spawning and they need heavy vegetation for protection. Shad are the number one choice for schooling bass. That's why bass move out to open water when bait fish start to spawn. Bass just can't reject the heavy schools of shad. The mere number really excites them and irritates them to the point that they are at their aggressive best.

You can't ask for much better fishing than aggressive bass. When bass turn on, you will turn on.

My best fishing days are when fish are schooling. Sometimes hundreds of bass will come to the top and chase and feed on shad. Other times the bass and bait fish will hit the side of your boat with a thump. Now you are really experiencing a shot of adrenalin that makes your blood come to a boiling point. The action is unbelievable and it is something that every fisherman should experience at least once in a life time.

The method and technique I use to help me catch trophy bass out of schooling fish are: **1-** Look for open water action– fish that are actually jumping out of the water and chasing and feeding on live shad. If this method does not work, then immediately look for bait fish schooling. If the water is a red color and the live shad are in a good concentration, you will notice them moving right along the top. They will make a small ripple like a "V." I call it "V" for victory mainly because it is only a matter of time before the bass observe them.

2- Locate open water fish by observing where the different types of wildlife are, watch the gulls and other birds that feed on bait fish. Look and see where the gulls are diving into the

115

water and circling and there is your guarantee that the bait fish are there, and most importantly, where the bass are. Bass will never lose control or sight of their food supply.

At the point where I observe surface water action and I'm sure that there are fish in the area, I immediately stop the boat and work the area where the water is exploding. The average fisherman will concentrate on the open water surface action and try to chase down or keep up with the schoolers. I would be the first to agree that this is super fun that offers a lot of action and excitement for any fisherman. You can catch a lot of good fish between two and four pounds and occasionally you will catch a trophy bass. But many years of hard knocks have helped me to establish better methods and techniques. I have come to realize that the trophy bass that most anglers search for definitely has different habits and actions than yearlings or schooling fish. Bass become bigger because they get smarter as they get bigger.

Another proven theory of mine is very simple but very meaningful. An adult will walk to the mail box but a child will run. Get the picture? So what do I do? I immediately concentrate on the area where the fish just went down. Even if they come up again, which they will, I will stay on the spot where they first came up. The reason is that when the smaller schooling fish charge into a massive school of bait fish, they automatically injure and kill dozens of bait fish because they are moving so fast. So the bass really have their work cut out.

The explosion of bass charging into the schools of bait fish injures and kills shad. They fall to the bottom where there is hydrilla, peppergrass, or coon-tail, perfect cover for the monster (trophy bass) that awaits the easy serving of bait fish. My technique goes right back to my dead bait technique. The only difference is I try to use as little weight as possible– or none. I like 8-10 pound test **Stren** line. The name of the game is to present your artificial bait in the most natural fashion. Then present your bait as close as possible to the real thing: in this case the injured and dead bait sinking to the bottom. What better way to fish than the dead bait technique, a bait that lies perfectly still on the bottom, just like one of the dead shad that sank to the bottom?

BASSING'S NOT SLOW WHEN THE WATER'S LOW

Casting with a figure eight underhanded twitch, I watched my weighted, quivering plastic crawfish plop into the muddy goo a foot up the incline of the sandy bank. I took up the slack on my casting reel, saw the life-like crawly imitation of a bass morsel turn toward the water and a second later it left a bit of dirt on the surface when it submerged from the 1/4 ounce lead in its tail. It zig-zagged toward the bottom that was three feet below. It never reached that expected destination. A bass was waiting.

Shocked from a thrill I usually experience from a strike on a topwater lure, I suddenly had a devil on the line that had exploded only moments after my crawfish was out of sight. It was close enough to the surface that the lunker largemouth's flopping tail had boiled the water with incredible action and the noise of the strike sent a tingle up my spine that made me think minnows were flouncing in my veins. It was the moment bassers live for.

There was no need to set the hook. The sharp 2/0 TruTurn hook that was embedded and buried in the two inch, motor oil colored soft plastic crawfish had done its job. It was firmly fastened in the upper lip of that bass the instant I had the line sufficiently tight with enough resistance to force the penetration.

A couple of runs and one jump later, all exciting and cherished moments as I awaited a better look at what I had fooled into striking a truly unappetizing mouthful, I reached down and lip-lifted a nice 5-pound bass over the gunnels. Again, the manufacturer of an artificial fishing lure had devised a bait that would prompt the challenging largemouths of the county to make a mistake and thus bring a degree of accomplishment and enjoyment to another angler. It was a revealing experience.

It meant something more to me on that memorable day when I caught a half dozen other bass before the day was done. It meant that there was a lure that is productive **when the water is low** and yards away from the weeping willow-draped covered and scenic shoreline of low country rivers and lakes. No longer

117

would I shy away from low water streams with barren, exposed shores, because now it was evident that these hungry fish were aware that most of their food supply came from the banks and not from the open water. Obviously, they kept an eye peeled for anything that moved at the water's edged and when a phony crawfish slipped through the mud and into the stream, where is there a bass smart enough to detect the counterfeit? It slinked into the water like the real thing.

In the long ago, I had caught dozens of fine bass with real live crawfish, scooped up or trapped under rocks, in drainage ditches and swamp bogs. I suffered through a few slightly painful pinches from the menacing claws of these critters that seriously objected to having a hook poked through their corrugated tail muscles. But in those fishing adventures, I sank the squirming creatures to the bottom of the stream in the deeper holes where the water was eddying and peaceful. A lead shot or two kept them weighted down and easy for bass to catch as well as other predators searching for a tell-tale tap-tap that signaled a live something was stalking my bait. Then a quick hook set often put a bass in the boat and topped off another successful fish hunt.

I had even had success in some Southern streams with live baby snapping turtles impaled through their rough tails and allowed to scramble around awkwardly on the bottom where there were abundant logs, rocks, limbs or other cover. Big bass relish these two inch turtles that tempt them in their territory and they will go after them with the enthusiasm of a red-shouldered hawk after a water moccasin. They can't digest the hard shell but they can keep the reptile in their stomach until all the nutrient is absorbed and then regurgitate the useless bone tissue.

I had also found artificial crawfish with hard plastic bodies that could be retrieved near the bottom moving backward in flicks, were productive bass baits. Manufactured in several sizes and in natural colors, this variation from a conventional crankbait will often bring lunkers a' running. Bass have a natural appetite for crawfish. They are clumsy, have little defense and are far more nutritious than shiners and other forage food in the school family. Bass sometimes will strike these lures when minnow-like artificials are ignored.

But I had unlocked a way to catch bass that I had never tried before. Generally, when droughts send water levels plummeting along the Florida lake fronts, I had resorted to plastic worms and crankbaits dropped in the holes. There was not much shoreline cover left when the water ebbed two or three feet from normal and presumably the largemouth moved into the main streams of these swampland wildernesses. But it was not necessarily so. Many kept an eye out for forage critters from the banks. And why not? Small snakes often dropped off overhanging bushes and wiggled into the water when I trolled along a few yards from the flora. Small turtles and frogs scrambled through the mud to apparent safety in the water. Even flying insects and fuzzy worms often lost their grips on the bushes, splashed in the mud and squirmed into the water. Yes, bass did have reason for lurking along the shoreline, ever-observant for a possible meal. The crawfish retrieved through the mud and eased into the water is a real attraction for hungry bass.

"Crawfish flipped on the hill and then reeled back in the water will murder bass. I have tried it when the water was low in many lakes and streams. It is a dynamite lure and you'll sure like it if you use it," says Glenn Lau, the celebrity largemouth film maker and avid student of bass behavior. Lau first tested this realistic, soft plastic crawfish lure in Central Florida in mid-1986. He recommended it highly to his friends. He was right. It's a great bass lure in the swampland area where the crawfish logically could be creeping out of hiding places in search of a receding water line. Maybe it would not work if you cast it against a rocky cliff, but it is practical, rational and productive along Florida shorelines.

Creepy critters all seem to attract bass. The life-like Snakebait by Burke is catching bass. The frog and eel has bass fighting for a chance to strike it. Flimsy, curly plastic eel, snake and worm replicas have proven their effectiveness. Lunkers have the instinct to watch for these foods at the spots they are most likely to be found. That's why they take a look along the swampland river shorelines. If there's something moving toward the water with a quivering claw and some shaky legs, it must be a crawfish. That's good eating for every hungry largemouth in the territory and they strike it with gusto. It's the first low water bait you can try when most anglers expect the fishing to be slow. Low doesn't mean slow for those bassers who go after shoreline bass with an humble crawfish. And you'll note another real fact: bass hit artificial crawfish hard, much more intensely than a plastic worm. You'll seldom miss a strike on a crawfish lure. The bass gobble down the crustacean quickly and run. Hook setting is often not necessary for the predator has swallowed the whole thing and is off to the races. They almost never mouth and fondle a crawfish, whether real or artificial, like they will a plastic worm.

This crawfish enticer is a coming bait, especially during dry seasons when the real thing gets marooned on the hill and has to wobble back to the water. Alert bass pick him up quickly—dinner is served.

CHALLENGE COLD FRONTS

After years of making a living from fishing, I have learned from experience that bass fishing is no different than any other sport. You have to establish a defense to get on the offensive. (A quote that many athletes hear.)

What is offense? In the case of fishing, it can be cold fronts. They are probably the most serious and most difficult of times to catch bass. This is when you immediately concentrate on your defense.

What is defense? It is presenting your artificial lure with the proper technique. The presentation is of the utmost importance to meet and challenge any condition. After this is accomplished, you should notice that your catches are increasing. When I fish during a moving front, I find that most of my fish are still pretty active. It's after the front has moved through that I find it really tough to get strikes.

During the active period, I use my bumping worm technique. The activity is there when you can see bait fish jumping to escape the predators and by observing the movement of aquatic vegetation. Fish moving through buggy whips, cattails, bullrushes, lily pads, peppergrass, hydrilla and milfoil leave telltale signs of feeding. The bumping worm is literally a plastic worm rigged up Texas-style with no more than 10 to 12 pound test line with a 1/16 or 1/8 ounce bullet slip sinker. Water depth should exceed 12 feet for this cast. Cast out about 50 feet and let your worm drop to the bottom then lie there perfectly still. At times, I have let it lie for up to 30 minutes. This is very important because during the front the bass have a case of lockjaw. Natural currents may move the worm, but don't you move it!

So, what better way to fish your bait? DEAD BAIT. The lure is behaving in the same manner as the dormant fish. Two words to adhere to: Patience and self-discipline. These virtues definitely separate the men from the boys. After the lift, the strike and the fight, release the fish gently. Remember, today's conservation practice means the difference between a healthy future or a total disaster. Catch and release is the only means I know that will save 10-pound bass

CHIP OFF THE OLD BLOCK

When Bud and Kathy's young son John was 2 1/2-years old and attending Sunday School at the First Baptist Church in Inverness, he was asked what he would like to thank God for. He quickly told his teacher, Linda Higdon, "Fish." Later that same day his mother was about to fillet a 2-pound bass that was dying in the holding tank. It would be their supper. The fish reminded Kathy of Johnny's answer to the Sunday School question.

"What else would you thank God for besides fish?" Kathy asked.

Without hesitation the youngster said, "Hooks."

It's obvious where Johnny's love is.

WHY WE MUST CHANGE LURES

Every sophisticated largemouth bass fisherman has witnessed a change in the striking preference of fish in lakes and streams where there has been an extended period of optimum angling pressure and successful landings. Often one or two lures will be highly productive for many months, even years, and then fishermen suddenly discover the bass are turned off. You can't buy a bite with that favorite lure that has been so miraculous for so long.

Typical of this phenomenon is the Sputterfuss, a noisy topwater spinner or buzzbait that once was remarkably successful almost everywhere that there was aquatic growth, especially in Florida. Around spatterdock lilies and scattered grass in Lake Orange or Lochloosa, it caught thousands of bass. Cast into the cover, the semi-weedless lure jumped from one obstacle to another when slowly retrieved to the angler's reel. From spring and well into winter, it caught limits of lunkers and yearlings. Bass couldn't leave it alone. It was the greatest artificial Florida bassers could cast in the 1970's.

Then shortly after the advent of the plastic worm, there was a combination spoon and worm introduced to fishermen called the "El Tango." This was a heavy, curved piece of metal to which you tied your line and an eight or six inch worm was attached to a hook on the novel-looking spoon. You could cast it a mile with spinning tackle or casting equipment. Plopped down around grass in shallow water where bass were feeding, and then quickly retrieved a few inches under the surface, every respectable bass in the territory would dive for it. It was almost irresistible for a year or two. It had one flaw. When the bass jumped and shook her head, the heavy spoon often dislodged the lure and the fish was unbuttoned. But the El Tango was so attractive to bass that I have seen the same lunker attack the bait three or four times within minutes and it was obvious this lure had something that turned bass on.

These are just two examples. Hundreds of artificials have had a heyday for a time and then suddenly the fish wouldn't strike for love or money. That's what happened to the Sputter-fuss and the El Tango. In Central Florida I haven't known anyone to use these baits for over a decade.

Then why do bass love a lure for awhile and then turn it down year after year in the same water when it is expertly cast and retrieved by the same experts who once were so happy with its performance?

The late Dr. John N. Hamlet, a renowned naturalist who captured the monkeys used in polio research, later a consultant at Sea World and the Homasassa Attraction in Florida, had the answer to why lures play out after proving successful.

"It's a matter of evolution," said Dr. Hamlet. "In any body of water there are bass with certain genetic characteristics. There may be a dozen different families of bass in that water and each of them has its own preference for food and eating habits. One or two of these families with similar genes may like to feed on frogs or snakes on the surface but frown on underwater forage. Those who like to eat the frogs and snakes see the Sputterfuss or buzzbait as something that they prefer and they strike it. The word gets around that this lure is deadly and catching a lot of bass. Then more and more fishermen buy the bait and start hauling in the lunkers. There is a great deal of pressure on the bass that like this lure. Every bit of habitat in the lake has a Sputterfuss splashing over it, by it, and around it many, many times. Lunkers are pulled over the gunnels as the bait is obviously fantastic.

"Then the bass quit and the once popular lure sags deeper and deeper into the tackle box where it rusts and fades. It has had its day. No longer will largemouths strike it in the grass, the lilies or anywhere else.

"In truth, fishermen have used the popular lure so efficiently and so often in the lake that they have literally caught out all or most of the bass that like that particular look and sound. It doesn't mean that there aren't plenty of bass still in the lake. There may be just as many as ever. But that family with the genes to like this kind of replica of their favorite live food has been caught or their numbers so drastically reduced that the fisherman can't get the strikes that he is accustomed to. He has to shift to something that the remaining bass families in the lake like or he is going to start believing that all the bass are gone from the favorite honey hole," reasoned Dr. Hamlet whose studies bear out his deductions.

"The bass change in hitting specific lures that are over used in specific waters is comparable to the evolution of the rattlesnake. Before man was tramping around all over America, the majority of rattlesnakes rattled. It was the way they frightened their enemies away. It was their protection from predators. But then along comes man who has been taught to dislike snakes, all snakes, since the time of Adam and Eve. When man got too close to the rattlesnake, he raised his tail and made that eerie rattle. Man picked up a stick and killed the snake or shot him if he was hunting and armed. Slowly over the centuries, the snake has given his position away by rattling. Instead of frightening the human away, it simply meant the death knell for the snake. Now there were always some rattlesnakes that did not rattle. They were quiet and simply slithered away when man approached their territory. Those snakes were not killed nearly as frequently as those noisy rattlers. And today, there are very few rattlesnakes that rattle when they are threatened by man. Those with the genes that told them to make a noise and scare the enemy away have almost disappeared. The noisy trait has been their undoing, "Dr. Hamlet reveals.

"That's exactly how it works with certain lures that catch fish for a time and then are useless. You catch the bass that like that sight and sound. When their number is drastically reduced, it gets few strikes and few fish. Anglers who want to be successful over the long haul must adapt to change and learn when to throw away a lure and shift to a new concept," said this brilliant scholar of nature.

Douglas Hannon, a protege of the late Dr. Hamlet and widely known for his bass research that earned him the title "Bass Professor," agrees with the summation of Hamlet. He further contends:

"Lures that make no noise, like the worm and spoon, are more likely to continue to attract bass over the years than those that buzz, rattle or spin. This awareness that it is the noise of the lure that runs its course and no longer produces, is one of the reasons that I developed the Snakebait, Swimming Worm, Skitterfish and other worm-type lures for Burke. They are quiet and will attract fish longer than some artificials.

"Even crankbaits and spinners make considerable noise when they are retrieved. Worms are noiseless and spoons with no moving parts are also noiseless. I believe this type of lure will keep bass interested longer than the Sputterfuss, for example.

125

"I believe that already the plastic worm has lasted longer than any other modern lure. It may be, with variations as to hookup, texture, reaction, length, etc., this imitation of a live eel will continue productive for bass anglers for decades. But most lures are successful for much shorter periods and the smart professional and lay anglers learn this by trial and error. I have learned to adapt to this change as you must do to keep catching fish," Hannon says. As a long time admirer of Hannon, I agree with his deductions.

ARCHIE BLOUNT WATCHED ME FISH

Archie Blount, an outdoor writer for *The Tampa Tribune* some years ago, came to Cypress Lodge and went fishing with me. He was very observant and wrote some interesting paragraphs about my techniques as follows: After analyzing Andrews' worm technique, I came to the conclusion that everything he did wouldn't necessarily apply to all worm fishermen.

Andrews' technique was matched to his particular style of fishing and, more importantly, to his tackle.

His practice of setting the hook hard enough to lengthen a fish by several inches was well suited to the way he buried his hook in the worm and his stiff baitcasting rod.

For the ultralight spinning tackle user, Andrews' Herculean lunge in setting the hook would accomplish nothing but a broken line.

Andrews' trick that may or may not work on lighter tackle involves the hooking of the worm.

He first buries the point of the hook in the worm, then pulls it out and repositions the hook in the hole he has just made in the plastic worm. The reasoning is that the point of the hook will come out of the worm easier when the fish is struck.

Other worm experts may not agree with his approach and say the barb of the hook should be inserted just under the "skin" of the worm so that the slightest strike will pop it out.

Obviously, light tackle users who fish 10-pound test line or lighter probably would favor the second method of hooking the worm lure. But this method probably hooks more bottom junk than the deeper-hooked lure.

Probably the biggest thing going for most successful worm fishermen is versatility.

Fish are supposed to be color blind, but the clarity of the water varies from lake to lake so darker or lighter colored lures probably do have an effect on the number of strikes a fisherman gets depending on his choice of color and the clarity of the water he fishes.

Andrews swears different colored lures get different results.

127

So, when one color isn't working, he switches.

Another variable that Andrews says pays off is his choice of lead.

"As a rule, the lighter the lead the better," he says.

Obviously, the size of the worm lure and the depth of the water the fish are in have a lot to do with the proper selection of lead.

The most common worm-lead rig is 1/8 ounce, fished with a six or seven inch worm. This rig is effective in water depths up to six or seven feet.

Most fishermen generally fish the same lake or river and getting the right combination of lead and worm is a matter of experimentation. The key to successful worm fishing, as Andrews points out, is confidence.

A fisherman should tailor his technique to his tackle and the fish size he is seeking. Once he gets the right combination, he should keep fishing it. Even though a previously proven combination doesn't produce strikes, it doesn't necessarily mean the fish aren't buying it. It may mean the fisherman just didn't put it in front of the fish.

DYNAMITE FOR FALL BASS

Having become bored with the long hot summer, "Mother Nature" has once again dispatched invisible fingers of cold through the night air to touch her lakes. A transformation begins that is so slight in the onset, detection by even the latest electronic wonder is almost impossible. But, for the finny creatures that abound in the underwater world, the change has ignited a renewal of activity.

Seizing advantage of this early seasonal upheaval requires a watchful eye and an alert ear for the first subtle signals. Extremely rabid bass may kick-off this feeding extravaganza by mid to late September, and the banquet could last until the surface thermometer dips below the 50 degree mark in late December or early January.

Due to overall shallower water and smaller size, areas farthest from the dam on most reservoirs are the first to be affected by any temperature change. Bass are drawn out of their deeper, well hidden summer homes to feed on abundant shad populations. For most knowledgeable fishermen, this metamorphosis causes restless nights complete with visions of exciting battles with schools of lunker-sized bass.

Some added knowledge of the thermal effects on most man-made lakes, especially deeper impoundments, is necessary to be able to share in this fall action.

The water becomes stratified or layered during the hot summer months. Cold water fish like trout, walleye, and yellow perch live in the cooler lower temperature layer, while most of the other fish remain in the oxygen rich, but warm, upper layer. However, as the nights become chilly, the layers begin to change. The surface is cooled by the night air, and since cooler water is denser and heavier than warmer water, the cold water sinks through the warmer water forcing more warm water to the surface to be exposed to the cooler air. The process is called lake turnover, and triggers the aforementioned renewal of aquatic activity. Understanding this fall phenomenon, and how to use **Lunker-TNT** can turn wasted time into hours of exciting autumn bassin' action!

129

THE JIG AND FAT ALBERT—
"LUNKER TNT"

Probably as many big bass are caught during the fall of the year on the jig and pig as on any bait. That's a pretty strong statement considering how many different lures are used at this time of the year. Unlike many other baits used during the fall season, the "jig and pig" actually resembles a big bass delicacy, the crawfish. His usual fare of shad is not as filling as an old crawdad. It's like having to eat hot dogs all week then being offered a big juicy steak.

The conventional "jig and pig" is in two parts. First is the "jig," which has a molded lead head that's usually painted and has some type of plastic or nylon guard coming out of it at an angle to protect the point of the hook from underwater brush or debris. Over the hook is a "living rubber" filament type skirt. Attached to the hook, is the "pig" portion, which is just a piece of cured pre-cut fat pork with the skin still on it. These pieces of pork come in many different shapes, sizes and colors, and are stored in small jars that contain a liquid preservative. A few anglers have learned a new wrinkle that saves both time and hassle. The secret is the "Jig and Fat Albert."

As everyone knows, pork baits tend to be messy, hard to handle, and the wife won't allow them in the house. Also , if the dyed piece of "fatback" is allowed out of the water for more than 15 minutes, it will become hard and shrivelled enough to require its removal with a pair of wire cutters. The problem can be solved by using Zoom Bait Company's chunky "Fat Albert" grub as a trailer instead of the unforgivable pork.

Now lots of the close-minded "Old Pro's" are going to frown on this bait. They'll say, "As soon as she takes it in her mouth, she'll spit it right back out because it doesn't taste right." That statement would have some merit for a normal grub, but not for "Fat Albert."

Outside of the fact that the pork chunk is naturally messy, the only other thing it has going for it is the salt curing process. Ah! But the folks at Zoom already thought about that aspect. The "Fat Albert" grub has extra salt embedded into the plastic during the molding process, and another ingredient they

130

refer to as "Plus." Except in extremely frigid water conditions, the "Fat Albert" grub has more action than pork because of the swimming tail. Another plus for bass anglers is that the grub doesn't dry out like the pork chunk when out of the water.

Structures that are productive with the "jig and Fat Albert" during the fall season might vary in depth from less than a foot to as much as 45 feet, and can be found from the dam areas all the way to the shoals of the rivers that feed the lake. Many of these will be the same ones that might be fished with the Texas-rigged worm. The "jig and Fat Albert" is more productive in larger structures.

Instead of man-made brush piles with smaller limbs, whole trees with bulkier limbs are better. Large stumps or huge boulders can be very good. On the upper end of a lake, blown-down trees or huge stumps and roots systems along the actual river channel hide many lunkers that can be lured out with the "jig and Fat Albert."

This rig can be fished in a more conventional manner than the Texas-rigged worm. The "jig and Fat Albert" can be cast or flipped into visible structure, but even when fishing invisible underwater bass havens, it's not usually done vertically. Don't make long casts, but keep the line at a 45 degree angle to the water, and move it slowly. Since this bait is more natural looking and tastier than the worm, the immediate hook set is not as critical, but don't wait too long.

Even though the "jig and Fat Albert" is effective all during the fall season, the most productive period is from October until late December. By using the **Lunker-TNT** properly, fall can prove to be an eruption of bassin' success!

BEFORE PERRY'S RECORD BASS

Prior to the world record bass landed by George Perry, the largest bass certified was caught by Fritz Freibel in Pasco County, Florida, in 1921. It was caught on a Rapala and weighed 20-pounds, 3-ounces. It's still the Florida record and was recognized years after W.A. Witt's 19-pounder was on the books as the biggest Florida bass. Witt caught his big bass on a live American eel in Lake Tarpon, and it was considered the state record for decades.

HOT TIPS FOR COLD WEATHER

Proper technique competes with the agony of defeat. Winter cold fronts can be a total disaster. Summer fronts are not nearly as serious because the water temperature doesn't fluctuate as much. In the winter the changes are sudden and drastic, resulting in bass lethargy. However, after five years of fishing the bass tournament circuits and nearly 15 years of guide service, I have discovered that there is a way to compete with the agony of defeat.

The water temperature of Florida can drop down into the 50's during severe cold fronts. When this occurs the fishes' conditions change considerably. Their metabolism and aggressive action is cut way down. When this condition exists, I immediately move to rivers that offer moving water. For one reason, the rivers offer steadier water temperatures. In the summer it's cool enough and in the winter warm enough. Another reason for river fishing is that temperature is stabilized and deters sudden drops.

I have noted that any spring fed river that has a limerock base in its main spring will produce a constant flow of 68 to 72 degree water temperature year round. This reading is considered prime for these rivers. Lake bass are prone to warmer waters and are active in waters above 75 degrees. During cold fronts, many lake bass have been seen lying dormant on the bottom.

The main reason why spring water offers a better pattern is because the temperature will remain the same no matter what the outside temperature. This means consistent results with the proper application of lures. Slow retrieves are recommended during cold snaps because the bass are less aggressive. Top water lures work, but not as well as slowly retrieved worms, crankbaits and spinners. A change of as little as two degrees can alter feeding habits. Florida waters which are relatively shallow are more susceptible to cold fronts. The thermoclime in deep reservoirs is constant as is the temperature below it. Pay attention to water temperature changes and fish accordingly.

GITZIT INVENTOR BOB GARLAND
'KEEP LOW PROFILE—AVOID EYEBALL CONTACT WITH BASS'

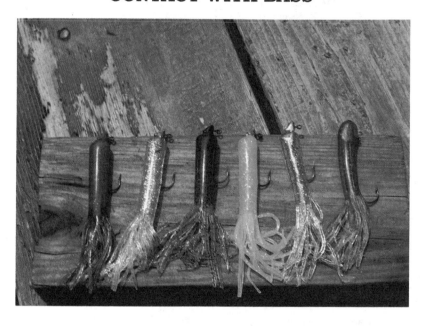

Lure Manufacturer Bob Garland, Washington, Utah, a 12 time qualifier for the U. S. Bass and Western Bass world championship, wins tournaments with his own artificial concoctions, and he has a big, ugly jig that he calls "Gitzit" that's bringing him more success. He says it is not pretty but he fishes it 90 percent of the time when he is competing for tournament dollars and no self-respecting bass will reject it when proper presentation puts it in the face of the fish.

"Fish can see you very well in clear water and you may stand there in the boat eyeball to eyeball with a big lunker that you are trying to catch. She will likely not bite if she looks you in the eye, but may just swim away and ignore your Gitzit or other lure. To catch bass in shallow water where you are only a few yards from the fish, you must keep a low profile, wear drab clothing, cast with a low trajectory and make no sudden moves that will send the bass a ' runnin' for deeper water and a hiding place," this veteran of bass tournament trails advises.

Garland says that lure presentation is critical in bass fishing and that the serious angler will start his cast with the rod tip near the water and never go overhead when he's after largemouths with a jig around docks, trees, stumps, steep banks and other cover where the water is relatively shallow. The fish will often spook from the angler's antics in the boat.

"If a boat dock is eight inches above the surface and I think there's a bass on the other side, I can hop-skip my Gitzit or other jig on the water so it will go under the dock and stop in the area where I want to give a bass a chance to hit it. I don't want it to fall right on the bass. I want it to skip near or past the bass and then give her a chance to strike as I bring it back over a short distance. You can present your lure to the bass many more times every day than if you are long casting and taking a minute to get your lure back to the boat. You have a better chance of winning with short, quick casts in and near the cover. You can't catch 'em with your hook out of the water.

"If I am fishing water that is five to ten feet deep, I often get my strikes when the jig is on the way down. If you are careless, you may get a hit and not know it. When I flip it into the hole and it starts down, I catch the line with my left hand and finger it. There may be a fish hanging on, and if you give the fish a split second advantage, she will spit it out and be gone. You learn the subtle touch of a bass and you can hook almost every one that bites when you gain experience.

"If I am fishing a target 30 or 40 feet away, I keep my eye glued on the spot I want to hit, and I stop the line with my left hand if I'm using spinning tackle when it gets at exactly the right spot. Accuracy is mighty important in fishing a jig in cover," says this astute veteran with enough savvy to outsmart most bass in or out of hiding.

The Gitzit is "ugly" by Garland's own admission, but it works. It's a three or four inch tube of rubber with the last inch and a half shredded into tentacles. You thread the hook from the tail so it comes to the head of the jig very straight with no curves that would make it twist and turn. You can add a small plastic worm to the jig that will make it bigger and change it's fall and vibration. You can vary the fall rate by using any of the different lead head weights. In water less than ten feet, Garland recommends the 1/16 ounce weight, but if the bass are fussy, he may change to 1/8 or 1/4 ounce that will put it on the bottom quicker and it sometimes triggers strikes on the fall.

In very shallow water, the Gitzit may need a little customizing and Garland often cuts off a part of the head. When it is fished deep, he may toothpick a small piece of cork or balsa wood in the hollow body of the jig so that it will float up slightly from the bottom. This is particularly advantageous when you use a split shot in front of the jig as some anglers do. It keeps the hook from hanging on bottom cover. It's an open hook that Garland uses, not particularly endorsing the weedless variations. If he is fishing a creek mouth and wants to dress up his invention a bit, he often slips on a spinner bait skirt to entice the bass to strike.

"Accuracy is important in jig fishing and you need to be able to underhand your lure into a six inch hole under a bush 30 feet away. Again you need to stop the line at just the right instant with your left hand if you are an open-faced spinning tackle fisherman like I am. If you are fishing submerged moss beds like you have in Lake Mead in Las Vegas, you use a do-nothing retrieve. You just swim it slowly over the moss bed. If you are fishing holes in the moss, then keep your rod tip high and yo-yo the jig in the pockets when you reel across them.

"If I'm fishing a moss bed, or grass patch where I am confident there are some bass holding in the cover, I cast right into the aquatic growth the first time. I cast my jig to the left and to the right, each time retrieving near the hideout and parallel to it. If I get no strike on the outside fringes, then I'll go to the heart of the cover and try to get the bass to strike. Often the bass will come up to a swimming jig and explode on the fringe of the cover.

"You have to play every cast and every fishing trip by ear. You learn from fishing and there are times when I find a good looking moss bed and I'll switch my weight to 1/32. I just might do better than 1/16 ounce. Bass are wise to lures and fishermen and there are times when a minute change may make the difference. I know they are extremely cautious in clear water and quick movement, rod and clothing colors and boat positions may spook the fish out of range," this knowledgeable fisherman and lure manufacturer reveals.

He says that in summer you may need more weight or you can hook on a grub jig or spider to the Gitzit and improve your catch success. You may want to twist the hook a fraction when fishing around brush cover to give it a little more action. You may be able to make the lure circle a bush on the fall. When flippin' in cover, a twist of the hook in the jig may trap some air and make it fall slower at first, and then as the air gets out, increase its rate of fall. That sometimes brings a bass strike, Garland conjectures. The twist in the hook may put a lot of curls in your line after a while and you need to watch for that problem.

"In winter time fishing a jig, I like to use a 1/2 ounce lead head and yo-yo my lure like a spoon off the bottom or crawl it. Where there are rocks or gravel on the bottom, the heavier jig being walked gives the lure an erratic motion and triggers fish tight on the bottom. In the open, I use 6 or 8 pound test line and if I'm casting in cover, I'll go to 10 or 12 pound test. But if I am flippin', I'll change to 20 pound test. You have to use something strong enough to horse a big one out of the hiding places if it is dense cover.

"The Gitzit is soft bait that is mighty subtle. Fish can hang on to it without sending you much of a signal. You have to be alert and intense to feel some of the fish. I feel them best with a medium action boron rod five feet and three inches long. I like a light reel. If there is wind or if I'm fishing deep water, I may prefer a six foot boron rod. It gives me more leverage to cast into the wind. I may use either 6 or 8 pound test line when not in heavy cover.

"I make the Gitzit in 40 or 50 different colors. I try to fish the one that looks the nearest to what bass in that particular lake are feeding on. I try to match the crawfish or the shad as near as possible, both by color and size of my jig that can be varied by adding various skirts, worms, frogs, etc. You are always trying to get the bass to make a mistake.

"Always I want to keep control of my line, even in the wind. You can't catch fish with a big, wind blown arc and slack line. I believe in casting past my targets and bringing the jig back to the spot. I may lift the rod, slack off, drop it in a hole, yo-yo and give it a lot of movement right in the home of the bass. The line may be a little slack in this maneuver, but watch it react when you think something is after it. I control the slack in my line.

"In winter I like creek mouths and the do-nothing retrieve. Crank slowly. Keep line tight. The tail tentacles of the Gitzit will vibrate like crazy. Bass can't stand it. Then in deep water, often in spots more than 30 feet deep, I vertical jig my Gitzit. I get right over the spot I want to fish and yo-yo the bait.

At that depth, you are not likely to spook the fish. Yet, there are times even in water with great depth that your trolling motor will spook fish.

"If you see a real honey hole where a bush has a deep shade along a bank where a bass would love to hide, don't toss your jig right in the spot where the fish may be holding. Cast beyond the shade and bring the bait back through the shadow. Keep the rod low because if there's a bass in that shade and you are in the sunshine, he has probably already seen you. He knows when you are looking at him. Quietly observe for a few moments before casting 10 or 12 feet from the spot and then bringing your bait close to the fish and make it so tempting she can't reject it. The wait for a moment may take the fright out of your prey.

"And if you are going to retrieve or jig a bait in deep water, make sure you are working it **ABOVE** the fish. Not many bass will ever go down to hit a jig, but many times they will shoot from their deeper suspended position and strike it. They'll come up but they won't go down," says this jig fisherman with a reputation for success.

Garland once made the Mini-Jig, the most copied jig in the world, and it still is a great bait for crappie, bluegills and small bass. Today he is concentrating on the Gitzit and praising its virtues as a largemouth and smallmouth bass catcher. In that he fishes it 90 percent of the time and has for the past nine years with noteworthy success, obviously this strange-looking man-made morsel is being eyed and eaten by bass in both shallow and deep water. It won't win any beauty contests but it may keep Garland and other pros in the winner's circle.

NOTHING SET IN CONCRETE

While almost every guide and professional angler will recommend big lures for big bass, it doesn't always work like that. I think I have the proof. My largest bass is a 10-pounder caught in Orange Lake in 1969. It hit a two-inch long Bayou Boogie cast around a tussock of grass in May. When I tied that lure on the line, my partner joked that I must be going after baby bass. He changed his tune when I reeled in the 10-pounder. It just goes to show that there are no absolutes in bass fishing.

W.H.C.

137

Kids Catch Bass Too

Lake Lochloosa Bass Haven

TINY JIGS TAKE BIG BASS

Late winter, early spring, late fall, and then throughout the winter, if a lake doesn't freeze over, there's excellent bass fishing if you use the right tactics and lures. During these times, tiny jigs are the single most effective lure for big bass.

The first step, as always, is locating fish. In the late winter, early spring period, or pre-spawn period, look for bass in the upper ends of tributaries and creeks leading into reservoirs. They will be located along the submerged channels, the exact location depending on the timing and water temperature. Channel bends are an excellent holding spot at that time as are channels leading close to flats or spawning areas. A good depth finder is great for locating these areas, as well as spotting fish.

During this time of the year small baits, worked extremely slowly, are most effective and a Blakemore Road Runner Turbo Tail, available in 1/16 and 1/8 ounces is hard to beat. The Road Runner Turbo Tail, features the best of all in one jig—a solid body welded to a serrated "tube" type tail, all fitted on the famous Road Runner lead head jig, complete with a tiny spinner—the ultimate cold water bass lure.

When the surface water temperature stays in the low forties, locate bass on the deeper structures of the creeks and tributaries, and vertically jig Road Runner Turbo Tails over them. As the water temperature rises into the low 50's cast these jigs over nearby flats, dragging them off the edges of the shallows into the deeper water, then hang onto your hat. Although retrieving must be ultra slow, bass will often hit these tiny baits hard.

Road Runner Turbo Tails come in several colors, but the single choice for this time of the year is the white/pearl color because of the first influx of shad into these areas. Believe it or not the smaller 1/16 ounce size works best this time of the year.

In late fall/early winter the same basic spots will produce as bass make feeding forays from the deeper water into the shallows before the onset of winter. These holding spots along the migratory routes will almost always produce again. The top lure choices are again tiny jigs such as the Road Runner Turbo Tail, only the techniques are a bit different. Bass are feeding heavily during this period and the retrieve should be faster. The larger 1/8 ounce size in white/pearl gives the impression of a first-of-the-year shad when cranked steadily through the water at a fairly fast rate—a deadly treat for big bass.

As fall turns into winter, bass go deeper and the fishing drops off—unless you use tiny jigs and vertically jig the deeper structures along these same migratory routes. Granted the fishing won't be fast, and you'll have to work for every bass, but even at this time tiny jigs produce.

Pro Harold Allen Jigs Yearling

ALABAMA'S L. J. BRASHER HAS CAUGHT A WAGON LOAD OF 10-POUND BASS IN POTHOLES, PONDS, LAKES

In sheer numbers, L. P. Brasher, of Opeleika, Alabama, may have caught more trophy bass 10-pounds and above than any man alive, but his extraordinary success includes lunkers on plugs, live baits and cane pole in many private ponds, swamp potholes, lakes and streams over almost three decades. In 1980, his detailed log book showed he had pulled in more than 1,000 trophy lunkers in a 17-year period, recording an astounding 89 in 1976.

There are many differences in the records compiled by Brasher and other trophy bass fishermen. He fishes every pothole and private pond he can find with the owner's permission within a 150 mile radius of Madison, Florida, in the panhandle. And he is such a dedicated, determined trophy hunter that he often fishes 72 hours nonstop without breaking to eat or sleep, when he locates a promising pond where he is virtually sure big bass are lurking. Big bass are an obsession.

Never accepting a guide assignment, Brasher insists that getting paid for finding and catching a trophy bass would take some of the thrill away from the effort. He makes his living as an auto transmission shop operator and pulling giants over the side is his passion.

This unique basser who fishes giant muskie-type, wooden Jitterbugs at night and huge live shiners in the daytime, generally tied out on a 20-foot cane pole, says that most people fail to catch big bass because they don't fish for big bass. For years he caught hundreds of 2 and 3-pound bass but it wasn't challenging enough. He decided the true test of a bassing man was to fish for the biggest, meanest and smartest largemouths available. And that's what he has fished for exclusively the last 27 years.

"Catching a trophy bass is a true accomplishment and it results from hard work, careful planning and devotion to your goal," Brasher says.

"The most important ingredient in taking trophy bass is the water you fish. Not all lakes in all areas of the country produce wallmount size bass. But some lakes in every state have really big bass. You learn how to find them and then fish for them. You need to locate these big bass ponds that are within a day's drive of your home," this veteran lunker hunter says.

Brasher first fished the legendary big bass Lake Jackson near Tallahassee when he began his assault on giant trophies. But before he started his search for lunkers, he talked with boat dock operators, tackle and bait shop clerks, and country store lay fishermen who often had stories to tell about the one that got away in some remote pothole or farm pond never publicized and not on any maps. Many of these holes were not much larger than Brasher's living room and often they would be completely covered with lilies and grass. But if he believed the story of how a giant was hooked here that broke a tough test line, he never rested easy until he got a hook in that spot. He made a mental note of the pond and it became a project.

Brasher says that there are from 500 to 1,000 of these potholes in the area of Northern Florida where he fishes. And while most people would call them private, he says they are private only because no one asked the owner for permission to fish there. He always asks for permission and has been turned down only a few times during his long bassing career.

"Anytime that I drive by a place and notice a hawg bass on the wall, I ask the owner, who doesn't usually mind talking, where he caught the wallmount. It probably has other big bass. And if I hear someone say old Mr. So-and-So has plenty of big bass in his pond but it is private and you can't fish it, I take note of that pond. I'll find Mr. So-and-So and get his permission. That's where I caught many of my big fish. I have found when you hear someone say a pond is private and 'no one can fish it' that the statement is generally untrue. I know right away that this is a spot that I want to explore after I have talked with the owner.

"I have found that the three to 15-acre ponds have more giant bass per acre than the larger ones. Many of them are hard to get to and I may have to wade or fish in the lilies and muck but I go after those lunkers in places where many other anglers would fear to tread. I actually look for ponds that have alligators. I know there are fish in places where the gators are found and they have never bothered me, not even when I stepped on one that I thought was a log," Brasher reveals some of his secrets.

"I like ponds with a lot of lilies and coontail. I pay attention to sounds in those potholes and ponds. There are definite

Brasher Hauls in Another Hawg Bass

sounds that a big bass makes when she is feeding or attempting to kill something. You may hear a giant bass roll over in the cover. When your senses assure you that there is a big bass there, stay put and fish hard. I'll stay in a little pond for two or three hours quiet and still. Then if I get no strike, I move to another pothole.

"I'll drop a big shiner in the holes in the lilies and have it tied on a 20-foot pole. When it gets a strike, I jerk with all my power and you can be sure it won't break the pole. I get that fish's head out of the water fast and get her to the boat.

"I use tackle that is made to catch big bass. On the cane pole with a shiner or on my Shakespeare Ugly Stick rod and heavy duty casting reel, I use 40-pound test monofilament or 50-pound test braided nylon. I use big No. 9 Eagle Claw hooks. I don't want to lose my trophy bass because of insufficient tackle," this veteran lay basser says and he adds: "My technique is simple—use the biggest lure or shiner you can find. Buy the heaviest tackle you can handle. Then outlast the bass when you get a monster on the line or when waiting for a strike."

Brasher likes to fish the dark nights. He says, "In three days and three nights of no moon, a big bass is going to feed. To catch that lunker, all you have to do is present a bait that she will take, have the equipment to put her in the boat and have the staying power to continue to fish until that bass gets hungry and decides to eat."

This patient and talented angler especially likes night fishing and he has found that the best time to catch trophy bass is in the wee hours of the morning between 2:45 and 3:15. That half hour is his favorite time and is based on his documented catch record.

When he stops to talk about lures that catch big bass, Brasher always gets back to the Jitterbug, but he also recommends others. Here's what he says about lures:

"Big bass seem to feed heavily at night and racket baits have proven to be deadly deceivers.

"The number one nocturnal big bass catcher is a black muskie Jitterbug. The big plug with the wobbling motor-boat sound creates a wake and a noise that drives bass out of their pond. The size of the bait is directly proportional to the size of the fish you anticipate taking. Big baits get fewer strikes but catch more lunkers. If you want smaller bass, use smaller lures.

"Plunkers, spinners, hoppers and draggers are excellent night-fishing lures. As long as the lure makes a noise, causes a disturbance or in some way irritates or entices, it is a good nocturnal lure for the bigmouths.

"My old standby lure is a homemade Jitterbug similar to the bass bamboozler manufactured for years by the Fred Arbogast Company. The factory Jitterbug is now made from plastic and is not as good as the big wooden plug.

"There are a number of other plugs that trick bass at night. Cordell's topwater Boy Howdy, a 3/8-ounce skinny minnow with slashing spinners, is a good lure. Arbogast's Sputterbug or Hula Hopper, and the Spin Scout and Prop Scout from Strike King are floating spinners that throw a spray when jerked and sound off with a slurping noise that calls bass. Heddon's Chugger Spook and Lucky 13 call hawgs up after dark.

"When the giants are buried in the pads at night, you can hear them rolling but can't reach them with a topwater plunker, I use the Moss-Hopper by Four Rivers or Heddon's Moss Boss. They hop across the weeds where other baits would foul.

"Big black snake plastic worms from nine to 14 inches, slipped across the pads give big bass the wigglin' willies. They can't leave it alone. I make my own twister-type worms and these sneaky snakes are fished behind the pads where nothing else will work.

"The Dalton Special is a good topwater at night. The Barracuda Company attached a lip to the plug similar to the Jitterbug's face plate and that has turned it into a dynamite nighttime lure. After dark, on some of those little out of the way ponds I fish, you hear it get hit like a surface explosion and it catches another wallmount," Brasher says.

Neither bad weather nor lack of sleep, can drive L. J. Brasher from his flat bottom boat when he is after another big bass. He is an unusual fisherman totally dedicated to catching big bass. He believes there is a world record in Northern Florida and this bass is within his reach. He simply has to fish constantly day and night until the monster gives up and flounces in his boat.

While searching diligently for this world record, this veteran basser has compiled some amazing records, like the 89 bass 10-pounds or over in 1976. Then there's the 15 1/2-pounder he landed in Carr Lake in 1974 and that August night in 1971 at Lake Jackson when he took five bass on his Jitterbug lure that weighed a total of 60-pounds, 4-ounces.

He is a likely candidate to catch that world record and it may come from some of the unfished potholes and so-called private lakes in that Madison, Florida, bass fishing mecca that he has made his bassing bailiwick.

145

Alabama Basser Shows Off Wallmounts

FLORIDA 'GATOR IS NIGHT FISHING EXPERT

There was a loud splash after the big spinner bait halted its flight through the darkness and plopped on the nearly invisible surface. The experienced angler stood on the front platform of his Stratos bass boat as the heavy lure began to sink toward the murky depths. He concentrated on the feel of the big blade of the spinner bait as it windmilled slowly toward the bottom. He could detect every rhythmic movement through the thin strand of monofilament line, magnified by the stiff graphite fishing rod in his hand.

Suddenly the big lure ceased its descent, and the fisherman noticed a slight thump. He immediately snapped the rod upward toward the rising moon, but the rod stopped at the 10 o'clock position and bent into an ever-increasing arc. Another huge bass had been lured out of hiding by Georgia's Lake Lanier's friendly "Gator."

An accomplished fishing guide, Van Robertson, or "Gator" as he's known to his friends, originally hailed from Lake Harbor, Florida, which is on the southern end of Lake Okeechobee. His "Gator" nickname certainly doesn't reflect a ferocious nature. On the contrary, it's an affectionate moniker given to him by his many friends because of his Florida roots.

Being so close to the world famous Lake Okeechobee gave Robertson an early love of fishing and the outdoors. By the age of 7, he was already paddling a small wooden boat around in the canals near his home and catching fish. Before he had reached the age of 14, he was running 6 miles of commercial catfish lines every day to make spending money, and after his high school days, Robertson guided part-time for bass out of Slim's Fish Camp on Lake Okeechobee before moving to Georgia.

As early as 1973, he was already learning to convert the lessons he had learned in the shallow lakes of south Florida into productive fishing at night on Lake Lanier. Because of both his fishing ability and his personality, it was only natural that he would again become a guide.

147

Partly due to the hours of his job as a firefighter, and partly because of his shallow water knowledge, "Gator" has become an acknowledged expert at catching lunkers at night. His techniques are certainly different, but unquestionably productive.

For most anglers, the spinner bait is thought of as a springtime, shallow water lure, but Robertson has invented some unique ways to produce big bass on summer nights. His methods lure both deep and shallow lunkers.

"For the deep water bass," said Robertson. "I use an extra large 5/8th ounce single-spin with a No. 6 Colorado blade. I paint the big blade flat black, and dress the black vinyl skirt with a pumpkin colored Zoom 'Fat Albert' grub for added action." He continued, "The best structures for this rig are points with huge stumps, blown-down trees along steeper banks, big underwater logs, or points with huge boulders."

After choosing one of the above bass havens, Robertson will position his boat on the deep water side of the structure, and cast toward it with a baitcasting reel with 14 to 17-pound test line. "I engage the reel as soon as the spinner hits the water and allow it to fall to the bottom on a tight line," he said. "If nothing happens during the fall, then I'll lift the rod tip quickly enough to cause the spinner to vibrate, and follow it back down again on the tight line." He continues this "yo-yoing" action until his lure is directly below the boat. The strikes usually come as the lure is falling near the debris or structure. Since the hook must be extremely sharp, he uses a Doug Hannon designed Hook-Hone-R to make them razor sharp.

Another productive area for spinner baits after dark is lighted boat docks, but both knowledge and the proper bait are essential for success.

Robertson revealed, "Approach a lighted dock quietly, and remain in the shadows to one side of it. Use a 1/4 ounce spinner with tandem, nickel plated Indiana blades and a white skirt. Carefully cast it beyond the other side of the dock opening. After allowing it to fall two to three feet, reel the spinner bait across the mouth of the dock at a faster than normal speed. If there is more than one bass under the dock, there will be a bone-jarring strike! If nothing happens after two or three casts, find another lighted dock."

After much experimentation, Van Robertson has discovered another neat trick for night fishing with a spinner bait, the

use of chemical light sticks. Shallow water bass in areas where there is little or no artificial light have proven to be the best victims for this method.

Robertson first learned of the unique LumaLure spinner bait last year. He said, "It has a little plastic holder for the chemical light sticks built into the shaft behind the Colorado blade. I fish these in the shallower areas." He makes long casts toward the rear of small coves off the creek channels, and makes a slow steady retrieve. "I've caught several largemouth over 6-pounds in the past year with this method," proclaimed Robertson.

His methods may seem a little unorthodox but this Florida "Gator" has proven he can catch mid-summer bass at night.

When the daytime temperatures creep near 100 degrees, many anglers end their fishing season. By taking the advice of this night-stalking "Gator," explosive summer bass action is just a cast away!

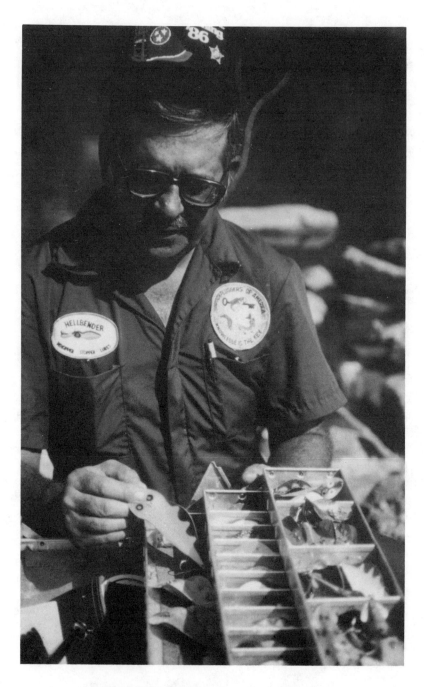

McAfee Looks Over Spoon Plugs

DOYLE McAFEE—SPOON PLUGS FOR BASS

Doyle McAfee maneuvered his ancient jonboat into the eddy area outside the waterfall that poured into East Tennessee's Caney Fork River and glanced up at the 100-foot high cliff where a wild kid goat was munching on tufts of grass that grew in the rocky crevices. Trickling water chattered as it detoured around a tree trunk in the rapids and tumbled over slick boulders. It was the kind of natural beauty, God's artistry, that you see all along 50 miles of mountain streams near Rock Island Rustic State Park.

"Mac," as he is known by all who have met him, transgressed from fishing a moment to admire the scenery that seemed far more important than putting another chubby mountain largemouth in the boat. The 54-year-old native of Coffee County has lived much of his life here in Warren County. He loves every inch of this Center Hill Lake where the Caney Fork merges with three other rivers and flows unconventionally northward through the Great Falls Gorge into the Cumberland watershed.

"There's 125 miles of shoreline along these rivers with towering, wooded and rocky cliffs along much of both banks. It is such a gorgeous part of East Tennessee that it often doesn't make much difference to me whether I catch fish or not," this articulate, energetic walking Chamber of Commerce expounds.

McAfee has fished numerous professional bass tournaments in sophisticated boats, and with the latest tackle, but today he has regressed to an humble jonboat, and a ten horsepower outboard with a steering lever on the stern. The ancient system is his by choice and he still catches fish.

"Bass can find hiding places from the big boats that the pros use today. I see some of them racing up and down the rivers with a six-foot-high outboard engine and every kind of accessory that science has devised. That's great if they want that kind of rig but I'll catch more bass with a flat bottom boat like this than they will in their high-powered fishing machines. Bass are not stupid enough to loll around in places that you can get to with a

151

battleship fishing machine," Mac expresses an opinion about the big fishing craft in widespread use today.

McAfee has fished with some of the leading professionals in his time, like Roland Martin, Ricky Clunn, Bill Dance and Tom Mann. He says they are talented.

"Today most of the pros are really semi-pros with stars in their eyes. Good pros are like cream and they come to the top year after year. Some of the fishermen casting for cash today couldn't catch a cold in a flu hospital," Mac says with a glint of humor in his eyes.

"Like some wag said years ago, fishing is a plug on one end of the line and jerk on the other. The fishermen are not going to catch all the fish out of the streams but pollution, wetland draining, straightened out rivers, and the like, is doing a lot of damage to bass habitat. It makes the gamefish struggle to survive except in isolated areas like this in Tennessee. It will be our carelessness in handling conservation and the ecology if the bass species is doomed," McAfee says.

"Many fishermen today only see lakes and rivers from the road beds and dams. Few ever really get into the wild waters where there is not a house in sight, no car and truck noises and where you feel the naturalness of the adventure. I like it here where it is scenic and there is not much evidence of man's intrusion. Dams, bridges and trestles cross the waterway at several places, but there are miles of undisturbed shoreline.

"This is one of the few good streams left in the country that is almost never too crowded to fish. You often can fish for hours without seeing another boat. You have fishing privacy here like Dan'l Boone had," the old mountain fisherman said with a touch of melancholy.

Then he shifted to the matter of lures, something he has felt strongly about for a lifetime.

"Some of today's young punks who call themselves outdoor writers ought to be baling hay. They try to doctor Buck Perry's fishing techniques with the spoon plug that he made famous. His expertise and technique can stand no tampering. Buck is the greatest and I'll always stick with his advice on largemouth bass fishing. He knows what he is talking about when he talks of structure and how it relates to the spoon plug that finds the fish. This structure-fishing originator is still my model basser and few if any anglers anywhere are as great as he is," Mac says.

"The spoon plug is a great finder of fish. Trolled in lakes and streams, it will get hits even when it doesn't catch a bass. But when you locate the fish with this trolled spoon plug, you can put it in the boat and catch some fine fish with worms, jigs, pig 'n' jig and other baits fished where you got the hit. You may have located a spot where the bass may hang out for days, even weeks. You can make an "X" where you got that spoon plug hit and maybe catch fish all season there. It's the greatest lure around for locating bass," or so says McAfee. "It's the way to find the mother lode."

Mac says, "I believe that fish bite all the time. I don't always find them and no one else does. You have to determine what depth to fish, what lure to cast, what speed to retrieve, among other variables. Once you unlock those secrets, you'll catch bass. I believe if you learn to be a good largemouth fisherman, you will have the expertise to catch all species. Good bass fishermen here at Center Hill Lake make good catches of all species.

"I have fished all over the Southern States. I have caught some big bass but, like everyone else, I remember the one that got away. I was fishing in Florida and I got my line tangled in the lilies. I had a plastic worm on tandem hooks with a 60-pound test leader. A monster bass hit that worm and before I could get untangled, she broke that heavy leader and was gone. Later that day, I caught an 8-pounder and reeled her in like she was just a yearling. She was a minnow compared to the one that I lost," McAfee laments.

"Yeah, I have fished almost everywhere and caught a lot of fish and got skunked plenty of times too. After all these years of fishing and trying to learn everything, the only way I am sure of getting a mess of fish for supper is when I go by Capt. D's," he concludes.

**IT'S YOUR ATTITUDE
NOT YOUR APTITUDE
THAT WILL DETERMINE YOUR
ALTITUDE
IN LIFE.**

Terry Nash With Orange Lake Lunker

BOB SMITH CAUGHT HUNDREDS OF TROPHY BASS

Bob Smith, a native of Hawthorne on the east bank of Lake Lochloosa in Alachua County, Florida, never fished a tournament, never had a trolling motor or an outboard larger than ten horsepower, and never owned a sophisticated fishing boat with electronic equipment. He fished from a small plywood boat made locally during most of his bassing life. He fished only one or two lures and had little need for an elaborate tackle box. He ate or gave away most of the bass he caught, the catch and release practice so popular today having few followers during his fishing career from the 1940's to the 1970's. Furthermore, he worked a night job and almost all of his hours on the water were from about ten a.m. until two p.m.

Yet, despite his humble equipment, mid-day fishing hours, and a skin cancer affliction that cut his outdoor career short, Smith caught literally thousands of largemouth bass in Central Florida, several hundred heavier than 10-pounds. Most of his success was in Orange and Lochloosa lakes, his home stomping grounds where he fished from childhood.

Smith's experience with bass fishing was before the introduction of hydrilla into the Florida lakes. He fished the natural cover of water hyacinths, spatterdock lilies, coontail and sawgrass that was plentiful along the shorelines of the lakes.

Smith eased his small boat out near a grass line or other cover, picked up a short paddle from the deck, and with one hand maneuvered to within 30 to 40 feet of the weeds. He usually then tied on a topwater lure, Devilhorse, Rapala or some other floater and he cast it astutely within inches of the cover. He let the ripples disappear, twitched it a time or two and retrieved it rapidly to the boat and was ready to cast again. He expected the strikes near the cover, not on the retrieve to the boat.

If the cover was not too dense, he might use an Arbogast Sputterfuss with a weedless hook that you could pull through the grass and lilies on top. It made a noise that would put most of today's buzzbaits to shame.

If these two bass-catchers failed, he went to the old reliable black or dark blue, eight-inch worm. Using little or no weight, he cast it near the grass and let it sink. A tap-tap was instantly recognized and he fished an era when you let the bass run and run and run before setting the hook. Smith knew just when to yank the line and he landed well over 90 percent of the bass that struck.

He would fish a line of cover for a couple of hundred yards, moving slowly by paddling from the stern of the boat. If he got no strikes or saw no tell-tale bumps or splashes, he cranked his little outboard and moved to a distant part of the lake. But invariably, he would find where the bass were and come in with huge trophies that got the attention of all who observed.

While he was not among the first bassers to recognize conservation, when Lake Lochloosa developed a sinkhole and went dry in the early 1950's he and other locals caught thousands of fish with their hands and seines, put them in 55-gallon drums and transplanted them into Lake Orange, a half mile away. When the sinkhole was filled with truck bodies, old appliances and assorted other junk that stopped the outflow, water returned to its normal level and the salvaged fish could swim Cross Creek and be back in their original habitat.

Bob Smith continued to catch big bass with his few selected lures, small boat and motor until the skin cancer made him quit fishing in the 1970's.

He was an expert with artificial lures, but he kept no diary and no one will ever know how many trophy bass he really caught. But it would have numbered way up in the hundreds.

THE UNEXPECTED LUNKER

Douglas Burleson, a 15-year-old avid outdoorsman from Lumberton, North Carolina, was fishing with a Super Jig on a B 'n' M telescopic pole in the deep lilies of Orange Lake in June. He was trying to entice some of the big shellcrackers that bed in the cow lilies to make a mistake and hit his little jig that he danced off the bottom in the holes.

Bingo! He felt a yank on the line and the limber pole bent. Something ran at full speed through the lilies, parting them as the line threatened to break. But it didn't. And moments later a bass surfaced, flared its gills and jumped. Douglas held on, excited but still keeping the line tight and the bass as near the top as he could.

The big fish surrendered and came to boatside. He went into the net and over the gunnels. The lunker was an 8-pounder that hit the tiny panfish jig. The lesson here—you can never be exactly sure of just what lure the lunkers want. Even a tiny morsel like the Super Jig did its job and the youngster fishing with the most humble tackle had put a bass of wallmount possibilities in the boat.

He held the big fish up a moment and admired his catch. Then he knelt on the deck, lifted the bass by the lip and gently turned her loose.

"Might as well let her live to bite somebody else's lure sometime," he said.

It was a remarkable sacrifice for a young man with his first 8-pounder.

A NOCTURNAL GIANT ON A POPPING BUG

Two couples were enjoying a few days and nights on a luxury houseboat up the Suwannee River after renting the home-on-the-water from Miller's Marina at the little town of Suwannee. They had been pleased with their catch of speckled trout in East Pass near the Gulf of Mexico that first afternoon, and after supper, decided to try their luck at bass fishing along the grassline of the main stream in the hope of landing some bluegills or redbreasts that are plentiful in the brackish water that supports fresh and saltwater species.

One of the husbands tied a chartreuse popping bug on a 12-pound test line and cast it into the dark current that swirled past some tussocks on the shoreline. He heard an explosion and then felt a strong yank on his spinning rod. He jerked and reeled. The water was in turmoil on the surface for a moment and then right at boatside the fisherman looked down into the open mouth of a 9-pound, 6-ounce largemouth bass. Carefully he lifted the trophy over the side. He forgot about the panfish. This was his dream fish.

While anglers may study lures, presentations, techniques and styles, you can never be completely sure what that big bucketmouth out there is searching for. Even a tiny popping bug enticed a wallmount on a calm night in the Suwannee.

A Big Florida Trophy

ACCIDENTAL BEND IN FISH HOOK LED TO TRUTURN DISCOVERY

Floating a live shiner under a cork along a weed-covered shoreline in the popular Davis pond near Montgomery, Alabama, in 1959, John Campbell was frustrated when he lost more than half of the bass that jumped on his bait, dived for the grass and then came unbuttoned. The best laid plans of this veteran and his partner, Warren Coggins, were thwarted by these lunkers that flaunted their Houdini tactics in the faces of fishermen. Expertise seemed to go for nought and Campbell and Coggins reached a head-shaking moment of indecision. What did they have to do to land these finny escape artists?

"As I was lamenting my bad luck in making hookups that memorable morning, my cork popped under again. The line split the water as the bass was moving like she was being chased by the devil. I set the hook with gusto! The struggle on the line relayed the message. I had a real trophy on the hook, maybe the wallmount lunker of my dreams. I gently played the giant minute after cautious minute, carefully working the bass closer and closer to the boat. She jumped and danced on the surface a dozen feet from the gunnels. She was indeed a beauty, the kind of catch you write home about. Coggins was excited as much as I was and he yelled:

'John, you got a whopper. Don't lose this one!'

"Alas! I cringed. The hook was stuck in a tiny corner of the bass' mouth. It was clearly a risky hangup that could be easily seen when the fish rolled on the surface. She struggled to dive once again. The hook fell out of her mouth." The trophy was loose and she fluttered downward as chagrin cloaked the faces of Campbell and Coggins.

"There must be a better mousetrap. Bass that strike like that are doing their part. The fishermen are the ones who come up short. Good anglers should land these strikers even if we do release the fish once we get them eyeball to eyeball and have a chance to admire their dimensions. To lose these big ones when you use all the acumen you have acquired over a generation of fishing, is discouraging. The right equipment plays a part in successful experiences and I must be lacking something," Campbell muttered. Then a thought popped in his mind that had been etched there since childhood. It changed his fishing career and his very life.

When Campbell was five years old and living with his grandparents on Choccolocco Creek near Anniston, Alabama, he was fishing with his grandmother in a clear, deep hole underneath the waterwheel that propelled the ancient family grist mill. John had been taught how to catch panfish by his grandma who sat with him on the creek bank many summer mornings and dangled worms and other baits near the bottom for redbreast bream as the wheel turned the grinder above that was operated by his grandfather.

"I was fishing with a cane pole that we had cut from the creek bank and had dried out to make a good, humble bream catching rig. I had a small hook tied to a lightweight linen line with a single shot above the hook and a tiny bobber suspended the bait just off the bottom. Bream were thick in the water wheel hole and when the cork popped under, I kept jerking. I hooked several fish, but I was losing two out of three. I missed on a hard jerk and the hook flew above my head, sticking tightly in the unpainted weather boarding of the mill house. I had no other hooks and feared that my fishing for the day was over. Hooks were hard to come by for country boys. I was not tall enough to reach the hook. I began winding my line around the cane pole until it was tight and only a few inches from the hook in the board. Then I pushed upward and fortunately the hook was jiggled loose.

"The hook had a terrible bend in it. But I didn't want to stop fishing. I poked the hook into a crack on the old millpond pier and tried to straighten out the bend. Instead of straightening, I put a second bend in the hook and it looked almost like there was an 'S' in the long shank.

"With no other hooks, I decided to try my mutilated Mustad. I impaled a wriggling wasp larvae bait and dropped it back in the slow creek current. That moment was the most astounding, revealing experience I have ever witnessed, before or after. Even at the tender age of five, I was impressed enough to recall it vividly half a lifetime later. I hung every fish that pulled my cork down the rest of the morning and grandma and I dragged a long stringer of redbreast up the hill to the house for several fine seafood meals. That crooked hook was a miracle, an accidental miracle. Somehow, the offset in the hook made it much more efficient. It struck back at the bream and hung every fish that attacked my bait that day and hundreds in the weeks that followed. The mutilated bend made an amazing difference," Campbell recalls from his Wetumpka, Alabama, Truturn office.

Stewing over the loss of that trophy bass on the Davis pond 40 years later, John dug out a long shank hook from his tackle box. With a pair of pliers, he put an offset in the big bass hook, much like the bends he inflicted on the bream hook at the millpond. Coggins looked on with mouth agape as it appeared his partner had lost his marbles and was wrecking fish hooks.

With the double bend to his satisfaction, Campbell impaled a nine-inch shiner under the dorsal fin and flipped the live bass bait near the cow lilies along the shoreline. Like magic, the cork disappeared. John snapped the rod tip up. The hook set! He reeled carefully. A fine 6-pound largemouth tumbled over the gunwale and onto the deck. That bass was held firmly by the altered hook. Quickly they bent another hook and tied it on Coggins' line. It was equally as productive and for the rest of the month, the bassing partners kept an accurate record. Out of 92 strikes, they put 91 bass in the boat. These good lay anglers knew they had unlocked a secret. An important discovery was proven—the proper offset in a hook would make it more efficient than conventionals.

While that discovery came when Campbell was using live shiners, a much more practical bait three decades ago than artificial lures, the crazy offset hook works equally as well with today's sophisticated artificials. Worms, bucktails, Gitzits, pig'n frog and Super Jigs seem to strike back at bass with better results than many of the conventional straight shank hooks. Giants of the species seem to hang on better with fewer escapees when the "TruTurn" hook, as Campbell's discovery is named, is on the line. It does strike back.

When Campbell was discharged from the service, he started working on his bent hook innovation. TruTurn grew up on his home workbench then, after having been born under the old water wheel and years later tested and proven by John and his partner at the Davis pond in 1959.

In 1960, Campbell bought a hook-bending machine from a Birmingham toolmaker. It had to be custom built, and for the first time, Campbell had a way of fashioning his crazy bend hooks that was many times faster than the handmade TruTurns he had produced for family and friends with pliers. He was ready to market his humble invention.

Soon he placed an order with Mustad after attending the AFTMA show in Chicago. He bought one million hooks. The first order arrived from Alburn, New York, (Mustad U.S.A..) in mid-August 1960. They came by rail.

The closely-knit Campbell family began packaging the hooks in John's home and their word-of-mouth advertising soon had Montgomery tackle shops busy selling the crooked hooks. TruTurn was on the way.

From the local market, TruTurn quickly became regional as avid angler after avid angler began swearing the crooked hook struck back and held bass, catfish, bream and crappie better than any hook previously tried.

Originally the TruTurns were available only in sizes 8 through 3/0, all bronze. In '67 they added a gold Aberdeen and a fine wire Aberdeen. Sales continued to boom and John became more concerned that he had never patented his crooked hook. He had tried in 1959 without success. His attorney had died and the patent had been forgotten.

In 1971, Campbell again applied for the patent. There were complications. The offset in the old No. 038 hook was further from the eye of the hook than in the newer ones. There was little consistency. The No. 047 hook had more specific dimensions, and test results by biologist Bill Phillips through the Anglers Research Associates certified that TruTurns were eight percent more likely to hook and land big bass than conventional hooks. The bend indeed was an advantage. Campbell, his son Wes, and patent attorney Mike Platt were convincing, and after personal demonstrations, the patent was granted. TruTurn was ready to go big time.

In 1977, TruTurn was introduced at the Kansas Ciity AFTMA show. John put two of his sons, Wes and Steve, through a baptism of fire, leaving them alone in the booth to demonstrate to potential buyers and outdoor writers how his crooked hook was an advancement in fishing technology.

Lady fishing professional Chris Houston was impressed. She showed the strange hooks to her popular touring professional bassing husband, Jimmy, an outdoor television showman. Houston liked what he saw and observed at the show. A few days later he was fishing with Cotton Cordell on Lake Sam

Rayburn in Texas. He picked up a big TruTurn hook from Chris' tacklebox and tied it on his line. He stuck on an eight-inch plastic worm and immediately began catching bass, three in a few minutes. Cordell remained skunked and skeptical

"What's going on here?" Cotton inquired. Jimmy showed the lure manufacturer the crazy bend hook that made his worm bait do odd maneuvers when he reeled it across acquatic growth or flipped it on the bottom. Both old pros were immediately convinced of the TruTurn advantage and they remain convinced today.

Two years after that, John gave Roland Martin and Bill Dance, among the all-time leaders in B.A.S.S. tournaments and popular outdoor TV notables, some of the TruTurn hooks. They tried them in a tournament on Lake Sardis in Mississippi and both came in with outstanding catches. Ricky Green, another prominent professional and showman, was converted too, and continues to be a TruTurn disciple today. These three pros, among many others have documented many big bass landings with Campbell's strange-looking hooks.

In 1977, Wes began full time work as Director of Sales and Marketing with TruTurn. Another of John's sons, Steve, finished college in '79 and became Production Manager. Still operating from his home, John moved TruTurn into a rented warehouse in 1981. The family, and some sub-contractors, were still packaging the hooks by hand in strips.

In 1982, the operation moved toward sophistication with more production and office space. With seven employees, TruTurn bought a hook-counting and packaging machine that for the first time put the crazy bend hooks in ziplock bags.

Production has skyrocketed since those early days with hooks made in more than a dozen styles, including two snelled, two weedless, a tough saltwater, a Brute for heavy tackle fishing and a bronze, along with some European models size 24 to 9/0.

In '83, two other children of the TruTurn founder joined the operation. They are Johnny Campbell and Patti Morgan. Both had worked tackle shows. They left their other jobs to be full time TruTurners. Another hook-counting and packaging machine was bought and production again soared.

Pattie Morgan became Comptroller and Patti Campbell, Johnny's wife, became Public Relations Director.

TruTurn is an All-American story. From that humble beginning when John bent hooks with a pair of pliers in his garage and home, the company today works 15 full timers, eight from his own family. Sales in 1987 topped $1.7 million and passed $2 million in 1988. TruTurns are sold in all 50 states, Canada, Europe, Australia and New Zealand.

Where else in the world can a man turn an accident into a successful invention that today provides a good life style for every member of his family, among others, and helps sportsmen the world over. Obviously, it does not rank with Eli Whitney's cotton gin or Thomas Edison's light bulb, but John Campbell invented a gadget that works and one that provides a myriad of outdoorsmen with a better mousetrap. TruTurn has helped put many trophies on den walls.

JOHN CAMPBELL AT HIS WORK

MANY FAVORITE TECHNIQUES FOR CATCHING BASS

As I have outlined in previous chapters here, my favorite way of catching big bass is patiently fishing a topwater or a plastic worm on the bottom until the lunkers get tired of observing the invader and attack the lure. But there are many fine lay anglers in Florida who have great records of success who fish entirely differently, 180 degrees in the other direction.

Consider the bassing life of Wilbur Haymaker, an 86-year-old outdoorsman who lives on Lake Lochloosa where I do some of my big bass guiding.

In 1953, Wilbur's doctor in Indiana pronounced him so physically exhausted that his life was nearing the end. He quit the cattle buying trade, moved to Lochloosa and he is still going strong, fishing several days a week and compiling an enviable record. He is still kicking vigorously more than 35 years after he listened to that death sentence.

Haymaker fishes in an old homemade, plywood boat that he had made for his bassing more than a quarter century ago. He says it is all the boat he needs. And how does he fish?

"I troll the deepest water in the lake with three rods, one on each side of the boat and one in the back. With that style of bassing, I have landed more than 3,000 bass in Lochloosa since I started here and at least 600 of them were lunkers that weighed 8-pounds or more. Five times I have had three bass hung at the same time and saved all three of them," this remarkable senior citizen recalls.

Wilbur has caught some of his bass on live baits but he generally trolls the largest size gold Hotspot lure he can find. He drags it near the bottom and he is satisfied that his system produces as many bass as any system you can devise.

Once he landed 80 bass in three weeks at the same springhead in Lochloosa. He discovered where the 72 degree water was flowing into the bottom of the lake and found that bass schooled there for days and days.

Haymaker has never owned a manufactured fishing boat and he has never had an outboard motor larger than the 9-1/2 hp

Evinrude he still has on his old boat. He feels his equipment is all that he needs to catch fish in Lochloosa.

His homemade rod holders, two strips of leather belting with a 20 penny nail as a stop in the gunnels, does the job for him that he wants. No store-bought rod holders are needed. He slips his 6-1/2 foot, medium stiff fiberglass rods in those holders, sets his Ambassadeur 6000 reels on free spool, and with a big Hotspot tied on a 17 or 20-pound test Stren line, he awaits the bass strikes. He gets them too. And he brings home the proof.

While he believes in conservation, he also believes in not going hungry. He and his wife of half a century have eaten most of the bass he caught. He has given many to a local Baptist Church for charitable fish fries.

"The best trolling lure that I ever fished with is a 2000 gold Hotspot, but other big crankbaits like brokenback Bassmasters, and Rebel, Norman and Storm lures catch fish trolling too. But the big old gold Hotspot is my favorite, especially for the trophy-size bass," Wilbur says.

Then he adds a little of his experience that makes a lot of listeners shake their heads.

"I can catch more bass on an old battered and bashed lure than I can a brand new one. Many times I have trolled a bright, new, shiny Hotspot and not gotten a strike for hours. I would put it in the tackle box, tie on one that was full of scars and cuts and bruises, and bingo! I started getting strikes again. It has happened far too many times for me to think it was accidental," says this astute old codger with a record of success you cannot challenge.

I have a 15-pound, 8-ounce bass on my wall and some others that weighed 12 and 14-pounds. But oddly enough, the largest one I ever caught weighed 17-pounds and I didn't catch her trolling, my favorite way of bassing. How then was she caught?

I caught her in the grass on an old Dalton Special when I was fishing with my daughter. I had hooked that giant several times before and always she broke off. But that Saturday we got her to the net and brought her in. I didn't have her mounted, but I still have the dried-out head of that monster to show people who ask about my biggest bass.

Haymaker's technique is far different from anything that I do to catch bass. But the system works for him. And as the saying goes, if it works, don't knock it. If it doesn't squeak, don't oil it. If it's not broke, don't fix it. He catches bass and I do too. We have contrasting styles and techniques. Bass fishermen everywhere to be successful must discover what method is best for them. Then stay with their specialty. When your confidence grows, so will your catch success. Confidence means a lot when you are after the largemouth bass that are old enough to outsmart the novices. Believe in your technique and perfect it. It will make you a winner too, like Wilbur Haymaker.

Haymaker Catches Another Bass On Rat-L-Trap

Bill Vanderford With Yearlings

SPOON FEEDING LUNKERS
IN DEEP WATER

The most successful bass guide on Lake Sidney Lanier near Gainesville, Georgia, is Bill Vanderford, a former European race car driver who now has a stable of fishing guides working for his Vanderford Guide Service, Lawrenceville, Georgia.

Vanderford is a veteran bassman on this 38,000 acre impoundment that is mostly deep water in the Peach State hill country. Fishing a reservoir like this for trophy-size bass is considerably different from bassing in shallow lakes with a lot of surface cover.

To cope with the deep water problem, Vanderford stalks big bass with the oldest of all fishing lures, the spoon that was once fished by Indians and Europeans. They were fashioned out of animal bones and wood for centuries.

Here's what Bill says about the spoon fishing for bass on Lanier:

The spoon is the proper fall lure to catch big bass on Lake Lanier, even if it is the oldest of lures. Ironically, it is a rather new bass catcher on Lanier and I was introduced to it about ten years ago by a Cartersville, Georgia, native, Charles Redding. He taught me how to properly use the Johnson and other popular spoons.

Charles had discovered the secret of locating and catching bass during and after a lake turnover, a period when the bottom comes to the top and usually results in poor fishing for days. He used his extensive knowledge of the lake's underwater channels, structures and hilltops, along with a good depthfinder, and some 3/4-ounce "Old Pal" spoons to establish the productive pattern of bassing in the reservoir.

Another famous Georgia fisherman, Tommy Shaw, had earlier captured my attention to spoon fishing back in the 1950's. I had read several articles about Shaw's unbelievable catches of big fish in the deep water of Lake Burton on a Daredevil "Imp" spoon. Coupling the vague information I had from Shaw, and the more up-to-date advice from Redding, I started experimenting with spoons above structure during the fall months. Spoon feeding the bass has been a rewarding experience for me since I learned it.

The most popular outfit for vertical spooning is a five to six foot medium action graphite rod with one of the old style baitcasting reels like Garcia's 5500C. I fill the spool with 12 to 15-pound test line.

169

Since bass in Lanier, and in any other deep water impoundment, may suspend at 25 feet where the water is 80 feet deep, it's necessary to accurately put the spoon where the fish are. The older type baitcasting reels have a level-wind guide that goes from side to side as the line leaves the spool. Measure the length of line that is released during one pass, usually five to seven feet per pass. Then multiply that until you establish the amount of line necessary to put the spoon in the face of the fish.

Choosing a spoon can be difficult as they come in many different weights, shapes and finishes. The ones that work the best for vertical spoon jigging are straight. Most of the action occurs in 20 feet of water or deeper, and a curved spoon flutters so much that the angler has problems controlling it.

More expensive spoons like the "Hopkins Shorty," or "Jack's Jigging Spoon" are hammered brass that is chrome plated.

Spoons like the Jim Bagley "Salty Dog" or "Mann-O-Lure" are either painted or plated with lead. Since the structure spoon is meant to imitate a two to three inch threadfin shad, 3/4-ounce is generally the most desirable weight.

I like the 3/4-ounce Jack's Jigging Spoon that is manufactured by the 1985 Bassmasters Classic Champion, Jack Chancellor. But I am sure that in 20 feet of water they all look like a sick or dying shad to a hungry bass.

After you have located a school of suspended bass with whatever fish finding equipment you have, fishing is academic. Drop the spoon straight down to where the flasher shows the fish. Then sharply yank it up so that it will bounce 12 to 24 inches on each jig. Watch the line movement when the jig falls. Most strikes come as the spoon falls and since bass usually hit it from below, slack line will be your only indication that you have had a strike.

Wherever you fish a spoon, look for narrow coves with a lot of trees, hopefully somewhere there is standing timber left when the dam stopped the water in the impoundment. If you have some knowledge of the terrain before the water was dammed, find some old homesites where a few shade trees were left and the tops still rise above the surface in 30 to 70 feet of water. Surrounding land was farmed and the fish cherish those remaining trees in the vast underwater clearing. I also often locate suspended bass over old creek channels.

Remember, spoon fishing is for fall and winter when bass are difficult to catch by any method. But if you have given up on killing a big buck this season, try spoon feeding the lunkers and you might catch a giant to write home about.

ROLAND MARTIN LIKES FLIPPING

A fellow Floridian of mine is Roland Martin, of Clewiston, on Lake Okeechobee, where he runs a guide service, motel and marina that carry his prestigious name. Nine times "Angler of the Year," the 20-year tournament veteran is among the all-time money winners on B.A.S.S. trails and he has popularized the vertical fishing presentation known as "flipping."

Martin, who began his professional guiding career in Santee-Cooper in South Carolina when he was in the Armed Forces and stationed at Fort Jackson, has qualified for the B.A.S.S. Masters Classic, the Superbowl of bass fishing, 17 times. He has won 16 B.A.S.S. tournaments.

This Maryland native is a versatile pro fisherman. He created the concept of pattern fishing, defined as a set of conditions such as depth, cover, water temperature and clarity, along with alkaline content, that attracts fish to specific locations.

Capitalizing upon his pattern fishing, this daddy rabbit of professional bassing has recorded a 13-pound, 4-ounce trophy as his largest bass. Here's what he says about his favorite way of catching lunkers:

The environment should be analyzed when pattern fishing. Most anglers simply define these areas as good places to catch fish. That is where all the right elements come together. I constantly evaluate the depth, water temperature, clarity and pH. All these factors and others affect the feeding and behavioral patterns of a bass and how it relates to a specific area.

My favorite type of fishing is flipping around heavy cover. It seems that no matter what the conditions, flipping produces fish. I use a long, heavy-action rod and my line varies from 20 to 40-pound test Stren. I go out and try several things, keying on four or five different patterns. I might be looking for specific boat docks, points or grass or lily pads, but they all have common components that are right for the bass on that particular day.

One of my favorite patterns is flipping a dark-colored jig with pork trailer in the shady areas beneath boat docks. Two key elements to producing fish with this technique are making sure the water is dingy or murky and you must drop the lure gently into the water. A noisy presentation on this pattern will spook the bass.

Water under boat docks is generally shallow and with little or no cover. A racket sends the bass a' running.

PATTERN FISHING FOR BASS

In recent years the where and how to catch bass in a given stream or lake has come to be known as "pattern fishing." It is an educated, designed plan to find fish around particular cover and to fish all similar areas, or patterns in the area for the fish. The idea is that if the bass congregate around a single stump on a shallow point, for instance, there will likely be other bass around a stump on another point where the water is similar in depth, current, etc.

I like the pattern of finding fish in deep water over submerged aquatic growth, and I know I can catch bass there with my dead worm technique. Another pattern is fishing on the surface circles along canal shorelines where there are cow lilies or hydrilla that hide the bass.

One of the all-times greatest professional bassers in the country is Roland Martin, of Clewiston, Florida.

He is generally acknowledged as the father of pattern fishing and he has dozens of productive patterns that he fishes all over the nation.

One of his more unusual patterns is what he calls his "garfish pattern." All Florida waters have a good population of gars or garfish. They are vicious predators that raid bream and bass nests, forage on the bait fish and anything else that they can swallow.

Martin says when he sees garfish swimming around, he knows that there are bass in the territory. They both feed on the creatures that live on the nest. Find the gars and you have found the bass, he says.

Over the years, I know that is truly a good pattern. The predators hang out together looking for the same kind of meal and several gars gliding around on the surface will mean there are bass lurking not far away. It's Martin's "garfish pattern" and it works.

Try it. You'll catch some lunkers.

Martin Is Daddy Rabbit Of Bass Fishing

JACK NAST HUNG TITLE ON ME

The late Jack Nast, a Suncoast outdoor writer for many years, once referred to me as the "Muhammad Ali of artificial bait bass fishing."

About the same time, Frank Sargeant, outdoor editor of *The Tampa Tribune*, tagged Douglas Hannon as "The Bass Professor."

Later we became friends and bass fishing partners. Some of the media described the association as a Muhammad Ali-Bass Professor relationship. An unholy alliance.

Douglas has caught more than 400 trophy bass over 10 pounds, mostly with live shiners, and I have landed 321 trophies on artificial baits. Together we have caught at least 721 trophy bass totalling more than 7,000 pounds. Almost all of them were released.

The first time I ever fished Lake Tarpon, I went there with Hannon, and I was lucky enough to land one of my 10-pounders on a dead worm bait. I caught several smaller bass the same day. It is one of my favorite lakes along the Suncoast, especially in the spring and summer when the yearling bass school in the open water.

BILL DANCE SAYS LEARNING FISH BEHAVIOR PARAMOUNT

Bill Dance, Memphis, Tennessee, was the first professional bass angler to become a national personality. His acumen with a rod and reel and infectious smile made him an idol of outdoorsmen more than 20 years ago when he enjoyed outstanding success on the cast-for-cash bass trails. He fished his first tournament in 1967 and during an era when winning purses were not nearly as substantial as they are today, he took home more than $150,000 in winnings.

He qualified for the Bassmasters Classic nine times before leaving the tour to teach angling on television. This 48-year-old expert basser has been as remarkably successful on television as he was on the lakes and streams of America as a tournament competitor.

Considered by millions as the All-American young man, here's what Dance says about catching bass:

There are three different areas to most lakes: upper, which is normally shallow, murky and has dense cover; middle, which has moderate depths, semi-clear water with some cover and open water; and finally the lower end, which is usually deep with clear water and little cover. By learning how to fish each of these distinctly contrasting sections, you expand your ability to catch bass.

Most anglers know that they can catch fish in certain areas of a lake or stream during specific times of the year, but they are always trapped in other places. Go to new places on a lake and learn how to fish them. When I did this, it forced me into learning how to locate fish on different structures and patterns. I became a better fisherman.

Knowing how your prey acts and behaves is one of the most important aspects of successful fishing. It is a long hard day when you don't know how the fish you are hunting behave and feed. When you know that, you can determine depth, type of lure, test of line and other information that is necessary for catch success.

It's important to try experiments with all types of lures. Using only one is like eating only cereal. Some of the time it will be good; the rest of the time it won't.

I like light spinning or spincast tackle for novice fishermen and a baitcasting outfit for the more experienced angler. I generally use 8 or 10-pound test line when bass fishing and Prime Plus is my favorite.

Anglers are creatures of habit and that unfortunately hurts their fishing. Too many people rely on certain types of lures and specific areas on lakes and streams. Break out of the routine. Try different approaches and you'll learn to be a better bass angler.

RICKY CLUNN TALKS TOPWATERS

Texan Ricky Clunn, for years a bass guide like I am, ranks among the top three all-time money winners in professional bassing. It is generally conceded by the best of the cast-for-cash anglers that his techniques, acumen and dedication to bass fishing stand atop the pedestal. Few fishermen in any era have better credentials than this young man from the Lone Star State.

Ricky fishes a variety of lures in being top drawer in performance in B.A.S.S. and on other pro trails. He spoke of topwaters at a United Bass Association tournament in Las Vegas. His analysis of topwaters coincides closely with my observations over the years as a guide and professional tourney fisherman.

Here's what Clunn thinks about topwater lures:

Tournament bassers succeed when they have experience coupled with confidence. Prowess of the pros for the proper lure selection, presentation and retrieve sets them apart.

I will not go so far as to say that topwater lures are the best bait of all, but I quickly agree that this old reliable artificial plays an important role in almost every tournament. Winners usually owe at least part of their victory to a topwater lure.

The winner may not have fished the topwater every day of the tourney, but a consequential portion of his weigh-in fell to the deadly topwater. It's a key bait that's excellent for tournament competition and it's always a dominant factor.

You catch more quality fish with topwaters. It's a sight bait that bass can see from some distance away, particularly in clear water like Lake Mead in Nevada. I don't believe it is quite as good a lure in murky water.

The first topwater that I remember was a Heddon's famous Lucky 13. It was a big plug, colored white and red, and when I was a little fellow and fishing with my Dad in Texas, I had to dodge those lure hooks many times when they sailed over my head from one of Dad's long casts.

The buzzbait is a simple topwater that makes a noise and it catches a lot of fish for me. You have to master the cast, learn the proper retrieve and it will put bass in the boat.

I remember back in 1972 when I was fishing an American Bass Association tournament in Illinois. I saw an especially ugly old topwater lure there in a bait and tackle shop. I bought two of them. I had never seen anything like them before. That same year I carried them to a tournament at Cordell Hull Lake in Tennessee where I fished a B.A.S.S. event. I cast one of those old uglies the first day and caught a 5-pounder. I then caught a nice 4-pounder and hooked another one that broke the line. That one went off with my old ugly lure. I had previously loaned my other unique topwater to my partner, but after he made three casts without a strike and knowing that I had lost the only other old ugly that I had, he gave it back to me. I tied it on a 20-pound test line and immediately I hung the lure in a tree. It broke off. I could see it and could have gotten it out of the tree but it was against the rules to leave the boat, even to climb a big maple. I had to leave it there and get another bait out of my tackle box. But I had lost my two unusual topwaters and I lost my luck, too. While I had a big lead the first day when I caught big bass on those ugly lures, I got only one fish the second day and lost the tournament by 12 ounces.

I came back the next year with a bunch of buzzbaits and won the tournament. It's a great lure in clear water when you fish it slowly. Bend the lure head down when you retrieve slowly through your target. I like my topwater lure to run to one side or the other, not straight. I make allowances for the way it runs and I make it pass by my target. I sometimes let it hit the target and then slip by. That gets the fish's attention.

When I was winning that tournament in 1972, 1/4-ounce buzzbaits were not common. They are now. I liked the 1/4-ounce but now, fishing clear water in the West, I prefer the 1/8 ounce. I fish it much faster than the heavier buzzbait. I go back to the heavier ones when the water is murky.

If I am fishing surface weeds, I use a 1/4-ounce without a skirt. It will hang up only half as much if you take the skirt off and you have to fish it fast. Sometimes you may miss a strike when the bass hits the spinner blade and not the hook. I have put on a smaller skirt after a miss and then caught the fish.

I use 17-pound test line and up. It's variable, depending upon cover, circumstances and water conditions. I do not believe the heavy line is any deterrent to bass strikes on buzzbaits. Line test is meaningless when fishing a topwater.

I use a 7-1/2 foot Daiwa fiberglass rod. I believe this is better than boron or graphite when topwater fishing.

A bass may strike and inhale a lure. When it does, something must give. The rod flexes when you are retrieving fast on the surface and you may be looking off, thinking ahead and planning. A good rod will help you save the fish when you have lost concentration. Don't point your rod at the fish. Hold it right or left so it can give to a strike.

*The better bass fisherman will miss more fish on a buzzbait than the **poorer** angler. The instinct to react quickly to a strike makes you lose some fish. You have to discipline yourself and wait to feel the pull of the fish.*

The Zara Spook is fished differently. It will get strikes. You need to use a short rod with wrist action. Feed it line and make it walk side to side. You must give a Spook line so it will have action.

The old Pop-R-Chugger by Rebel is a topwater that excels. It darts, walks on the water and dives. It will catch what I call "in-between bass." There are some active fish, some inactive and some that are neither. Those are the "in-betweens." This bait will make bass bite when they are not hungry. The fish hits the invader because the bass thinks it is a predator or a weak, catchable prey. It has erratic action that generates hits. You can make it imitate an injured bait fish that something else has already struck.

I used to guide a lot and sometimes I fished the Chugger with a bucktail tied on behind it. It worked great at high speeds. I believe that topwaters should be fished very fast in hot, clear water and the warmer the water, the better surface lures work. I concentrated on topwaters on Lake Mead in 1983 and I won the U. S. Open.

I do not pretend to be a topwater expert, but it is a tool that I do a job with. Match your tools to the water and the line. The

179

buzzbait is made for vegetation. You can make the nose of the bait run under the water. You may also have success with it with a trailing jig. It rarely makes a difference, but sometimes it is a lifesaver. I was fishing a tournament at Percy Priest Lake in 1977 and needed a 10-fish limit with one big bass to win. I caught a 4-pounder on a trailer. It was the key fish and I won the tournament. I caught most of my fish on a spinner bait but that topwater trailer was my key that day. It's easy to use a rigid trailer so that it doesn't hang up much..

Sound is irrelevant on buzzbaits, but not odor. I went to using fish formula years ago. I began to believe and endorsed it. What works for me? What works for you? The results may be different but a buzzbait may bring an active fish from a long distance to strike. One strike may win a tournament.

When you cast a topwater, make contact with the cover. If it's a bush, stump, rock or grass, hit it with the bait on the cast and then start your retrieve.

There are three dominant lures and all are tools of the angler. There's the spinner baits in one to five feet of water; crankbaits in almost any depth that doesn't have dense cover and then worms. I find worms to be successful at all depths when fished by experts, many finding it the favorite all-time artificial. It's hard to question that.

The old time topwater bait is a complementary lure that serves two functions—it will locate fish and let you cover a lot of water hunting them and it will also catch bass when properly presented. They are usually quality size.

Spinner baits are great for some fishermen like Guy Eaker and Jimmy Houston. They throw spinners in places where no one else would dare to cast. They catch bass in those seldom hit spots in the deep cover. Fishing pressure often puts bass in hard-to-hit places in the brush and grass. And some bass won't hit anything unless you put it right in their faces. Eaker and Houston can do that.

Bobby Murray is another good spinner fisherman. He won the first B.A.S.S. Classic on Lake Mead throwing a spinner from the back of the boat.

The old topwaters have helped me win tournaments. I can even recall times when I caught bass with a total reflex action. Bass watch the lure in the air and without thinking, pounce on it the instant it hits the surface. Topwaters have a history of forcing largemouths into making mistakes.

KEN COOK—A SCIENTIST
WHO LIKES SPINNERS

Ken Cook, of Meers, Oklahoma, blends professional bass angling with his fisheries scientist's education to be among the most astute bassers in the game. Combining education with skill has made a winner out of the personable fisherman who has placed in the money in 70 percent of the tournaments he has entered. He is a Skeeter boat, Trilene line proponent.

His biggest payoff was in 1983 when he won the Super Bass Tournament and the $100,000 first place money at Palatka, Florida. He came from eighth to first on the last day of that tournament to win.

Cook likes to talk about the 12-pound, 11-ounce beauty he landed in Texas' Sam Rayburn Lake and the time he caught 77 bass in three hours, releasing them all. Another time he caught five bass that weighed 25 pounds, a real success with lunkers.

While he is versatile and has to be to win as often as he does, Cook swears by the spinner bait. Here's what he says about baits:

My favorite method of fishing is with a 3/8- ounce spinner bait with a No. 4 Colorado blade and a chartreuse and blue skirt in shallow water. I believe all fishermen should learn as much as possible about the bass they are seeking. It will make you a better bass angler.

Spinner baits are the most versatile of the bass lures. You can change head size, colors of skirts, trailers and blades. While one spinner bait cannot be fished effectively under all conditions, a "set" of spinner baits can. The depth the bass are residing determines how I rig my spinner bait and why I choose that lure over others.

How do you reach a starting point? Water clarity is step one. When you can see two to three feet, that's muddy or stained. More than three feet visibility is clear.

When fishing the medium clarity, start with a medium size spinner bait, 3/8-ounce weight, a single spinner with a No. 4 Colorado blade or a No. 4 or 5 Willow Leaf. Couple this spinner with a tri-colored white, chartreuse and blue skirt or a metal flake skirt.

Bass tend to like big blades in muddy water. When the visibility is less than two feet, go with the bigger blades. The fish like the extra vibration when the water is dingy or even muddy. You can get more vibration by taking the front blade off a tandem spin. Use the larger Colorado blades instead of Willow leaf in off-color water. The former thumps better.

In clear water, go with tandem, smaller blades and I prefer the Willow Leaf. Be subtle with skirt selection. Skirts should be attached to the spinner hooks in clear or translucent water.

If the water is cold, the bass will want a slower moving spinner. A top technique is attaching a big blade to allow for a slow fall alongside cover where you think bass are holding.

With regard to the weight of the lead head on the spinner bait, you have to select a size and shape that will balance the package. During the retrieve, all spinner baits should come through the water straight—not with the lead head above or below the hook point. The spinner should be directly above the hook point, not tilted to one side.

The Color-C-Lector should be relied upon when choosing skirts. Instead of going with only one color the Color-C-Lector suggests, go with three colors, preferably the main color plus two on either side. The combo of white, chartreuse and blue fits a wide spectrum of visibility. Skirts of these three shades are popular among pro anglers.

HAROLD ALLEN LIKES
TOPWATERS, JIGS AND WORMS

East Texan Harold Allen, a 45-year-old guide and professional basser, has moved around the country extensively and
wherever he is, he enjoys fishing. He has loved fishing all his life
from the time his grandmother first carried him on Lake Sam
Rayburn. In his late teens, he got really serious about bassing
and became a guide on Rayburn in 1970.

Later he moved to Toledo Bend, a newer, more productive
reservoir, where he found every challenge existed on the one impoundment, including timber, depth, open water, coves, channels, boat lanes and aquatic growth. It taught him how to fish.
And in 1977 Allen joined the pro bass trails. He had two top-10
finishes his first year and made the Bassmaster Classic. He
made the Classic again his second year, barely missed the third,

and generally has been a successful pro. He fishes from a Skeeter boat.

Allen likes topwaters, jigs and worms and handles each of these lures effectively to catch lunkers.

Here's his testimony about lures that work for him:

Casting topwater plugs is the most traditional of all bass fishing techniques. It is also one of the most exciting ways to go after largemouths. There's a lot more to success with a topwater than merely chunking and reeling. You must fool the fish, sucker her out of the cover, make her strike something that doesn't even look like food that she normally eats. If you win, you have a feeling of accomplishment.

Slow down if you want to catch fish with a topwater. Let the mood of the fish and the water conditions dictate the type of lure you use on top. If the bass are timid or moody, switch off the larger topwaters and tie on a smaller one. With bass in a more aggressive mood, use a larger plug, work it faster and with more fuss. It will pay off.

Water surface condition also is a factor. The calmer the water the more subtle the plug presentation. Smaller lures attract more strikes in calm water. The more ripple on the surface, the more you have to thrash the bait. Work it! Draw the fish up!

In clear lakes, use stick-type lures, the style that doesn't make much noise but has action. Zara Spook works well. Lip baits like Rapala, Rogues, Bang-O-Lure and others are excellent. If the bass won't come after a chugger, then feed them the lip baits. Within a couple of feet of grass line cover, lip baits are great bass lures.

The jigging spoon is a productive bait for catching active bass. A jig will often catch several bass out of the same school. Bass may strike a jigging spoon not from hunger, but to keep other bass from getting it. Ripping the jigging spoon up off the bottom and letting it flutter and fall back like an injured bait fish will bring strikes from any bass in the territory.

The plastic worm is the versatile lure. It will catch fish from two feet to 42. And it works winter, summer, spring and fall. It works in the grass, on a gravel bar or in stick-ups. You can use it on any tackle as long as the rod has some backbone and any reel that will crank.

You can catch bass with topwaters, jigs and worms. It's all a matter of experience and confidence, plus fishing where the bass are.

SKIPPING LURE TECHNIQUE HELPS SHAW GRIGSBY

Shaw Grigsby, of Gainesville, Florida, is one of the best of the current crop of young professional anglers. I have fished with Shaw in tournaments several times and know him to be a fine tournament competitor and gentleman as well.

In 1984 he walked off with the $100,000 first prize in the Red Man All-American Tournament and more recently in 1989 he took home $76,000 for second place in the Megabucks Tournament at Leesburg, Florida, after having been the front runner all the first three opening days. He is a B.A.S.S. Classic qualifier and at only 33 years of age, ranks among the best of the cast-for-cash bass professionals.

Grigsby likes to skip a worm under docks and other cover for big bass, and he has perfected the technique enough to impress all the other professionals who have observed his successful system.

Here's how he describes his technique of lure skipping;

Most of us have skipped pebbles and rocks off the surface of small lakes or ponds when we were growing up. I remember those days and I now apply that skipping technique to my arsenal of tactics for catching nice bass.

I have found that bass suspend under boat docks, over-hanging trees and heavy brush cover. Skipping a worm on the surface to those hard-to-reach spots is the only way to present a lure in a "light" manner that will tempt the bass.

To be effective, the lure must be cast all the way back near the end of the dock or the bank, but it must enter the water with as little splash as possible. Noise is what you don't want when sneaking up on one of these shoreline bass.

I like to rig a worm Texas-style with a pegged weight to make it all one unit and weedless. If all the equipment is rigged correctly, with some practice, you can cast back 15 to 20 feet under these docks or overhanging cover. That's the area that is loaded with fish, sometimes real giants.

I use a 5-1/2 or 6-foot spinning rod with heavy action for this kind of skip fishing. The heavy action also makes setting the hook and playing the fish out of heavy cover easier. I use a small spinning reel spooled with 12 or 14-pound Stren line. Spinning gear is mandatory to prevent backlashes with this skipping technique.

To do it right, you must cast side-arm for a low level presenta-tion. Sweep the rod back and bring it forward with the lure as close to the water as possible. The worm should skip a couple of times and stop right near the target. It really is an effective way to coax fish out of hiding in heavy cover. You must try it a few times to get the feel.

I have won tournaments with this skip bait fishing and pulled some lunkers out of those hideouts that were over 10-pounds. It's productive and it's fun, too.

BURMA THOMAS—SHALLOW WATER WINNER

Professional Bass 'N Gal and Lady Bass angler Burma Thomas, Rainsville, Alabama, known affectionately as "Burning Burma" for her hot fishing streaks when she can't seem to lose, attributes her fishing success to catching bass in shallow water. That's where she is the most skillful. Here's what she says about how she catches bass:

It's easier to catch bass when they are not so deep and most anytime there are some fish near the bank. I prefer to use topwater lures but the water temperature really needs to be 65 degrees or above for best catches on top.

I'll use a spinner bait or crankbait to find fish. Then I bear down with the topwater. The best topwater lure for me is the 1/4-ounce buzzbait. I adjust the blades sometimes but generally they will work right out of the package.

I work the lure slowly, concentrating upon the available cover. I like the white skirt on my lure with a chartreuse grub trailer to help with hookups when bass strike short.

Bass strike harder on top than they do deep so you must use good line. I prefer 17-pound test because I can hook them quickly and get them out of the cover. You cannot do much with a line that stretches a lot.

I work just as hard when I am fishing for fun as I do when I'm fishing for money. When I go leisure fishing, I'm really keeping in shape for the competition later. I love to compete. That's really the reason I fish, to test my skills, not only against other fishermen, but against the bass, too.

But I really like to compete with other bassers in the Bass 'N Gal and Lady Bass tournaments all around the country. Using my shallow water bassing experience, I have been fortunate enough to be a winner and I am thankful for that.

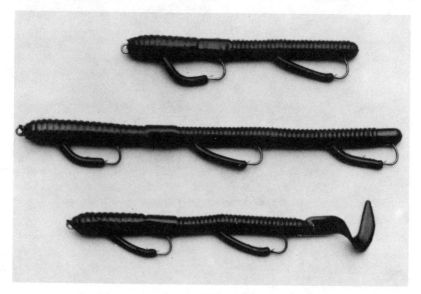

CHRIS HOUSTON'S
SPINNER BAIT TACTICS

There is no better spinner bait bass angler in the country than Chris Houston, wife of the professional basser and television showman Jimmy Houston, with whom I have made a number of fishing shows. While Jimmy taught Chris about spinner baits, she has been so successful on the Bass 'N Gal circuit and others that she is accepted as the superior angler with spinner baits.

Part of Chris' success with spinner baits comes from her unceasing effort over hours and hours on the water in tournaments all over the country. She flips

her spinners along the shoreline at the rate of a cast every ten seconds, sometimes every eight seconds. That's six casts every minute, 360 an hour or more. It's easy to see how she could have a very weary arm by weigh-in time. Six or seven hours on the water during a tournament fishing day, means she is casting that spinner 3,000 times at least. She gives the bass ample opportunity to get on the hook.

Chris fishes her spinner so fast that she never lets it get out of sight. She flips it with a talented, effortless figure eight cast to within inches of the shoreline or weed cover. She starts the retrieve only fractions of seconds after it splashes down. The bass must hit it running rapidly either on the surface or barely submerged, if it is struck at all; she never lets it sink.

A strike brings her rod tip up quickly, and unless it is a giant bass, the fish is flouncing on the deck in moments. She handles the lunkers carefully, astutely, and it takes a bit more time.

This lady bass professional has always been among the top money winners in the Bass 'N Gal circuit. Much of her success has hinged on her expert handling of spinner baits in shoreline shallows.

She likes yellow, chartreuse and white skirts on spinners, sometimes in combination.

Bass have little time to come unbuttoned when she gets a strike. Before the bass has time to think, Chris has the fish in the boat. She loses very few strikes.

A TOURNAMENT DAY WITH THE SPINNER BAIT QUEEN

By W. Horace Carter

It was a cool, overcast October morning, the first practice day of the 6th Annual Bass 'N Gal Classic, the Super Bowl of ladies' professional bass fishing. We were bassing on the relatively new Bob Sandlin impoundment at Mt. Pleasant, Texas, a reservoir covered with standing trees, that abounds with largemouths. Stickups dotted most of the lake and there was no scarcity of cover for the healthy bass. Often the cover was so dense that only the most daring of lady bassers ventured into the trees where the faint hearted feared to tread.

I was the press observer paired with Chris Houston, the petite and talented lady angler from Cookson, Oklahoma, mother of two, and wife of the TV renowned, jovial professional basser, Jimmy Houston. I looked forward to fishing the practice day with this greatest of all professional lady anglers, who at that time had been named "Lady Angler of the Year" five out of nine times. Even then (five years ago) she had earned $103,855 in tournaments and was the acknowledged master of spinner bait casting. (Later in 1985 she was again named "Lady Angler of the Year" and her earnings jumped to $124,642. She was the all-time BNG leading money winner at that time.)

Practice days are fun on the Bass 'N Gal tournament trail. The rules are not strict and the contender and press observer explore the water in search of honey holes where the contestant may land some lunkers when tourney days start and the big money is at stake. Pounds then mean dollars and prestige. It's a test of your acumen and stamina and only the best succeed.

A sleek vehicle with a trailer hitch pulled up to the dock. Chris's sophisticated Ranger boat was loaded on the trailer. I got in the car with the Houstons and Jimmy drove about 30 miles, crossed over a bridge and stopped at a launching ramp. It was dawn and the starting horn in Bob Ferris' hand blurted, "Go get 'em."

Jimmy had climbed out of bed early this morning because he wanted his talented wife to have as much time as possible to scout the territory. By driving her around the lake to this launching ramp, she would be only minutes from the area they believed was the most productive. It would have taken a great deal of time to get here by water as she would have had to run around thousands of obstacles.

Jimmy was showing Chris that she really had his support as she always did, whether it was with vehicle transportation or the selection of rods, reels and lures. And lures here is the key word. He had long been known as the most devout of the spinner bait casters on the B.A.S.S. circuit. That expertise had been passed along to his wife and it had earned her the unofficial title of "Spinner Bait Queen."

A few putt-putt minutes away from the landing, Chris cut the big outboard, lowered the trolling motor and eyed a bushy area where dozens of huge trees lay half-submerged in the cider-colored Texas water. She eased along 35 feet from the cover, picked up a bevy of open-faced spinning reels on limber rods that were neatly filed on the deck rack, and she was ready for action. She chose a bait that had a white skirt and double silver blades. The reel was full of 14-pound test Trilene, the monofilament choice of the Houstons.

Standing on the bow of the bass boat with the pedestal seat removed, because this lady angler never sits down when she is fishing, Chris began underhanding that spinner bait into pork 'n' beans size holes in a dead tree top. She was the acme of accuracy. Expressionless, she retrieved the spinner with its semi-weedless hook back to the boat, and in one motion had it out over the water and headed toward another likely spot just an arm's length from the first splashdown. Every cast was fantastic. Her little figure-eight motion with the rod tip near the surface flipped the spinner where she wanted it time after time. The spinner skims along just inches off the water. She makes no rainbow casts.

The brush pile was a good spot. Chris put a 3-pounder in the boat. Then tenderly, carefully she unhooked the bass and slipped it back in the water. Maybe it would bite again on a tournament day.

Chris moved the boat a dozen yards. Again she flipped in a tree top, changing the white skirt on the spinner to a chartreuse, and shortly thereafter substituting a yellow and black combination. She was testing these bass for color. Did it really make a difference what color skirt she threw at them?

She put that spinner bait in hundreds of the coziest pockets in the trees you can imagine all morning long and by noon she had caught and released seven nice bass, all keeper size. She released them so gently that you could see she was inviting them to stay there and strike again when she came back the next day.

She even put the boat in spots where I could catch a bass or two with my awkward cast that only splashed the spinner down in the general vicinity of the cover where I had aimed.

Not so with Chris. Always she cast accurately and quickly. She was so fast , in fact, that it became my point to ponder for the day. She cast short distances, never more that 40 feet, and she continually averaged eight to ten casts a minute, all the time trolling slowly along a fallen tree line. The reeling and retrieving were so fast that the spinner was never out of sight. It either buzzed along the surface or sputtered life-like a few inches under the water. It was enticing to the bass that must have calculated the bait fish that day were active on top, maybe because of the overcast sky. She never made a slow retrieve.

She sometimes flipped the spinner as much as 500 times an hour, never less than 350, and during the day that added up to as many as 3,500-5,000 opportunities that bass had to strike.

That's a lot of casts for any angler of any sex. Yet, she had the stamina to continue and to accurately and confidently hit the holes where she believed the bass lurked in the Sandlin reservoir. Accuracy and speed in casting and retrieving are the criteria of the Houston spinner bait success.

They handle other baits too. Chris had one rod and reel on the deck with a blue plastic worm. Another had a diving crankbait and still another a buzzbait. She tried them all from time to time when the spinner went cold. She could handle them like the professional that she was but always she went back to the tackle with the spinner. It was her grits and gravy lure.

Every successful pro angler must be able to adapt to various waters and determine the preference of the bass. Chris did that day and, as usual, she always returned to her specialty—the spinner bait. It's the old reliable that the Houstons bet on, all other lures just taking up the slack when strikes are few and far between.

How does Chris pick her places for casting that spinner bait? It's a matter of experience for the pros and luck for the amateurs. Chris likes to fish the shallow shorelines of lakes where there is some aquatic growth, a few limbs, stumps, rocks or other cover. She looks for quiet coves where the shoreline is inviting and she eases past the bank, scarcely making a ripple. She seems to know that bass are here and when she fishes 20 yards of shoreline without a strike, she may be undaunted, reversing her course and going back to fish the same pattern again and again.

If there is no action along the bank, she looks for other likely spots. That day on Bob Sandlin she first tried the deeper water, well out in the lake where there was a distinct tree line. She fishes the tree line like she does a shoreline. Later in the morning when she had established a pattern in trees, she spotted an old submerged roadway with bushes lining what was once the shoulders of a farm-to-market road. It had sharp dropoffs on both sides and the bass were hanging out on those drops. She worked it far enough to know that keepers could be caught in the area, filed it in her mind and moved on.

Like all good bassing pros, she looks for current. Bass food is swept along in water where there is movement and many lunkers spend a lifetime lurking in the eddies near currents that swish by cover. Forage fish congregate in the eddies awaiting helpless insects that are caught in the swirl and bass make meals off the schooling bait fish. A shiny, attractive spinner flipped near the current and reeled in fast enough to resemble a shiner, prompts strikes when predators are in the neighborhood. Bass make mistakes and succumb to a piece of metal, adorned with octopus-like tentacles of plastic that looks like something alive and nourishing.

Chris often customizes her spinner offering. She doctors it a bit by cutting a plastic worm in two and impaling a piece on the spinner hook that trails an inch or two behind the normal skirt. This makes it a bigger bait and at times it will entice larger fish to strike than the smaller spinner without the trailer.

Spinners come in a variety of colors, sizes and weights. They have gold leaves as well as chrome, black and even multi-colored. There is a time and a place for all the variations. But Chris is a

193

disciple of single blades, silver spinners with either white, chartreuse or yellow skirts and light weight.

Different kinds of water and different seasons require changes in spinner baits. There's no one combination that will work every day and everywhere. That's why Chris always has a tackle box full of spinner baits that she changes and tries in different combinations. She stays with the selection that gets strikes, tailored for the time and place. It's a trial and error system.

Jimmy and Chris do not always win the tournaments. But they win often enough to place among the elite of professional bassers. Chris didn't win the three-day event at Bob Sandlin. Those fish she located in practice had lockjaw on Thursday, Friday and Saturday, the tournament days. Someone found more fish than Chris did on on the days that counted. But the obvious fact remains, the Houstons know how to fish spinner baits as well as anyone in the country, and they have proven it year after successful year.

It's practice, patience and experience that have earned this husband-wife the accolade, "King and Queen of Spinner Baits."

Chris and Jimmy are more than outstanding bass professionals. They are an All-American, church-going family. A daughter and son are close to their parents. And the Houstons, when on the tournament trail and casting those spinners for lunkers, still find a Baptist Church to attend on Sunday morning. That's an indication of the character of this fishing family that's successful both on and off the water.

194

HANK PARKER'S SPINNERS
WAKE FISH UP

Hank Parker, the Denver, North Carolina, professional with a record of exceptional success in the B.A.S.S. tournaments, including a Classic title in 1979 at Texoma in Texas, casts spinner baits part of every day he is competing. Long ago he decided the spinner was a productive lure along cover lines, and he turns to it frequently when fishing near the bank or cover in shallow waters.

Fishing the B.A.S.S. Classic in Arkansas a few years ago, Hank tied on a big, two-bladed spinner with a yellow skirt and as he trolled slowly along a line of half-submerged pilings a few yards from the launching ramp, he plopped it down so hard that you could have heard the splash a football field away. Quickly he raced it back across the surface and flipped it quietly back in the same spot near the piling. This time it barely splashed when it hit the water so softly. Why the contrasts in the casts?

"I made that first noisy cast just to wake the bass up. Sometimes in the hot weather they are mighty sluggish, lazy. I figure if I make a big noise with the spinner hitting the water, it will get their attention. They will come around to take a look and I'll have the quiet spinner drop right in their faces," Hank grinned, but only half jesting.

Unbelievably, on that practice day the quiet spinner moved only a yard away from the piling before a loud explosion buried it in the waves. Hank popped the rod tip up and came in with a 4 1/2-pounder that he indeed had awakened.

JIM BITTER USES JERK-BAIT PATTERN THEN TURNS TO FLIPPIN' FOR LUNKERS

Jim Bitter, of Fruit-land Park, Florida, is a professional basser and guide who went after big money three successive years in the B.A.S.S. MegaBucks tournaments at Leesburg, Florida, 1987, '88 and '89. He finished 11th the first two years but in MegaBucks IV he carried home the top bag of money with a first place payoff of $108,000.

A member of the Yamaha Pro Angler team, Bitter fought six days of weather extremes, first with fair skies and sun-burning temperatures that turned to high winds and icy fishing lines the last two days of the competition. Bitter faced the adversary and overtook a number of other professionals who were ahead of him until the last weigh-in. Here is what Bitter says about catching bass his way:

"I fished a jerk bait pattern, tossing a floating bait near cover and then jerking it down under the water. Bass would charge the jerk bait. But when I went after larger fish, I shifted to flipping. Bigger bass are in the heavier cover."

TIRCUIT DEPENDS ON PLASTIC WORM

Claudette Tircuit, 13 times a qualifier for the Bass'N Gal Classic and a first place winner in 1979, declares that she uses all the bread and butter lures to compete in the cast-for-cash lady angler circuit. But in the end, the plastic worm is the winner.

This Denham Springs, Louisiana, angler has been fishing the professional circuit since 1976. In addition to winning the Classic in '79, she was second in 1980, and won the Ranger Powder Puff and the U.S. Bass 'N Gal Invitational in 1983. She is acknowledged a winner by her associates in BNG.

Here's what she says about the lures that catch winning bass:

I'll almost always start out with a spinner bait. I can cover a lot of water with the spinner and when I find fish, I can slow down and concentrate on fishing a worm. I use all the other lures and have even won tournaments with crankbaits. But when it comes right down to it, I depend upon the good old plastic worm to keep me in the money.

I find most of my fish in less than 15 feet of water around some kind of cover. Often the bass will not come out of the cover for some lures, but with a worm I can fish in the heaviest cover, getting inside the strike zone of the fish.

If the fish are in the grass, you can use a worm to get right down in the holes. In the timber, like stumps and fallen trees, you can work the worm right in among the roots. Worms are particularly effective in the colder weather.

No matter how much worm fishing you do, knowing how and when to set the hook is difficult. Most anglers hit them quickly, but there are times when you need to let them run a little.

Generally, anglers think they have to set the hook with all their might. I disagree. The trick of setting the hook is simple. First, get the slack line out. Then lower your rod tip. With a small loop in your line, come back with a short, quick pop. That gives you a good set. I don't miss many fish and I don't break off either.

You must be able to feel what's going on when you get a strike on a worm. When you set the hook, the last thing in the world that you need is a line with a lot of stretch. I think I feel everthing that is going on down there and I get good hook sets. Line is critical for me whether I am in a tournament or fishing for fun.

Spinner baits and the plastic worm are the bread and butter lures for me. They are what I depend upon to be a winner and the worm gets a little nod over the spinner. But I love to fish them both.

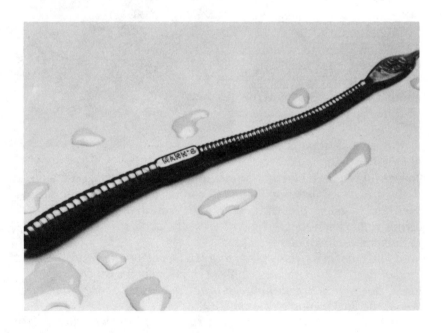

LINDA ENGLAND
JIG AND FROG ANGLER

With more than $180,000 in career winnings as a lady bass professional, Linda England, of Old Hickory, Tennessee, is among the elite fishing women in America. Six times since 1981 she has been a first place winner, four in Bass 'N Gal competition and two with Lady Bass.

In 1981, she won the Bass 'N Gal National Championship, the Bass 'N Gal Classic and was named Bass 'N Gal Angler of the Year. In 1987, she again won the Bass'N Gal Classic and the Lady Bass Arkansas Invitational. In 1988, she was named Lady Bass Angler of the Year. Her credentials are fantastic and when she tells you she likes to fish spinner baits, big crankbaits and jig and frog lures, you know she is versatile and can catch bass. She has a 12-pound, 4-ounce trophy to prove she can catch big bass.

Here's what this remarkable lady bass professional says about how she catches bass:

When I fished my first tournament in 1978, it was an ordeal. I fished it on a lark with no thought of being a professional. On the opening day, I was so nervous that I backlashed my reel on practically every cast. With 178 other women in the event, I quickly learned that I didn't know the tricks of the business. But I learned that day. The following day I moved from dead last to 51st place. I finished out of the money but with a respectable catch for a newcomer on the trail.

I enjoy fishing but I also like competition. There is a difference. Fishing for just fishing's sake is fun but fishing for money requires 100 percent intensity and effort. You have to hone your skills and fish with determination.

My favorite way of fishing is pitching a jig and frog. I look for heavy cover in one to five feet of water. I work the cover from 30 feet away and expect a strike any moment.

A lot of fish stay shallow all year. You never know what's going to happen when you drop that bait in heavy cover. To me, there is nothing more exciting than having a big ol' bass on the line in shallow water.

I fish these shallows with visible cover and in that type of water, you need a line with good abrasion resistance and one that will not do a lot of stretching. I like for my line to have sensitivity and when I'm pitching that jig and frog, I back off the drag a little. Good line helps me set the hook and if you are not careful, you'll straighten the hook or rip it from the mouth of the fish.

Pitting my skills and wit against the big largemouths is a major part of my life but I want to keep bassing in perspective. I have tasted some success but I remember that more often than not, bass make a fool of me.

BOBBY MURRAY
ACE OF PRO JIG FISHERMEN

Of all the astute jig fishermen on the professional circuits today and in the past, Bobby Murray, of Arkansas, a B.A.S.S.

Classic champion and great competitor before his retirement, was generally regarded as the greatest of the bass jig anglers. The jig was, and is today, his favorite lure and he knew how to handle it in all kinds of conditions.

Much of Murray's tournament success was attributed to his acumen with various jigs that he could use in heavy cover and in deep holes when the bass were hard to entice with the more popular crankbaits, topwaters, spoons and plastic worms.

Murray frequently spent about half his tournament time with a jig on a light Stren line, open-face reel and limber six-foot rod. He twitched the lure with the expertise of the knowledgeable professional he was and largemouths, smallmouths and spotted bass struck his jigs with consistency in dozens of tournaments from coast to coast.

He was frequently quoted as saying the "Jig Is Big" and indeed it was a big part of Bobby Murray's fishing career.

Murray borrowed money from his wife Mildred's piggy bank to enter his first bass tournament. Fortunately, he won and replaced the funds. He might not have won had he not twitched a black jig in the face of those Arkansas lunkers that gave him the weigh-in victory. He never forgot that memorable event that turned him to full-time pro bassing. And he didn't forsake the jig that helped him be a winner. It was always BIG in his tackle box

KATHY MAGERS—THREE LUNKERS
WINS TOURNAMENT

Kathy Magers is a Texas transplant to Arkansas and she was the winner of the 1989 Bagley's Silver Thread/ Bass 'N Gal Florida Invitational on the St. Johns River. After competing for ten years, it was her first professional circuit victory. It earned her a fully-rigged Ranger Boat along with other merchandise and cash totalling $40,000.

The remarkable thing about Kathy's victory over 158 other of the world's greatest women bassers, was how she did it with big fish. On her first competition day, she landed a 5.29 and a 5.09 lunker. On the final day, she put a 6.19 bass in the boat. The three big fish brought her the victory.

She caught each of the lunkers on a different lure. The first one hit a black/blue C&M Incredible Crawler and the second struck a No. 2 Mepps Bass Killer spinner. The third big bass was caught on a Bang-O-Lure.

"It was that third one that nailed down the victory for me," Kathy said. "I knew I had to do something different that last day and I tried the Bang-O-Lure. It worked.

"I was nervous that bluebird morning because I looked across Dunn's Creek and saw Chris Houston fishing. I had to change my tactics from the day before. I did with the Bang-O-Lure and caught the winning lunker," Kathy grinned.

JOHN TORIAN
CRANKBAITS NOT FOR DUMMIES

Dropping out of college at the age of 20 in 1968 to pursue the vagabond life of a professional bass fisherman set the wheels in motion that John Torian hoped would lead to a secure life as one of America's top bassers.

A Louisiana native, Torian moved back to the Toledo Bend Reservoir—the hottest bass lake in the country—and began guiding for a living. After guiding over 250 days a year for two years, Torian felt he had paid his dues. He was ready for the pro circuit. He was 22.

Today at 32, Torian is among the country's best pros. He has qualified for the B.A.S.S. Classic three times. He won a U.S. Bass event in 1986, the Louisiana World's Fair Tournament in 1984 and three Red Man tournaments.

A proponent of crankbaits for lunker bass, here is what John says about these minnow-like lures:

Crankbaits have been called "dummy baits" because of the ease with which these diving lures can be fished. Simply toss it out and turn the reel handle to bring it back and the built-in action will do the rest. Crankbait success is more than that. They are not for dummies.

Better bass anglers understand the lures. Fishing a crankbait takes some sophistication and refinement. My system for cranking will work for all skill levels on waters located all over the country.

I utilize three types of crankbaits and I understand what each will do. The lipless crankbaits, like the Cordell Spot and Bill Lewis' Rat-L-Trap, do not reach significant depths when cranked quickly, make a great deal of noise and that's why many pros use these lures as "draw baits." With these versatile lures, you can cover a lot of water quickly and you draw bass out of hiding when they attack the rattling noise. Depth can be controlled with the position of the rod tip.

I also like the shallow-running diving lures like Bill Norman's Little N that runs down to about five feet. This type crankbait will also cover a lot of water but can be fished as a finesse bait around targets, stumps, treetops and rocks.

The relatively new super-deep crankbaits have opened up a new area for bass anglers. This new breed of crankbaits reach depths of 10 feet or more. It makes it possible to fish situations that once were limited to plastic worms, jigs or jigged spoons.

I use the deep-diving lures primarily in open water situations, like an isolated underwater hump or island. Getting a lure to dive 15 feet among tree limbs and brush is impractical. I use other tools in those places.

I have an unorthodox technique that has paid big dividends. I bounce a lipped diving bait off the lake bottom, kicking up silt that resembles a disturbed crawfish. It triggers strikes.

I tell people to use a crankbait that runs a foot deeper than the bottom. That way you are sure of using a bait that will dig up the bottom without much effort.

GUY EAKER
KING OF SPINNER BAIT BASSERS

Recently I invented a new style spinner bait that I believe will eventually be quite successful and may replace some of the older models of this fine bass-catching artificial. My new spinner has a 180-degree bend in the blade that makes it noisy when retrieved. The field testing that I have done, along with my guides at Tsala Apopka, indicates this innovation in spinners will be a considerable improvement over the conventional lures.

Spinner baits have long been the favorite of some of the best professional bass anglers and tournaments have been won with this fluttering bait that sometimes brings bass a' runnin' when everything else is ignored.

One of the most successful spinner bait specialists on the tournament trails is Guy Eaker, of Cherryville, North Carolina. Eaker has been a consistent money winner and has made the B.A.S.S. Classic event several times, usually qualifying for that prestigious event by catching bass on some kind of spinner.

Eaker says that Roland Martin introduced him to spinner bait bassing almost a quarter of a century ago at Santee-Cooper in the South Carolina Low Country.

"My success with spinner baits came from my own experiences and study over the years, but Roland and some other fine pros taught me the difference in spinners. You have to learn the differences in the myriad types of baits on the market to really fish them successfully," Eaker says.

"There are hundreds of different kinds of spinners, many that are proven winners, but others just take up space in your tackle box. My experience has shown me that the small wire, Bagley Switch Blade, that I helped design, is the best of the spinners that I have tried. The Diamond Head spinner and the Blade Man with a yellow head and white skirt and a Burke tail is a bass catcher. But you must be experienced in how to handle this bait. Casting and retrieving even the best spinners only pays off when you have the expertise to fish it with some knowledge of its capabilities.

"I fish spinner baits both deep and shallow, contrary to some other professionals, and I fish them both rapidly and slowly. That is part of the secret. I keep the spinner always in sight when I am fishing over brush or tree tops, but when it pulls free of the cover, I slow down the retrieve and let the bait sink. I have caught so many good bass in shallow water where there was good cover that I know this technique is best for me," Guy reveals his methods.

"Usually I fish a double spinner, but when I am in heavy cover like hydrilla, milfoil, lily pads and pepper grass, I shift to a single blade.

"I think color makes a big difference. I believe that two colors of blades, gold and silver, will entice more bass strikes than the single color when the water is muddy.

"Casting accurately has much to do with success. I know that I am more successful when I use short, underhanded casts than I am on long heaves. I put the bait where the bass are better with that technique. You can also cast two or three times faster with that flipping system than you can with long casts. You can almost throw the spinner in a pork 'n' bean can under overhanging willows, in hat-size holes in the cow lilies and between trees and stumps where the cover is heavy with the underhanded flip," this 47-year-old veteran basser who fishes both for fun and cash says.

Eaker fishes the shorelines with spinners and he is sure that bass prefer the habitat along the banks to open water structure cover. He says when he does fish open water, there is some scattered grass around and that is the only time that he uses an overhead cast.

**Whisper Spinner
by Blue Fox**

When he fishes muddy or cider-colored water, he is inclined to get closer to the bank than when the water is clear. It makes sense that the bass see you too well when it is clear and you are in the shallows near the shoreline. In near the bank, he uses that under-hand flip cast that takes only seconds. In the murky water along these banks, he likes a yellow and white skirt on the spinner and then changes to a blue and white when it gets clearer. But he would rather fish his spinner baits in the murky water because he can get closer to where the bass are hanging out.

"I get 70 percent of my spinner bait strikes by feel and the other 30 percent by line sight. It seems that the real lunkers, the 9 and 10-pounders, I catch by line sight and the yearlings I catch by feel. The really big fish move the bait around without much of a tell-tale bump-bump. The yearlings hit hard and you feel it immediately.

"You do not have to set the hook when you are fishing a spinner. It's entirely different from fishing a worm. You have no slack line when spinner fishing.

"If I were not a shoreline fisherman, I suppose I would forget spinners. But I like to fish the banks and I have been doing it with confidence ever since Roland Martin gave me a spinner and a lesson. He made it himself 25 years ago. I fish spinners now the year around but I believe it is a better bait in the spring and fall," this personable professional with no reluctance to share his secrets, talks on.

He caught his largest bass on a spinner at Santee-Cooper. It weighed 10-pounds, 12-ounces. It was caught on a Diamond Head spinner with a yellow and white skirt nearly 15 years ago.

You wonder what Eaker would fish with if there were no spinner baits and he is quick to note that he fishes Tom Mann's Jelly Worms and many of Bagley's crankbaits.

When Eaker talks about color, he says, "Each color shows a different gray combination to a fish like it appears to a color-blind fisherman."

He differs with many other veterans when you discuss cloth-ing that should be worn when bass fishing. While some students of the sport consider a white shirt a no-no, Eaker consistently wears a white shirt. He says it blends in with the blue and white sky better than any other color.

"Spinner baits are better on overcast days than clear days because that's when the bass are more active. Sunny days put the bass in deeper water and tight on brush and stumps. I love to flip a spinner bait right beside a stump along a shoreline. I'll drop the spinner around it four or five times quickly. I don't just cast once to a stump and move on," he points out details of his system.

Like Doug Hannon, Eaker is a great believer in the solunar tables. Bass feed on those major and minor phases of the moon and when they are feeding, that means they will strike a spinner when it is properly presented. They make mistakes and that's why fishermen put them in the boat, this articulate professional believes.

This Tar Heel angler uses 20-pound test Stren line usually when he is casting spinners but occasionally changes to 14-pound test when the water is clear. He likes the Lew Childres & Sons Speed Reel and the Lew's G56X graphite 6-foot rod.

"I'm not the only pro who has won tournaments with spinner baits. In 1970, Jimmy Houston of Cookson, Oklahoma, won some big tournaments with spinners and Hank Parker, of Denver, North Carolina, was among the leading money winners in 1978 and '79 with his spinner baits. In 1977 I won a national tournament in Lake Seminole with spinners and was the point champion that year with more money on the cast-for-cash trail than anyone else. Spinner baits have certainly been good to me," Eaker remembers some of his successful experiences.

"Everyone can reminisce about some special occasion he recalls in the past. Fishermen are adept at telling of those exciting moments. I certainly remember my most unforgettable fishing adventure. It was in 1978 and I was fishing with a friend on the Santee-Cooper lakes. We were in Lake Moultrie, the lower lake, and both of us were flipping spinners in the 'stump field.' That day we landed more than 100 largemouth bass, the biggest a 10-pound, 8-ounce giant. We had five others over 8-pounds and one 9-pounder. Our ten fish limit at the end of the day weighed almost 100 pounds.

"But the memorable event of that day that I will never forget is the one that got away, a classic story. I hung this monster bass that both of us saw four times. I still believe the fish would have been larger than the 16-pound, 2-ounce South Carolina record. When I saw the fish the first time, I yelled that this was the biggest *bass I had ever seen. Four times I played that fish right to boatside, but the fifth time, she went down, wrapped around a stump and broke off. I was so upset that I had to sit down and try to calm myself for half an hour. It was such a shame that we could never get that big mama in the net," Eaker tells the story with understandable chagrin.*

A last bit of advice to spinner bait proponents is passed along. Eaker believes that spinners made with 28,000 and 30,000 wire are more productive than those made from larger, heavier material. A lot of big bass suck the whole spinner bait in with one strike. When you set the hook with the lighter wire, the bait slides down past the hook easily. Also, you do not need to fish a stringer hook on the small wire that is necessary on the heavy stuff.

The much-discussed "how-to" catch bass is a variable that stretches over wide expanses and from lake to lake, Eaker believes. What is a great bait and great technique for one angler isn't necessarily that for another, even in the same lake. There are no absolutes, no positive patterns that work for everyone. The individual must seek out and explore the "how-to" that works best for him and adapt to it.

While today Eaker is a great advocate of catch and release, he has a prized possession over his mantel that he had mounted before the era of turning bass loose became the vogue. It's a string of eight bass between the weights of 12-pounds, 2-ounces and 10-pounds, 12-ounces. All were caught in North and South Carolina except one that he landed in Florida in 1975. He caught that one in the Kissimmee River and it weighed 9-pounds, 14-ounces. "I had the big fish for that tournament and won the bass boat and trailer. My experience with spinner baits certainly put that big bass in the boat," Eaker recalls.

"I like to fish for the fellowship and just to get together with other fishing people to talk about bassing at different lakes and streams around the country. I like to learn the habits of other successful bass anglers and unlock their secrets and techniques for catching fish. Then I like to take my knowledge of bass fishing, humble that it may be, and share it with younger people so they, too, can enjoy bassing and perhaps win big tournaments in the future," Eaker shares a bit of his personal philosophy.

Spinner baits have been a big part of Guy Eaker's life. While it may not be the panacea for everyone fishing for fun or cash, it has been the grits and gravy for this Carolinian and he is not reluctant to share his experience and expertise with others. Spinner baits are big with Eaker.

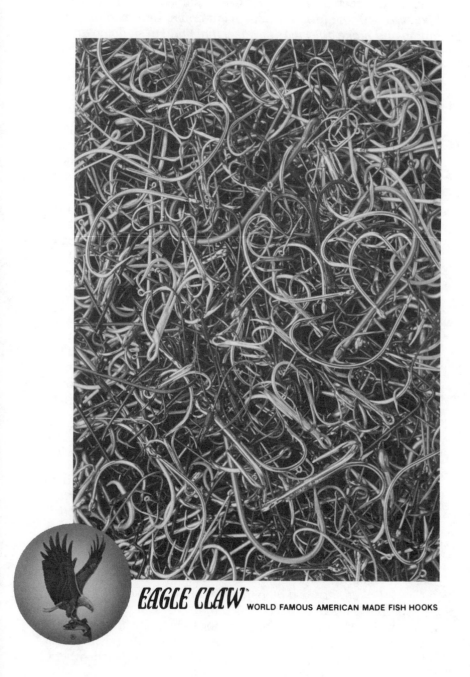

EAGLE CLAW™ WORLD FAMOUS AMERICAN MADE FISH HOOKS

DENNY BRAUER
LIKES JIGS AND FLIPPING

Denny Brauer, Cramerton, Missouri, 1987 Angler of the Year, is sold on jigs and says flipping for bass wins tournaments. He ought to know. He has won seven major tournaments and qualified for the Bassmasters Classic five times and the U.S. Open year after year.

This veteran of the tournament trail shares his expertise on tackle and techniques that put lunkers in the boat:

When I hear a professional basser at a seminar, it sometimes makes me feel like a ventriloquist, but I do know that you can learn from listening. Professional bass fishermen do not know it all, but I can tell you how I catch nice bass on jigs. Then it's up to you to master your own technique and fish the jig or some other lure that you believe in and in which you have confidence. I have great confidence in flipping for bass and in the jig as a lure.

When you are flipping a jig, you are in close proximity to the bass. She isn't 100 feet away. Hooking a bass long distance gives her a lot better chance to come unbuttoned.

Sometimes I'll get ten strikes flipping a jig and catch all ten fish. You can do that when you have the right equipment and hang them at close range. You need a strong line and a long rod. I prefer a 7-1/2-foot flipping rod but a shorter person might do better with a 7-footer.

Many fishermen want a stiff flipping stick, but I prefer one that will bend. When I'm using a stiff rod, I tend to set the hook too hard. I use too much force and the hook flies right out of the fish's mouth.

I do not use a special flipping reel. I use a regular casting reel like I would with any other lure in my tackle box. Flipping does not require special equipment. I remember fishing the mud flats of the Ohio River in Cincinnati. Bass were concentrated on these flats and they were striking a white jig. I could not get real close to them so I began casting the jig well past their holding pattern. I then made the jig ski by a submerged log. After four or five casts and by my walking that jig over the log, they got mad and began to strike. To get the jig in the right spot to pull it past them, I needed a versatile casting reel, not a flippin' reel, and it is such an experience that makes me stick with regular tackle.

I'm persnickity about my line. Weather weakens monofilament, particularly hot, direct sunlight and a backlash may damage the line. When I am fishing a tournament, I change my line every night. I always use a line that I can see. In clear or stained water, I use clear line because it is visible. I see far more strikes than I feel. When the jig is falling, I jerk it at three feet if the water is five feet. I may jerk 30 times when there is no fish after the jig, but I catch some bass without any tap-tap feel.

I normally use 25 or 30-pound test line and never anything lighter than 17-pound when flipping. In grass I may use a plastic worm but still with heavy line. It gets me just as many strikes as the lighter line.

While many veteran pros find flipping an exhaustive and nerve-wracking method of bassing, I think it is the easiest kind of fishing with artificial lures. I get lazy flipping, but to be successful you must stay alert. Keep the rod tip low near the water, skip the jig underhanded around cover and let it splash softly. A gentle splash is necessary in every kind of lure presentation. Or so I say.

I remember an experience I had fishing with an Oklahoma man in Toledo Bend. We found an underwater hump off a point. I had *been spinner bait fishing for three days and had weighed in only nine pounds of bass. Then I drew the Oklahoma fisherman for a partner. He hadn't done well either. I was flipping a small jig with a tiny spinner. He was using a big, heavy line and lure. He got a rise and came in with a 3-pound fish. I noticed he didn't set the hook. The next cast he caught another 3-pounder. Again he didn't set the hook. He just wasn't fishing right. I pulled in a little keeper and we moved to another hump. The water was deeper so I showed him how to rig a jig and frog. He had never used that arrangement before. He didn't know much about jig fishing. I told him how to let the bass run and then set the hook. He didn't pay much attention, but quickly came in with a 4-pounder. I hadn't gotten a bite and I was a little upset.*

We moved to a grass patch and I managed to catch a little fellow. My partner pulled another 3-pounder over the side. I flipped in a hole in the grass and lost five strikes in a row. That Oklahoma man made a high amateurish rainbow cast with the jig and frog and it plopped down hard and noisy in the hole. Bingo! In he comes with another big bass. He wasn't doing anything right. That was in the era when we had ten fish limits in tournaments. I turned around to look at him in the back of the boat and he was playing with his nine big bass in the livewell. I had three little keepers. So, you might do better to fish everything exactly opposite from the way Denny Brauer fishes. That guy from Oklahoma did nothing right and never set the hook, but he surely showed me up.

When I am pitching, I stay a little further from the boat and the fish. I keep everything low to the water and I am quiet, cast faster and keep my lure in the water. Fishing around docks, willows and overhead cover, I circle cast off the end of the rod and I get more distance. I try to get the jig in hard-to-reach places.

I like to use a big mouth hook when I'm in the shallows. I want it sharp and heavy and I'll hook most of the bass in the tough part of their mouths. In deep water, I want a lighter wire hook. Sometimes I may use a weed guard but I'll spread it out, maybe cut part of it off with my scissors, making it the same length as my hook. I may trim off some of the rubber too. I want to make it fall slowly by making it lighter and more buoyant. I may use a trailer hook in cold water with a 3/8-ounce jig. In 45 to 57 degree water, I catch more fish with this rigging.

I use no pork in warm water, only plastic. The hook tends to get set in the pork. Plastic doesn't foul the hook as often. I use a

Gator Tail-type worm when the water really warms up. A Snaketrix also works well in warm water.

Bob Garland's Gitzit is a big, ugly lure but bass go after it in deep and shallow water. Flipped in the right places, it's a winner. I fish it with a weedless trailer in some cover.

When stream fishing, the crawdad with a weed guard is productive. And as I move West, I fish smaller jigs. Bass are frequently smaller and I use a lighter line and midget jigs. On Truman Lake, I like live rubber jigs with a rattler and I believe the rattle helps. When I am using a pork frog, I put the fatty side down because the natural forage fish that the bass eat are always whiter on the bottom. A rattling jig does well on Truman around trees where the bass spawn. Spawning fish are spooky, but if you pitch over branches and shake the rattler as it descends, bass can't stand it. It may take two or three minutes but then you feel the line get heavy. Reel down! Set the Hook! Big fish with heavy line can be caught with rattlers in that heavy cover.

In summer when bass suspend around tree tops, the Spin-Jig is a good lure. Let it flutter down at the edge of the trees where you need to pitch it accurately. A combination of rubber skirt and gold spinner draws strikes from big fish. Color is some concern. I like black and other dark colors. Chartreuse is sometimes effective in murky water. There are lakes in the North where brown is a good color. I use white only when I know the bass are feeding on shad.

I sometimes make a weed guard out of a soft rubber band. I also may toothpick my sinker to keep it from sliding down but it weakens the line and it may make you lose the feel of the jig.

Flipping is the high percentage way to catch bass the year 'round in deep and shallow, clear and dingy water and in all kinds of cover.

The Spin-Jig, made in Missouri, allowed to helicopter down in the cover is a good bait. A twin-tail jig pays off for me too.

Wacky-looking baits often are surprisingly effective. I have taken a plain plastic worm and hooked it through the mid-section so it floated down in a "U" shape and bass wouldn't let it alone. Obviously, it looked real on the fall.

You can learn about catching bass even when you are not catching them. I have seen a fish hit a buzzbait and run off 20 feet when I pushed the release button by accident. I still caught the fish and it kind of proves you don't have to jerk the fish's head off the instant you get the strike. Often there is plenty of time and even if I miss the connection, it teaches me something about how big bass hit.

214

JOE THOMAS
FISHING RIVER-LAKES,
MUDDY WATER AND BLUEBIRD DAYS

Hailing from Cincinnati, Ohio, professional bassers like Joe Thomas must learn about fishing rivers with impoundments that are the only waters available in some areas of his home state. Coming up through the ranks of B.A.S.S. Federation competi-

tion, first winning the Ohio Federation Tournament in 1980, this 27-year-old pro is aware that thousands of bass anglers live along major rivers that have been dammed to create reservoirs. Fishing those river-lakes differs from much of the other waters where anglers stalk big bass.

This Bassmasters Classic qualifier at an early age, calls the Ohio River his local waters as it flows through his hometown. These river-lakes have unique personalities and Joe shares some of his expertise for fishing those waters:

With river-lakes, you have three basic options. Each option has its own season:

Option one: Fishing the upper end of a reservoir where the influence of manmade current is the greatest, you pattern the bass on points and bars affected by the flow. My tools here are crankbaits and Carolina-rigged worms. There is no consistency here because if the management stops pulling water, the action stops.

Option two: Fishing the backed up tributaries is productive in the spring when the fish are spawning in shallow water. I fish large areas of shallow water with a 1/4-ounce or 3/8-ounce white spinner with a No. 5 Colorado blade. I found that flipping in heavy cover in the shallows with a jig and pork frog on 25-pound test line is best for me.

Option three: Summer means that big bass will concentrate on main lake structure in the lower one-third of the reservoir. I focus my attention on patches of aquatic vegetation using a topwater plug early and late in the day and I'll also use a 5-inch worm with a 1/8-ounce weight and 10-pound test line in the middle of the day.

Vegetation is the savior of bass fishing in most river-lake systems. If you didn't have current in the upper portion of the lakes, they would be almost worthless. Creeks are good only during a short few weeks in the spring. The aquatic growth saves the fishery the rest of the year. It shelters the baitfish and the fry and aids the food chain. Guntersville and Chickamauga are examples of river-lakes that are great for bass because of the vegetation.

I fish a lot of muddy water in the river-lakes complexes. The most difficult time to fish muddy water is when it is cold. The metabolism of the fish has been slowed down and the fish's ability to sense objects with its lateral lines is reduced plus its vision is limited. Bass have trouble catching enough food to survive.

My best success in this circumstance is to use a lure that displaces a lot of water, yet moves slowly. The jig 'n pig and a 3/4 -ounce spinner bait with huge Colorado blades are good lures. I usually go with the pig 'n jig. I try a lightweight 1/4 to 3/8-ounce living rubber jig and a minimum of a No. 1 pork frog. This bigger frog displaces a lot of water as it falls, plus it sinks slowly because of the light jig. Black is the best color in muddy water. It provides the largest silhouette. Browns and greens are the poorest colors to use.

When the muddy water starts to warm up, a huge slow-rolled spinner bait is a good choice. The gold No. 6, 7 or 8 Colorado blade with a white and chartreuse skirt is best and I never fish it deeper than five feet.

After the muddy water gets really warm, it can be the best bassing condition of all. The bass' sight is not any better and your lure is camouflaged in the dingy water. The warm water stimulates the bass to feed and she becomes more aggressive. Her lateral line passes along a bundle of information.

Under these conditions I go to lighter spinner baits, 1/4, 3/8 or 1/2-ounce. I use the No. 4 or 5 Colorado blade and I slow roll it on the bottom in shallow water. Chartreuse and white skirts make an excellent imitator of a shad. In water two feet deep or less, I switch to Willow-leaf spinners and look for logs. Bass like to take up positions against the warm log, plus it offers good structure and a good ambush point.

A pulsating spinner is ideal in the warm, muddy water. I seldom use a worm in these circumstances, but I will tie on a Ditto Gatortail occasionally. It has a wide sweeping action. This movement and the worm's larger size displace a lot of water. I fish the darker colors, black grapes and black. I do not like the thin diameter worms or worms that do not have a wave or curl in the tail.

My other advice to bass fishermen has to do with bluebird days. That's when the sky is clear, there is no wind and the surface of the lake is a mirror. The best technique then is to go to topwaters and stay with them.

The slickness of the water combined with little or no wind allows a bass to see the lure much easier than when there is a chop or ripple. These slick, calm days with bright skies offer anglers a chance to catch fish on the surface all day long, especially in deep water.

A bass looking up from 20-30 feet below will often rise to the lure and she will feed on anything dead or alive that looks like a meal. A slow moving bait that closely resembles an injured bait fish will bring strikes. The Dalton Special may call bass from cover on bluebird days. It creates racket and churning of the water that bass can see from great distances.

A bluebird day on a clear lake is a highly productive time to catch lunker bass, at least it is for me.

RICH TAUBER—BASS IN CLEAR WATER AND ON TOP

At the age of 20, Rich Tauber, of Woodland Hills, California, was the Angler of the Year on the Western bass circuit and gained more national acclaim in 1982 when he won the U.S. Open and became the Western Bass champion. Since then, in 1986 and

1988, he qualified for the B.A.S.S. Classic.

Tauber has caught two bass that were an ounce short of 10-pounds and he is still searching for that magic weight, but he is generally considered a quality bass catcher on the pro circuits.

Catching lunkers in clear water with topwater lures is his specialty. Here's what he says about catching bass on top:

No other type of bass fishing is as universally revered as surface action where aggressive fish attack the human senses with a torpedo-like charge. Unlike sub-surface strikes, the topwater explosion of a charging bass startles the sight, sound and feel of the fisherman and leaves a lasting impression. It's a thrill you remember.

Like so many good experiences in life, surface plug fishing success is unpredictable. In the West, I like May through October for topwaters in clear reservoirs. Clear water and temperatures above 70 degrees are important ingredients in topwater casting. I concentrate on fishing submerged cover, vegetation, rocks and wood, in four to 12 feet of water. I also like cracks in the canyon walls and shady areas.

The perfect topwater lure in clear water is the Zara Spook. It is the best lure of all for catching quality bass. I work it fast, trying to imitate a feeding fish. It's an impulse or reaction-type bait and there is nothing better for catching bass in deep water or in heavy cover. Bass are particularly active from summer into fall in the West and there are days when you can catch fish on topwaters, like the Spook, all day long.

I use a six-foot, medium action graphite baitcasting rod and 14-pound test line for most of my Spook situations. I also add a split ring to the nose of the Spook to give it more action. I like to fish from my Skeeter boat.

Accuracy is critical in clear water fishing. I wear polarized glasses so I can look into the water and cast directly to the cover. If I see a dark spot in front of my boat, I don't have to know what it is. It's cover and I cast to it from as far away as I can. I presume that there may be bass hanging out around it.

One of the biggest mistakes an angler makes is when he finds cover, runs his boat right to it and looks down to see if there's a bass holding there. If you can see a bass, she sees you and the game is over.

JOHN DEAN GOES FOR TOPWATERS

John Dean Jr., has a fulltime guide service on Toledo Bend Reservoir in Zwolle, Louisiana, where his father and mother run a marina on the huge impoundment. This 39-year-old fisherman has an engineering degree from Kansas State University, but after working with an engineering company in Houston after graduation, he decided he wanted to go back to Toledo Bend to help his parents and start a guiding career.

That was in 1972 and Dean is vice president of the 12-man Toledo Bend Guide Service, Inc. He managed it successfully full time until 1980 when he entered his first tournament. He came in fourth and was immediately bitten by the cast-for-cash bug. While he still operates the guide service, he has fished B.A.S.S. trails and others frequently and in 1983 he made the Bassmasters Classic. That was his very first full year of fishing the circuit, a noteworthy accomplishment.

Dean's specialty is fishing vegetation and he has learned how

221

to relate time of the year, water temperature and other factors to fishing behind grass, in front of grass and how deep in the grass.

Here's his message to other bass anglers who want to put lunkers in the boat:

I use four tools like a golfer might select certain clubs for different situations. The most effective topwaters for me, and they catch the bigger fish, are the Rebel Pop-R, Heddon Zara Spook and the Devilhorse and Rogue by Smithwick.

No single topwater bait will handle all situations. You handicap yourself if you stick to a single lure. I make my choice of a topwater at a particular time by trying to match the plug's size to the available bait fish that season of the year. I like to make color selections based on that same observation.

When the bass are feeding on bream or large shad, I fish the Spook. If they are feeding on small shad and minnows, I use the Pop-R.

The Devilhorse is my prime spring-time choice for active fish that have finally shaken the winter doldrums. The Rogue, that has a small plastic lip, is also excellent in the spring because it dives and you can cover a wider range of depths than with a strict surface lure.

There are times when I am interested only in catching a large bass that I need to win a tournament. That's when I use the largest topwater and leave the Pop-R in the tackle box. I bring it out when I need a quick limit.

You can use a topwater anywhere—around logs, vegetation, stumps, pilings, docks and even bluff walls in 100 feet of water. Bass in the deep, clear lakes like those in northern Missouri and western lakes like Mead, will often suspend in as much as 100 feet of water. But they will come up to hit a Zara Spook, Pop-R and Devilhorse.

I don't think line size has much to do with the number of strikes you get with a surface plug. That's unlike my experience with other lures. The line floats on the surface and doesn't attract much attention. I use no line less than 15-pound test and in dense cover I will use 20-pound.

I replace the factory hooks on my over-the-counter lures. I like the wide-throat hook from VMC, Inc. It saves a lot of big bass for me.

GARY KLEIN IS ANOTHER FLIPPING SPECIALIST

Personable Gary Klein began his tournament fishing in California when he was only 15 and while he did reasonably well, he had to work in a bait and tackle shop to make the ends meet. But he was in love with professional bass fishing and in 1979 he made his big leap and began fishing the B.A.S.S. national tournament trail. Living the itinerant and costly gypsy life, he soon faced financial disaster. He was down to his last $20. Miraculously, he won the B.A.S.S. Arizona Invitational at Lake Powell that week at the age of 21, the youngest tournament winner ever. He pocketed the first place money and was on the way to bass fishing prominence that has earned him more than $250,000 from the Bass Anglers Sportsman Society events. He has qualified for seven Classics and has fin-

ished in the money in 50 of 64 B.A.S.S. tourneys. He lost Angler of the Year honors to Roland Martin in 1979 by a mere 24 ounces.

He is a proponent of the flipping technique when going after big bass and here's what he says about successful fishing for the lunkers:

I believe that flipping produces bigger fish than any other method of angling. Usually the larger fish are not the most aggressive fish, and they always hold next to or in some type of heavy cover. Most anglers are not able to reach these big fish with conventional casts. Flipping lets an angler be precise with his lure presentation and put the bait right where the big bass are holding.

Flipping movements originate from the wrist and here's how I recommend you use the basic technique:

Hold the seven to eight foot rod and baitcasting reel in your right hand. Use a weedless bait like a pig & jig or a plastic worm. Use a 5/0 or 6/0 hook. Allow the bait to fall seven or eight feet from the tip of the rod. Take three or four feet of line in your left hand between your thumb and index finger and hold it away from the rod. Drop your rod tip without moving your arm or body that would cause the bait to move forward. Don't try to make flips of more than 18 to 22 feet. Feather the bait into the water gently. Hold just enough tension in the line to allow the bait to enter the water softly and quietly. When the bait touches the water, pull back on the line enough to prevent the lure from dropping. Do not set the hook until you feel the fish. The bass will generally hit the lure as it falls and on a slack line you don't want to set the hook too quickly.

I am also a proponent of finesse fishing. That is a method of fishing light lines and small lures. It's a great way to compete in crowded waters where there are a lot of fishermen at the same time.

A finesse bait fished slowly and subtly is often the answer to fishing in a crowd. It requires some skill with light line but I learned that fishing the deep reservoirs in the West where I grew up.

In this finesse fishing, I like the small Gitzit. This lure is effective because it is small, about the size of the average bait fish, one and a half inches long. It's great in clear water. The only disadvantage of the Gitzit is you have to fish it on light line; six-pound test is best. That may let some of the giants break off but a good bass fisherman often can land even big fish on that light line in open water.

While much of the Gitzit's success in the South has come in shallow water, I have learned to fish it around deep structures vertically. That's the very best way to fish this small lure. The key to its attractiveness to a big bass is the spiral fall that produces small air bubbles that turn lunkers on.

The most effective way to catch bass on a Gitzit is on its initial drop. In shallow waters it doesn't usually fall more than three feet before a fish hits it. But I do catch some nice bass on the Gitzit. It takes patience to let that little bait fall 30 to 40 feet, but once I get it down, I drag it or let it drift with the boat and that catches bass for me.

CHARLIE CAMPBELL—EXPERT WITH ZARA SPOOK

Charlie Campbell was a part-time professional basser and full-time associate of Bass Pro Shops in Missouri until he went all pro in 1986. Long accepted as among the very best topwater bassers in the country, Charlie once could almost make a Zara

Spook talk. He most certainly made it walk and that's how he landed many of his trophy-size bass over the years.

He now has his own company that makes a stick bait that he walks around surface cover.

The Heddon Zara Spook is a big bait and Charlie cast this lure around overhanging bushes, and with a novel technique of tipping the rod tip astutely, he made the topwater come from the shoreline, cross in front of the bush and then back to the shoreline again, covering three of the four sides. It is a way of bringing big bass out of the cover with a single cast that would otherwise require three and possibly would spook the lunker under the bush.

It's called "walking the bait" and other pros have perfected the technique but Campbell was one of the original walkers of topwater lures, especially the Zara Spook that was his specialty. Few fishermen anywhere have greater control of a topwater than this veteran midwesterner.

Here's what Campbell has to say about his expertise with topwaters:

I don't have any secrets. It's so simple I don't see why everyone can't catch big fish on these lures just about anytime they want. At 57, this old pro continues to catch fish on topwaters better than almost anyone else in the country.

Most any lake that has a water temperature above 60 degrees has bass that can be caught on topwater lures. I fish back in the coves and cover early in the season. Those big old bass will teach you the rest that you need to know. There's nothing more exciting in fishing than seeing a big old trophy bass blow up on a lure. When fish hit the surface, you can count on a jump or two. The fish will jump and fight. Nine times out of ten you'll be fishing cover. Your casting must be accurate and it puts a lot of demand on your line. Use good line. I use Prime Plus. It takes a lot of punishment, has excellent sensitivity and nothing I've seen casts any better.

I prefer a cigar-shaped lure. I put most action in it myself. By jerking the lure with my wrist rather than my arm, the topwater makes a lot of commotion without moving very far.

The only hard thing to get into people's heads about fishing topwater baits is that you don't set the hook until you actually feel the fish on the line. When they get that big strike, they seem to lose control.

226

GEORGE COCHRAN LIKES WORMS AND SPINNERS

My associate in writing this book was the press observer with George Cochran on the second tournament day of the 1987 Bassmasters Classic. George caught his seven fish limit that day and it was obvious this veteran professional knew how to handle a plastic worm in aquatic growth. That's how he won the Classic. He fished it almost exclusively.

A native of Little Rock, Arkansas, this 30-year-old pro is a quiet winner who has qualified for the Classic six times.

Here's what he says about catching big bass:

I look for the ends of the lakes and wherever the heaviest cover can be found. Around heavy cover, there is usually dingy water and fish will feed in those areas. I use a 5-1/2 foot medium-action rod and cast a spinner bait or worm as close to the cover as I can. Ninety percent of the time a bass will hit the lure in the first two feet of the retrieve from where the bait landed if she is going to hit at all.

I prefer a 1/4-ounce spinner bait with a No. 4 willow leaf blade. When worm fishing, I rig it with a 1/4-ounce slip sinker and tie the worm on Texas-style for weedless water. Cover determines what line test I use. I try as light a line as I can, but structure dictates how heavy a line I'll need. In heavy cover, I do not use less than 14-pound Stren. Sometimes I may go up to 25-pound and I use Prime Plus line part of the time. In dingy water, I use clear blue and fluorescent.

During a full day of bassing, I will cast more than 1,500 times. That's why I have shifted to left-handed baitcasting tackle. By casting with my right hand and reeling with my left I have reduced the wasted motion and energy.

My shallow water technique won the 1986 Match Fishing Championship and I finished in the top 20 of all contestants in every Bassmasters Classic I have fished. I know the technique pays off.

The spinner bait and worm have given me confidence on the bass tournament trail. Confidence in your ability to select the right location, equipment and technique means the difference between filling the livewell and going home empty handed.

Lady Gets A Lunker

REST OF THE PACK. . .

WHAT OTHER EXPERTS SAY ABOUT LURES FOR LUNKERS

Other anglers with reputations for catching big bass with artificial lures are scattered all over the country and they have specific ideas about what works best in their communities. Here is what a few of them say:

Stan Fagerstom, Silver Lake, Washington, a fisherman who has caught six bass weighing between eight and nine pounds in the last ten years in that Far West corner of the country where most people would doubt that such lunkers even existed, says:

Big bass hang around in deep water near cover and sometimes they can be caught by fishing deep and slow. Bomber's Water Dog is a good lure in the Northwest territory for trophy bass. Sometimes I remove the spinner and put on a standard white pork rind. It makes it hard to cast and it hangs up around brush. I cast just beyond cover and stop. I let it rise and then jerk it, letting it fall back again. Big spinner baits will catch lunkers in my home lakes too.

Steve Daniel, professional guide at Okeechobee, Florida, with Roland Martin's Marina, and a young man who qualified for the B.A.S.S. Classic in Richmond, Virginia in 1988, says:

If the water has color and is not clear, I like big spinner baits and big jigs retrieved slowly. If the water is clear, I prefer the topwaters like the Devil's Horse. I like to trick bass with artificials and I have caught three over 10-pounds with lures at Okeechobee.

Stanley Mitchell, a young Georgia professional angler who won the B.A.S.S. Classic the first time he qualified, has caught his share of lunkers in the same area that George Perry landed the world record bass. He has three 10-pounders on artificial lures, one a 10-pound, 8-ounce bass. He says:

When I go after trophy size fish, I want the biggest bait I can find. I like big crankbaits, spinners or worms that are six to seven inches long. I like to cast a jig 'n worm or a big buzzbait in the cover. I like to go after the lunkers in the Ocmulgee River. Farm ponds in my Georgia neighborhood have a lot of big bass too.

Guido Hibdon, a Missourian who won the 1988 B.A.S.S. Classic and a guide on Table Rock and Lake of the Ozarks, has landed two trophy bass over 11-pounds and three others over 10-pounds. His choice lures for lunkers are:

I catch most of my big fish with a G-2 lure made by Lucky Strike. It looks somewhat like a Gitzit. The Gitzit is good too.

Lonnie Stanley, Texas professional and the maker of Stanley Jigs, used by bass fishermen everywhere, likes his big jigs for big bass and he has put many trophy size in the boat himself. He says:

Big fish are lazy and they are slow movers. I want a big rubber jig that will imitate a salamander. I use the regular rubber jig in winter but change to the metal flake jig in summer. Using that lure, one August I caught ten fish that weighed 38 pounds. It was obviously a good lure and I had a good day. The Uncle Josh 100 or Jumbo Frog is a good lunker lure. I also like the plastic crawler in summer with no pork rind and a 5/16 or 7/16-ounce weight.

Paul Elias, Laurel, Mississippi, is among the most successful professionals. He has a 12 1/2-pound trophy to his credit that he caught on a Mann's blue worm. He has this advice for trophy fishermen:

Fish thick vegetation and channel dropoffs if there is no vegetation. Do your homework on the lake and learn where the biggest fish hang out. Then work a jig 'n pig slowly on the drops or in the cover. Flipping in the cover is a good method for catching these lunkers.

Ken Cook, a Meers, Oklahoma professional with plenty of credentials on the cast-for-cash circuits, relates his advice on catching big bass to the seasons:

In the pre-spawn period, he would look for them in the shallows where they go after moving out of the deeper water earlier in search of food. At that time, he likes a big bait, like the jig 'n frog pitched near the cover. I might prefer to flip with a 25-pound test line in clear water. I also like a big spinner, an ideal spring lure.

In summer, I fish where there is overhead cover, wood or grass and I fish both shallow and deep water, usually flipping a worm.

In the fall, I look for bait fish in water below 70 degrees and I fish up creeks and rivers. The spinner is my No. 1 fall lunker catcher.

Then, in the winter, I find vertical structure. The fish are not aggressive and I shift to a jig that I hope the bass will mistake for a crawfish. A crawfish replica is also a good winter lunker lure.

Hoot Gibson, another B.A.S.S. Classic fisherman from Mississippi, with some lunker catches, says:

I would fish a big topwater lure for a big fish, probably a buzzbait and I would be fishing the spring of the year. I like the triple-wing buzzbait. I also like to float a weightless worm down through the cover. Bagley's Bang-O-Lure is a good big bass catcher too.

Steve Lloyd is a veteran guide with Roland Martin's Marina, in Clewiston, Florida. He also fishes several of the professional circuits. Here's what he says about the best lures for catching bass, large or small:

I believe the best of all artificial lures for bass is the plastic worm and in the tournaments, about 90 percent of the bass that are weighed in are caught on plastic worms.

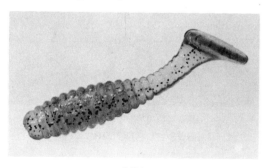

Basser Drags in Another Trophy Bass

HOMEMADE LURES CATCH LUNKER BASS TOO

Max Clarke is a Cross Creek, Florida, bass angler who makes his own lures in a tiny workshop in his backyard. His first customized lure was a replica of the Devilhorse, but a bit shorter, and he caught hundreds of bass in Lochloosa and Orange lakes with his wooden copy.

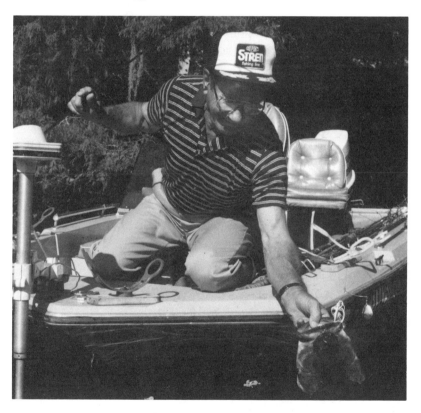

Later he began making a torpedo-shaped short plug that looks like some of the manufactured chuggers. Fished on top and twitched so that it dives and is noisy, it catches fish today when many other artificial baits are ignored.

It doesn't just work in the Florida waters. In '88 he went to Alabama and fished with Dr. Henry Gwaltney and quickly convinced his host that his homemade lure was great. He landed a 9-pounder. Many smaller bass took the chugger too, while he was there.

Later he was invited to Minnesota and despite the cold weather and unusual bassing circumstances for him, Clarke put dozens of nice bass in the boat from a half dozen Minnesota lakes and ponds.

He continues to catch lunkers and yearlings with his backyard torpedo bait virtually the year around in Central Florida.

Ed Lindsey, a veteran bass angler and guide at the huge Santee-Cooper impoundment in the South Carolina Low Country, has retired a homemade lure after catching an even 500 largemouths on the same bait.

"I leave that lure in the tackle box now because it has done its work for me over two decades when I pulled in 500 bass on that same lure that was made for me by a fisherman in Charleston, South Carolina. The inventor designed it somewhat after a Dalton Special but he called it a 'Dolly Jumper' and that's what I call it.

"I caught a lot of big fish on the lure up to 12-pounds and I once lost one that I had in the boat, but it flounced over the side and got away that I am sure was in the 15 to 17-pound range. The Dolly Jumper was a great lure for me.

"Seven times I hung this bait on the bottom and I thought so much of it that I jumped in, dived down and retrieved it rather than lose it. That's one reason I do not fish it any more. I am afraid I

Dr. Henry Gwaltney
A 9-Pounder On A Homemade Lure

234

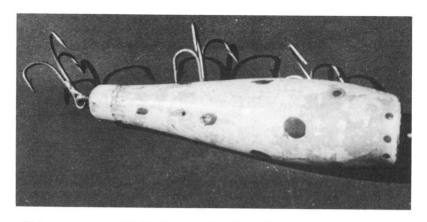

This homemade Dolly Jumper has been retired by Ed Lindsey, of Santee-Cooper after catching 500 largemouth bass.

might lose it on the cover and it is too much of a hero for me to lose," Lindsey says with nostalgia.

Five hundred bass on the same lure! That must be some kind of record, but unfortunately there are no statistics on those kinds of bassing results.

Max Clarke Reels In Another Cross Creek Giant

UNCLE JOSH PORK RIND LURES

These baits create an illusion that something alive is around and bass think it is good to eat. The forms closely resemble forage food and big bass chomp on them when flipped in their territory.

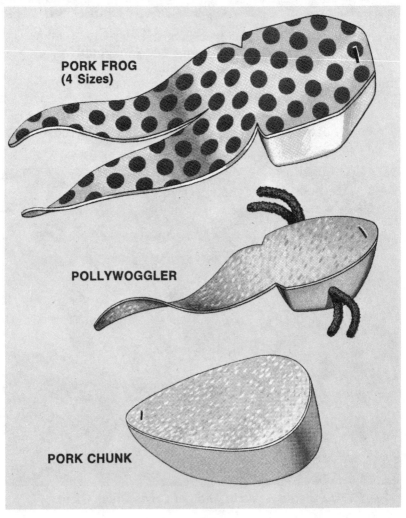

PORK FROG
(4 Sizes)

POLLYWOGGLER

PORK CHUNK

REBEL HAS WIDE VARIETY OF BIG BASS LURES

Deep Sinking Crawfish: It has a weighted paddle for countdown type fishing. The deep sinking crawfish bumps and digs the bottom at eight feet on the retrieve. The unique action proves irresistible to the lunkers.

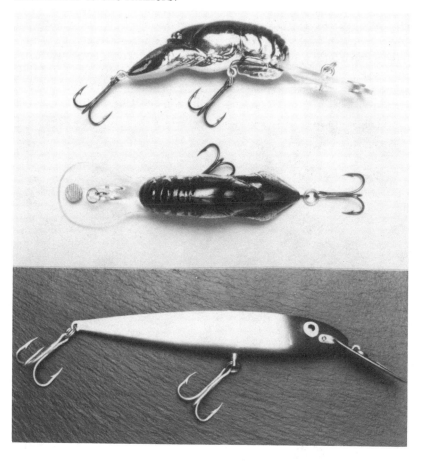

Jawbreaker: Molded of a new, space age material, the Jawbreaker features a continuous wire form, and a deep diving metal bill. The barrel swivel on the first hook allows a pivoting action for sure hook of the largest fish. This seven inch beauty is perfect for trolling or casting.

RAPALA'S NEW BASS CATCHER

Culminated after three years of research, the sinking Rattl'n Rap features the addition of low frequency sound to a balanced swimming lure that makes a difference causing gamefish to strike.

This, the 'newest addition to the Rapala line, has seen countless hours of testing and redesigning until it met the exacting requirements of that famous Rapala swimming action. The added attraction of sound (custom-balanced) creates a most effective rattle—alerting and arousing the attack instinct of big bass. Top quality, gleaming metallic finishes in six fish-catching colors reflect the real quality of this lure. Its custom-designed bill allows slow or fast retrieve without skipping or broaching. Two large razor-sharp treble hooks assure a good hook-up.

BOMBER CATCHES LUNKERS

The Bomber is a deep-diving, fast wiggling lure used with equal success by both novice and expert. Even though all but the 100 series are floating lures, Bombers will run deeper than most sinking baits. The broad bill serves two purposes: it drives the Bomber deep and it acts as a guard to prevent excessive hang-ups on brush. This feature allows you to fish at great depths with a minimum of lost lures—and it also makes the Bomber ideal for trolling. The Bomber is also an excellent casting or spinning bait. The pulling link on all series is adjustable to make the Bomber run true. It's a great big bass lure.

BOMBER'S LONG "A" (MINNOW)

Bombers' Long "A" (Minnow Type) Lure is designed for shallow water or deep water fishing. It has the buoyancy of Balsa wood and has a molded-in lip for strength and true performance. The Long "A" has a built-in tight wiggle with a roll to give it a truer swimming action. This lure is destined to revolutionize "Minnow Type" lure fishing, just as the Model "A" has set new standards in "Crank Bait" fishing. The Bomber is a big bass catcher.

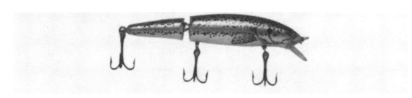

239

STORM'S WART LURES

In response to the continuing surge of interest and enthusiasm for STORM'S "Wiggle Wart" series of crankbaits, STORM add the **"Short Wart"** to fulfill the fisherman's need for a lure that's loaded with the famous "Wiggle Wart" action while operating at a shallower running depth.

This wiggler's movement is achieved by the combination of the **"Short Wart's"** own special stubby, squared-off diving lip with the classic "Wiggle Wart" body design. It produces some of its best results when worked along shorelines, under fish-havens such as lily pads, and above natural or man-made structure. Its shallower action will allow for low-water river fishing for big bass.

The **"Short Wart"** possesses great versatility with its floater/diver body style. As a casting bait, it will reach depths of approximately 2-4 feet on a retrieve, making it a high-yielding surface lure for schooling fish or for predators searching in the shallows at dinner time. If trolling is the preferred method of fishing, the **"Short Wart"** is stable enough to be trouble-free when flat-lining and can easily be utilized with downriggers to cover vast stretches of water at exact depths. Since it does not dive extremely deep, a downrigger can be positioned at the desired depth and the **"Short Wart"** will dive only slightly lower than the downrigger ball. No guesswork is involved with the **"Short Wart"**—it will be just where you want it to be.

" SHORT WART "

HAWG BOSS SUPER TOAD

The Hawg Boss Super Toad, a deep diving crankbait manufactured by Yakima Bait Co., is available in six new colors. The

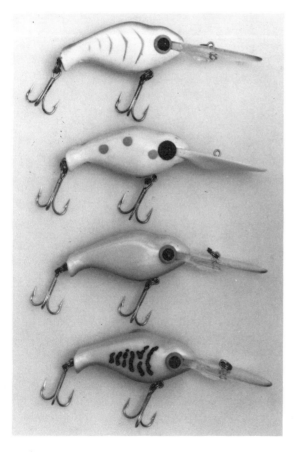

new colors are: clown, bone crawdad, rainbow, bone/ orange belly, chartreuse/lime green herringbone and chartreuse/flame red herringbone, and field testers are lauding their big bass success.

The new colors were added to the line after being successfully field tested on salmon, steelhead and bass in different parts of the country.

With the addition of the six new colors, the Super Toad is now available in 44 different fish catching colors.

All 44 colors are also available in the Hawg Boss Super Toad II, a smaller-billed version of the Super Toad that dives quicker to medium depths.

MISTER TWISTER'S SPINNER BAITS

In addition to the famous Thunderworm, Skinny Dipper and Trico worms made by Mister Twister, that prominent bass professionals like Tommy Martin swear by, this lure maker is now turning out a wide variety of buzz and spinner baits that have fast become popular. Techniques vary with spinner anglers, but these lunker catchers are effctive from the surface to hugging the bottom. They are effective in clear as well as turbid water and their vibrations pique the interest of marauding bass.

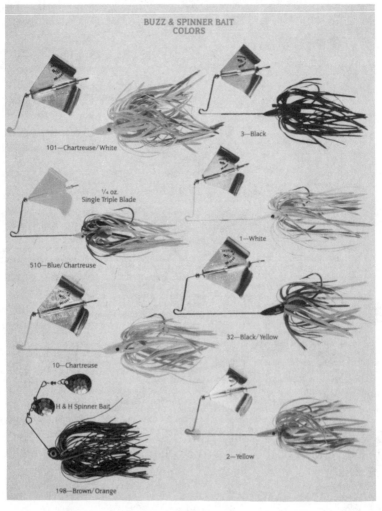

BUZZ & SPINNER BAIT COLORS

101—Chartreuse/White

3—Black

1/4 oz. Single Triple Blade

510—Blue/Chartreuse

1—White

10—Chartreuse

32—Black/Yellow

H & H Spinner Bait

2—Yellow

198—Brown/Orange

CLUNN'S SHAD BY POE IS A FAVORITE

Rick Clunn introduced his secret lure, RC 3 in 1988 and the cedar wood crankbait has taken many fishermen by storm. Manufactured by Poe, this imitation of a shad in many colors has claimed testimonials for the quality fish it catches. The LRC 3 is hand-crafted from California cedar wood, has natural buoyancy great body vibrations, castability, strength and durability. Many avid anglers believe it is unmatched among crankbaits marketed today.

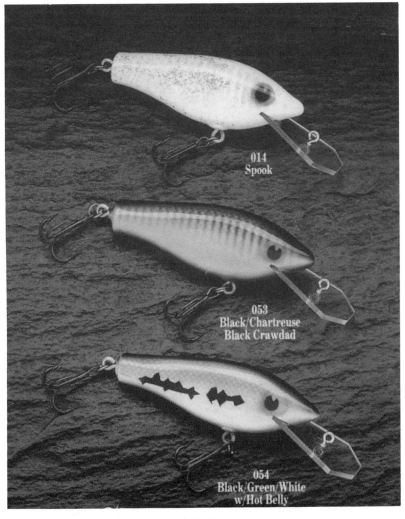

014
Spook

053
Black/Chartreuse
Black Crawdad

054
Black/Green/White
w/Hot Belly

BAGLEY'S OUT-O-SITE BASS LURES

Bagley's famed Bang-O-Lure has been many bass anglers' favorite for years and it still catches its share of quality fish. Now Bagley has the Chug-o-lure, Pop 'n B and Mighty Minnow series that are making big waves among fishermen when cast in calm waters. These bite-size lures are intimidating bass and prompting strikes at times when the fish wasn't really hungry.

SWIVEL-HIP
BANG-O-LURE

Diving Bang-o-lure

HEDDON LURES PROVEN OVER 30 YEARS

LUCKY 13

ZARA SPOOK

RIVER RUNT

MANN'S BAITS ARE LEGENDARY

From the soft plastic jelly worms made famous two decades ago to a wide assortment of crankbaits that make a tackle box selection complete, Mann's Bait Company today markets artificials for anglers with a myriad of preferences. From the bottom to the surface in all kinds of cover and many depths, Mann has a bass lure that satisfies everyone.

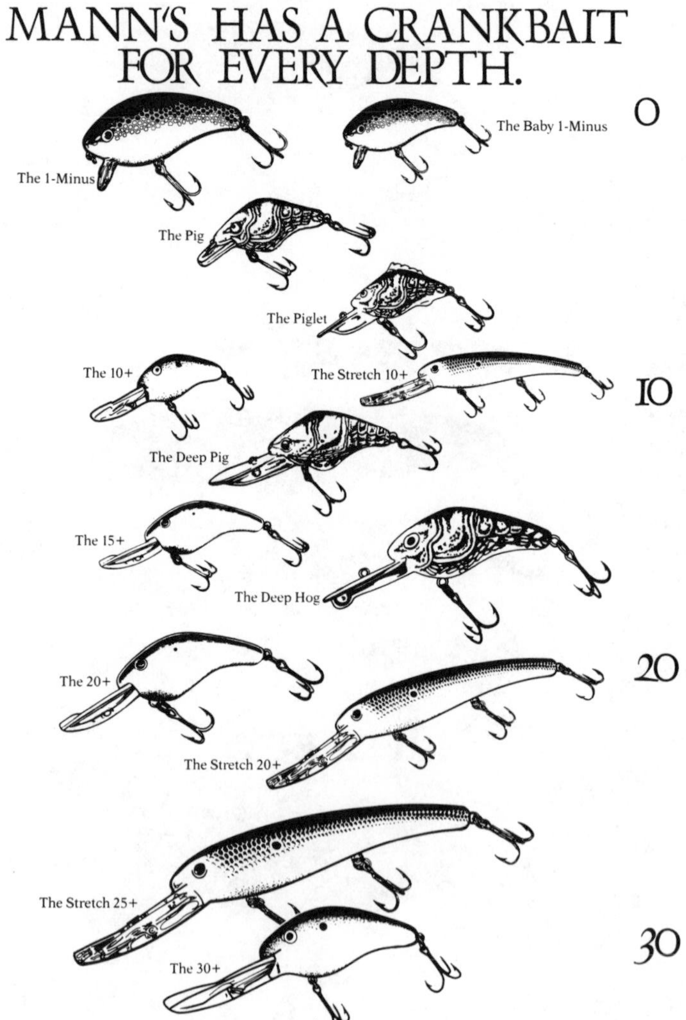

MANN'S HAS A CRANKBAIT FOR EVERY DEPTH.

The Baby 1-Minus

O

The 1-Minus

The Pig

The Piglet

The 10+

The Stretch 10+

IO

The Deep Pig

The 15+

The Deep Hog

The 20+

20

The Stretch 20+

The Stretch 25+

The 30+

30

STORM HAS BIG BASS VARIETY

An old company with young and creative ideas, Storm Manufacturing has introduced some new concepts in bass lures for lunkers. Storm has brought bass fishermen a successful series of original lures, all designed for specific purposes and constructed in detail to produce many hours of fine fishing for anglers.

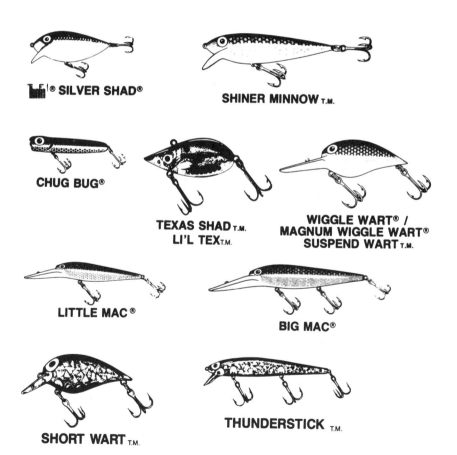

SILVER SHAD®

SHINER MINNOW T.M.

CHUG BUG®

TEXAS SHAD T.M.
LI'L TEX T.M.

**WIGGLE WART® /
MAGNUM WIGGLE WART®
SUSPEND WART** T.M.

LITTLE MAC®

BIG MAC®

SHORT WART T.M.

THUNDERSTICK T.M.

STRIKE KING

Big bass often fall to the wide variety of spinner baits made by Strike King Lure Company of Collierville, Tennessee. Strike King is the World's number one spinner bait manufacturer and is endorsed widely by the pros, including Bill Dance and Jimmy Houston.

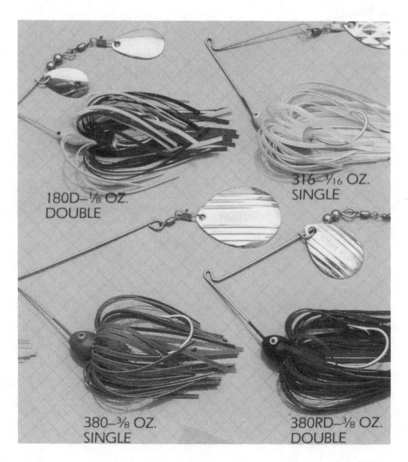

180D–⅛ OZ.
DOUBLE

316–³⁄₁₆ OZ.
SINGLE

380–⅜ OZ.
SINGLE

380RD–⅜ OZ.
DOUBLE

CABELA'S
WALKING JIG SYSTEM

The most popular sinker shape in the history of livebait fishing has been incorporated in a new Walking Jig System that covers the entire spectrum of walleye fishing. Doug Stange, Executive Editor of *In-Fisherman* magazine , calls the Walking Jig System, "An impressive new wrinkle in a rigging-and -jigging game that has meant billions of fish for millions of fishermen."

Cabela's Walking Jig System retains the shape and non-snag characteristics of the reliable walking sinker. As a result, the Walking Jig can be fished in places you wouldn't dare use a standard jig. This new jig can be fished using the traditional method of tipping it with livebait. This favorite jig and livebait combination results in a natural, low-key presentation.

But Cabela's has taken this new concept even further to entail a variety of bass fishing situations.

The Walking Jig System also includes accessory trailer hooks, spinner blades and soft-grub retainer pins, all of which attach to the Walking Jib via a built-in snap on each jig. So, when sluggish bass are hitting short, simply attach a trailing treble hook. When the fish display a preference for a livelier action, or in stained water, when fish need more vibration to zero-in on, simply attach a spinner blade or a soft, Cabela's Action-Tail Grub. In addition, the Walking Jig can be used as a good ol' walking sinker when double rigged with your favorite trailer.

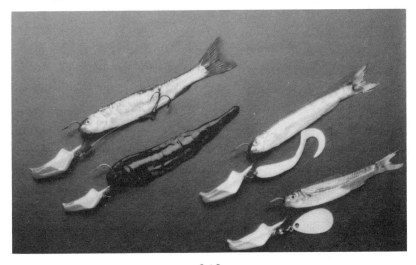

BASS PRO SHOPS
CAJUN RATTLER

The new Cajun Rattler from Bass Pro Shops is a unique aluminum blade with built-in rattle chamber that lets you throw this bait into cover you wouldn't go near with other favorite rattling crankbaits. No matter what speed you retrieve this bait, the chamber of the aluminum blade taps out a big bass calling rhythm. The double "R" bend of the stainless steel wire shaft and a simple rubber band make the Cajun Rattler virtually weed and snag proof. Just loop the rubber band around the inside curve of the wire, then stretch it back to slip behind the barb of the hook. The rubber band deflects brush and weeds, yet is easily knocked free of the barb by striking fish. Other features include a tough acrylic finished alloy head, with large viper eyes and scale pattern; sure holding trailer barb; Eagle Claw Lazer Sharp hook; living rubber skirt; and Sampo ball bearing swivel. Available in single-spin only, in 1/4, 3/8 and 1/2 ounce weights. It's a great new big bass catcher.

WEEDLESS *KLIPR* BY VORTEX

When you have to fish in, through, or around stumps, grass, weed pads, trees, slime, pilings or moss, you don't want to be spending time picking the weeds off your lure or the lure off the weeds. The **KLIPR** works well for big bass in cover that anglers might otherwise have to skip. The weedless model of the **KLIPR** has a patented innovative concept in hooks that allows bassers to fish instead of picking off weeds.

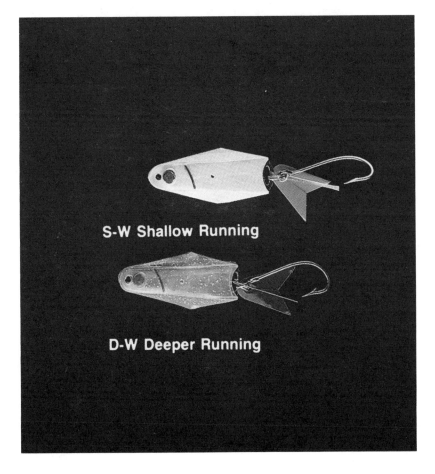

S-W Shallow Running

D-W Deeper Running

STANLEY JIGS

Stanley's Vibra-Shaft Spinner Bait has been a big bass catcher since 1985 when Tommy Martin finished second in the B.A.S.S. Classic using the innovative discovery.

26 professionals out of 40 contenders in that Classic used Stanley bass baits, including Rickky Clunn and Larry Nixon.

BILL NORMAN'S WEED WALKER

THE BIG BASS CAN'T HIDE ANY MORE!

On hot summer days when the really big bass hole up in cover, Norman's weed walker is a great lunker catcher.

ARBOGAST SPUTTERBUZZ®

The all-around bass lure for fishing all around the clock.

Fish it under the stars or under the sun. In open water or through the weeds. Retrieve it slowly across the surface or buzz it straight back—hard. Any time of day or night the Sputterbuzz gets their attention of big bass.

CREME'S GLO WORM
IT'S CATCHING

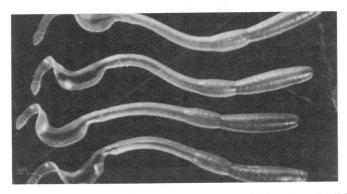

This big bass catcher is two worms in one—the outer shell both attracts and reflects light, giving the solid-color inner core a unique, fish-attracting glow.

Creme invented the first plastic worm in 1949 and it remains a great bass catcher today. It's the original. Glo colors are purple, green, blue and gold.

MANN'S LITTLE GEORGE IS
ALWAYS A BIG SUCCESS

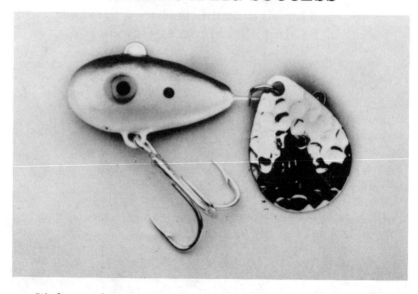

It's been a long time since Mann's Bait Company introduced the Little George back in 1959. But 30 years and many lures later, don't try to tell the nation's top fishermen that this lure is outdated. The little George is still going strong.

Just ask Randy Behringer, winner of the 1986 B.A.S.S. Georgia Invitational Tournament. "The Little George had a lot to do with my winning," said Behringer, whose winning catch was hooked with the Mann's lure.

Just ask Mike Johnson, whose Little George hooked a 10-pound, 3-ounce bass and won him the "biggest fish" prize in the same tournament.

When it was introduced 30 years ago, the Little George was revolutionary in design, with its lead body that allows for excellent castability. Its tear-drop shape and center line balance cause it to parachute downward in the water with the spinner tail whirling, creating a wiggle that fish cannot resist.

Mann's has added a new 1-ounce size to its line of 1/8-ounce, 1/4-ounce, 1/2-ounce and 3/4-ounce Georges. Also Mann's has added Gold Chrome to its variety of Little George colors, including Chartreuse, White/Pink Eye, Hammered Chrome and more.

The success of the Little George is no surprise to anyone. It's a classic lure that continues to bring in the big ones!

FRITTS LIKES POE'S CRANKBAITS

David Fritts, of Lexington, North Carolina, has earned the right to fish in four consecutive Red Man All-Americans, the only professional angler ever to do that, and he competed in the $100,000 event the fourth time in June of 1989.

Fritts made other history with the Red Man regional classic that he won the third time in four years in '88. He was third in '86 but won in '85, '87 and '88 for his record. Fritts has earned more money in regional classic competitioon than any other angler, more than $107,000.

How has this 4-wheel drive mechanic from the Tar Heel State made these marks? He says he is a crankbait enthusiast and his success is attributed to astute handling of Poe's cedar-bodied crankbaits that catch quality bass. It's hard to argue with success.

SMALL LURE—BIG BASS

It was May 3, 1969. I was fishing in the River Styx section of Orange Lake with a medical doctor from Indiana who was a friend of my son-in-law, Rowell Burleson. We were not getting any strikes with topwaters, worms or anything else in the shallow water around the grass beds.

"I'm about to give up," I complained. "I'll give this old Bayou Boogie a try and then quit."

You are not going to catch any bass on a little old lure like that," Rowell yelled from his boat nearby.

Ignoring his advice, I tied on that little inch and a half diving lure with a red face and gray back. I cast it a few yards with little confidence. Then it throbbed a bit and the line took off. A giant bass tore up the surface and I knew this was a memorable moment. I had a trophy on the line.

"I'll never get this fish in," I yelled. "It's too big for this little spinning tackle."

"Ah, you can do it!" my partner encouraged.

Five minutes later he put a net under the wallmount fish, lifted it aboard, and I sighed with pleasure. On the scales a few minutes later, the bass weighed an even 10-pounds. It's on my wall. It's the largest bass I have ever put in the boat with either live bait or artificials. And it was caught on a tiny plug that my cohorts joked about.

W.H.C.

HOOK DRAWINGS AND DESCRIPTIONS

All Styles Feature the Tru-Turn Cam- Action Offset

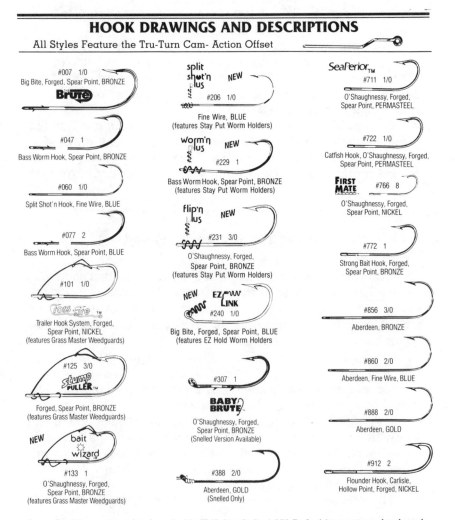

#007 1/0
Big Bite, Forged, Spear Point, BRONZE
BRUTE

#047 1
Bass Worm Hook, Spear Point, BRONZE

#060 1/0
Split Shot'n Hook, Fine Wire, BLUE

#077 2
Bass Worm Hook, Spear Point, BLUE

#101 1/0
Cross Fire ™
Trailer Hook System, Forged,
Spear Point, NICKEL
(features Grass Master Weedguards)

#125 3/0
Stump PULLER ™
Forged, Spear Point, BRONZE
(features Grass Master Weedguards)

NEW bait wizard
#133 1
O'Shaughnessy, Forged,
Spear Point, BRONZE
(features Grass Master Weedguards)

split shot'n plus NEW
#206 1/0
Fine Wire, BLUE
(features Stay Put Worm Holders)

worm'n plus NEW
#229 1
Bass Worm Hook, Spear Point, BRONZE
(features Stay Put Worm Holders)

Flip'n plus NEW
#231 3/0
O'Shaughnessy, Forged,
Spear Point, BRONZE
(features Stay Put Worm Holders)

NEW EZ LINK
#240 1/0
Big Bite, Forged, Spear Point, BLUE
(features EZ Hold Worm Holders

#307 1

BABY BRUTE
O'Shaughnessy, Forged,
Spear Point, BRONZE
(Snelled Version Available)

#388 2/0
Aberdeen, GOLD
(Snelled Only)

SeaPerior ™
#711 1/0
O'Shaughnessy, Forged,
Spear Point, PERMASTEEL

#722 1/0
Catfish Hook, O'Shaughnessy, Forged,
Spear Point, PERMASTEEL

FIRST MATE #766 8
O'Shaughnessy, Forged,
Spear Point, NICKEL

#772 1
Strong Bait Hook, Forged,
Spear Point, BRONZE

#856 3/0
Aberdeen, BRONZE

#860 2/0
Aberdeen, Fine Wire, BLUE

#888 2/0
Aberdeen, GOLD

#912 2
Flounder Hook, Carlisle,
Hollow Point, Forged, NICKEL

Perma Steel® is a registered trademark of the VMC, Inc., St. Paul, MN. Zip Lock® is a registered trademark of the Dow Chemical Co.; First Mate is a registered trademark of Precise, International, Suffern, NY.

**Culprit Worm Traps A 12 1/2-Pound Trophy
On Tsala Apopka Chain**

Little John Andrews and Mother Kathy Fish From The Pier

NO TIME FOR BASSING

Running a busy fish camp like Cypress Lodge, in Inverness, Florida, where as many as 1,000 anglers are guided to bass every year by her husband and his associates, and raising a four year old offspring who delights in fishing off the launching area piers where he must be watched carefully, keeps Kathy Andrews from doing much bassing. Even though her husband has been proclaimed the World Champion artificial bait largemouth catcher.

While he guides tourists from around the nation to sensational big bass catches, Kathy's bass fishing is temporarily curtailed. She doesn't have a 10-pounder on the wall and doesn't know just when she'll get around to trying for one again.

Her husband has personally landed and can verify 321 bass weighing over 10-pounds. All were caught on artificial baits and in public waters. He doesn't believe it is "challenging" to catch these monsters with any kind of live bait.

"I don't fish with Bud much now. I used to, but the Lodge and my son, John, take up most of my time. I have caught some five and six pound bass when I had time to fish but I have never yet landed a trophy over 10-pounds. I like to bass fish and maybe I'll get back to it sometime, but right now I'm too busy to fish," says the cordial, always smiling lady who came here from New Jersey with her husband back in 1975.

Helping to document the many catches of large bass on artificial lures, Kathy has seen most of Bud's big fish weighed in at Cypress Lodge. The actual weighing has been done by Bud's sponsor, John (Jake) Chastain, who declares that Andrews has actually caught more than 321 trophy size bass.

John, the energetic son of the Andrews, grabs his Zebco rod and reel and heads for the dock to fish at every opportunity. The cypress clad shoreline, ramp and docks along Lake Henderson is the tot's playground and Kathy gives him a free rein (most of the time) to pursue his outdoorsmanship. So far, his fishing doesn't amount to much, he seldom has a hook with a barb and his lures are not likely to entice a lunker. But he is starting early and with a mom and dad oriented to bass fishing and living on a Florida lake, young John appears to be a likely candidate to become a bass angling champion in the future.

259

Kathy and Bud are true conservationists. They mounted a dozen bass. Most lunkers, except those that were gut hooked, were released to fight again.

Only when the fish are hurt too badly to survive do the Andrews eat bass. They prefer to eat some of the several panfish species that are available and plentiful in the Tsala Apopka chain of 50 lakes. The entire chain covers more than 24,000 acres and includes some of Florida's most scenic waterways.

Bud's 321 fish came mostly from Central Florida, with 60 percent coming from the Tsala Apopka chain where Cypress Lodge is located. Six of the monsters came from Okeechobee, some from Rousseau, Orange and Lochloosa, Jackson and other nearby lakes. The St. Johns, Oklawaha, Homosassa, Crystal, Hall and Withlacoochee rivers are other choice spots of Andrews.

Kathy and Bud have made thousands of Florida's tourist fishermen happy over the last 15 years. They have made it possible for over half a hundred anglers to land nice bass over 10-pounds and virtually all clients have had some success when fishing with Bud or one of his guiding associates.

"I have never been skunked on a bass guiding day yet," says Andrews. "Maybe tomorrow I will be, but to date, we have always come in with some kind of bass catch."

Kathy is passing up some of the bass fishing adventures today but lets you know she still likes to catch fish and in the not too distant future she will accompany her husband and land a real trophy on "waggle-tail worms" or the silver Rapalas that Bud declares are his favorites.   *W.H.C.*

The Andrews Family at Cypress Lodge

ANDREWS AND SPONSOR JAKE CHASTAIN

ROYAL BONNYL
GREAT LINE IN COLORED WATER

While I use clear Stren line in streams like the Crystal, Homossassa and Rainbow rivers, among others, my monofilament preference in the tannic acid colored waters like that in the Tsala Apopka chain, is Royal Bonnyl. This tan tinted line is camouflaged in these lakes and almost invisible. I believe that makes it a better line for big bass fishing my style, with long delays without moving the lure.

I have also found this line to be as strong as any, test for test. It resists nicks that weaken monofilament and its stretch resistance compares with the other lines that I have used since starting my guiding career.

Royal Bonnyl is not one of the more popular advertised brands but when you are fishing cider-colored water, I believe it is the finest line you can buy. It has certainly been good for me.

FUTURE OF LUNKER BASS

February and March are the big bedding months for large-mouth bass in Florida, but whether you fish in the Sunshine State or elsewhere in America, there's plenty of reason for you to consider the ethics of taking bedding bass off the beds. It's really a great tragedy.

Good sportsmen should think of future generations and never purposely catch the bedding mama, turn her loose quickly and gently. She may be able to return and save her family.

There's nothing wrong with catching a few yearling bass and eating them for dinner. But you can normally get those without fishing the beds and without disturbing the reproductive process. At least, if you are a three or four day a week angler, you don't need to keep your fish every day. Keep what you honestly need and let the rest live.

Research has shown that the 2 to 4-pounders are the best spawners. Particular attention should be given to those in this weight range in February and March in Florida. The bass population is decreasing rapidly in almost every lake and stream in Florida. Unless good conservation is practiced now, soon there will be few fish to catch. That's a shame.

Florida Game and Freshwater Fish Commission does not stock largemouth bass in the streams of the state. They contend that it is not necessary, but the heavy pressure on the resource is destroying bass fishing everywhere. Size and numbers of bass are decreasing rapidly. Everyone knows that.

Every two-pound bass that is released during the bedding season may provide 12 to 20 two-pounders the following year. It's easy to see the potential gain in bass population.

There's a growing feeling that bass clubs and tournaments hurt bass fishing. But fishermen are going to fish whether they have organized events or not. Tournament anglers do not catch any more fish than you and your neighbors catch. Clubs sponsoring most tournaments do a fine job of catch and release of bass. It's questionable whether a good portion of the lay anglers do as much toward preserving the species. It does not appear to be so.

Current laws on the books on bass bag limits are not being enforced very well. There are no Florida bass size limits. Many conservationists believe that is a mistake. Enforcement officers say they can't do any more about creel limit checks with the manpower and funds available. Accepting this as fact, it is all the more important that bass fishermen police themselves and protect the species, at least during the bedding season.

The spawning season for bass starts in late fall for Southern Florida. Okeechobee bass fishermen report beds as early as mid-November. Around the Lake Placid area it will start in December and in Central Florida in February. The panhandle lakes have bedding bass as late as April. By my own records I have found in my territory, Inverness and Panasofkee, that the height of the bedding is during February and March, just around the full moon period. This is especially true on the Tsala Apopka Chain of Lakes. Many of the forest and grove lakes have earlier bedding cycles, generally late December to mid-January.

This brings up the question of whether or not bass should be kept when caught off the beds. I honestly feel that any good sports person should take an interest in the future and not keep the fish he catches during the spawning cycle. Taking a few for dinner with a sensible quota doesn't harm the overall bass population. But this is not to say that keeping the limit four or five times a week is all right.

On my last trip with Paul Andrea, publisher of *Woods & Waters Protector*, I watched him release fish without even taking them out of the water. If he wants to weigh one he takes a quick measurement of girth and length. The formula for weight is: girth squared, multiplied by the length and this figure divided by 800 gives you the weight.

Photographing a lunker can injure the fish if it is out of the water for a long time and is laid on the bottom of the boat or in the grass. The protective slime coating that covers the fish resists bacteria and diseases and when removed can kill the fish.

Since the Florida Game and Fresh Water Fish Commission has stopped stocking bass in our lakes and rivers, it is even more important for fishermen to practice good conservation. The commission is still stocking Sunshine Bass, a hybrid fish, that doesn't multiply. This species and others do compete with the largemouth bass for food. Our bass populations are decreasing rapidly both in size and numbers. Lord only knows how man is hurting our bass with the spraying and polluting. Sportsmen

264

should do all they can to preserve this valuable resource.

I have heard of instances where big spawners are speared at night while on their beds. It would be nice if the officers could survey these areas on a 24-hour basis, but we all know it is impossible. So do the poachers. They will use their ladders, snatch hooks, jugs and spears as long as they can get away with it.

Slob fishermen will deliberately fish the beds just to get a big mama to show off, even stooping to snagging the bedding bass with snare hooks after spotting the nests from step ladders and lights in boats at night. Just such callous disregard for wildlife is what destroyed the buffalo herds. Do you want to be one of those selfish bass anglers that your grandchildren can point back to and say, "I would have largemouth bass to catch had not my grandpaw caught them all"?

The future of bass fishing depends on sports fishermen. We must do something to protect our bass. Stricter laws to protect the bedding bass would be a good start. Until this happens, fishermen should put into practice their own conservation measures. . .before it's too late.

THE ORIGINAL CULPRIT®

The Original Culprit is truly the mainstay of soft plastic lures. It comes in over 50 color combinations and 4 lengths that will fit any fishing condition. As with all our baits the Originals have Culprit's own special flavor enhancements and protein is impregnated right into the soft plastic body.

This lure is a proven big bass motivator. Time after time again, it has consistently caught bigger and better bass with its unique tail action and tail flotation response.

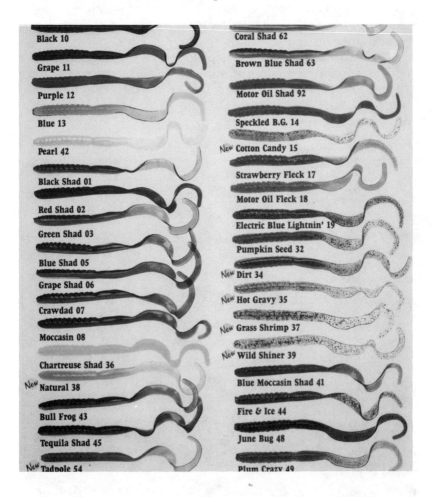

Black 10
Grape 11
Purple 12
Blue 13
Pearl 42
Black Shad 01
Red Shad 02
Green Shad 03
Blue Shad 05
Grape Shad 06
Crawdad 07
Moccasin 08
Chartreuse Shad 36
New Natural 38
Bull Frog 43
Tequila Shad 45
New Tadpole 54

Coral Shad 62
Brown Blue Shad 63
Motor Oil Shad 92
Speckled B.G. 14
New Cotton Candy 15
Strawberry Fleck 17
Motor Oil Fleck 18
Electric Blue Lightnin' 19
Pumpkin Seed 32
New Dirt 34
New Hot Gravy 35
New Grass Shrimp 37
New Wild Shiner 39
Blue Moccasin Shad 41
Fire & Ice 44
June Bug 48
Plum Crazy 49

Convenient Order Form

I would like to have additional copies of this book,

Lures for Lunker Bass

Please mail me_____copies to the address below:

Name:_____

Address:_____

_____

Enclosed please find check or money order in the amount of $16.95, that includes postage and handling, for each book.

Please mail to:
W. Horace Carter
Atlantic Publishing Company
P.O. Box 67
Tabor City, N.C. 28463

(Tear out & mail this sheet to publisher.)
Please ship me one copy of Atlantic Book checked below:

Hannon's Field Guide for Bass Fishing $9.95
Creatures & Chronicles From Cross Creek $9.30
Land That I Love (Hard Bound) **$14.50**
Wild & Wonderful Santee-Cooper Country $8.30
Return to Cross Creek $9.30
Nature's Masterpiece at Homosassa $9.30
Catch Bass $8.30
Hannon's Big Bass Magic $13.50
A Man Called Raleigh $9.30
Damn The Allegators $10.95
Bird Hunters Handbook $11.50
Hunting Boar, Hogs and Javelina $9.95
Deer and Fixin's $9.95
Shiner Fishing $9.95